Understanding Greek Warfare

This is a hugely impressive, and just as importantly, enjoyable book that offers the reader much more than the usual general survey of this fascinating subject. Its pages are packed with the author's evaluation of evidence, discussions about scholarly debates, and explanations of the evolving art of war, all the way from the Mycenaeans to the Macedonians. This is, then, a fresh new look at a topic that continues to captivate a wide audience that transcends the boundaries of academia.

Jason Crowley, *Manchester Metropolitan University, UK*

Understanding Greek Warfare offers a wide-ranging survey of Greek warfare, from the Mycenaeans through to the Hellenistic kingdoms' clashes with Rome. Each chapter provides an overview of a particular theme and historical period, and a detailed discussion of the relevant sources, both ancient and modern. This volume covers not only the development of equipment, tactics, strategy, and the major wars of Greek history – the "drums and trumpets" – it also examines the political, social, and cultural importance of warfare in each period. Each chapter outlines major scholarly debates, such as the true nature of hoplite battle and whether Alexander the Great had a strategic vision beyond conquest, and includes several short selections from the primary literary evidence.

Readable yet scholarly, this book is an ideal companion to courses on Greek warfare and society, and offers detailed suggestions for further reading and research. *Understanding Greek Warfare* will be a crucial resource for students of war in the ancient Greek world, and of the ancient Greeks in general.

Matthew A. Sears is an Associate Professor of Classics and Ancient History at the University of New Brunswick in Canada. He writes on ancient Greek history, society, and culture, and is the author of *Athens, Thrace, and the Shaping of Athenian Leadership* (2013) and co-author of *Battles and Battlefields of Ancient Greece: A Guide to their History, Topography, and Archaeology* (forthcoming).

Understanding the Ancient World

Understanding Greek Religion
Jennifer Larson

Understanding Greek Tragic Theatre
Second Edition
Rush Rehm

Understanding Latin Literature
Second Edition
Susanna Morton Braund

Understanding Greek Warfare
Matthew A. Sears

For more information about this series, please visit: www.routledge.com/classicalstudies/series/UAW

FSC
MIX
Paper from
responsible sources
FSC™ C013985
www.fsc.org

Printed in the United Kingdom
by Henry Ling Limited

Understanding Greek Warfare

Matthew A. Sears

Routledge
Taylor & Francis Group

LONDON AND NEW YORK

First published 2019
by Routledge
2 Park Square, Milton Park, Abingdon, Oxon OX14 4RN

and by Routledge
52 Vanderbilt Avenue, New York, NY 10017

Routledge is an imprint of the Taylor & Francis Group, an informa business

British Library Cataloguing-in-Publication Data
A catalogue record for this book is available from the British Library

Library of Congress Cataloging-in-Publication Data
Names: Sears, Matthew A., author.
Title: Understanding Greek warfare/Matthew A. Sears.
Description: Abingdon, Oxon, New York, NY: Routledge, [2019] | Series:
Understanding the ancient world | Includes bibliographical references and
index.
Identifiers: LCCN 2018044924 (print) | LCCN 2018046282 (ebook) |
ISBN 9781315267791 (ebook) | ISBN 9781351974134 (web pdf) | ISBN
9781351974127 (epub) | ISBN 9781351974110 (mobi/kindle) | ISBN
9781138288607 (hardback : alk. paper)
Subjects: LCSH: Greece–History, Military–To 146 B.C. | Military art and
science–Greece–History–To 1500.
Classification: LCC DF89 (ebook) | LCC DF89 .S46 2019 (print) | DDC
355.020938–dc23
LC record available at https://lccn.loc.gov/2018044924

ISBN: 978-1-138-28860-7 (hbk)
ISBN: 978-1-138-28861-4 (pbk)
ISBN: 978-1-315-26779-1 (ebk)

Typeset in Times New Roman
by Wearset Ltd, Boldon, Tyne and Wear

For Barry Strauss

Contents

Figures

Maps

Preface and acknowledgments

As this book's title suggests, I hope readers will gain not only a deeper knowledge of ancient Greek strategy, tactics, and equipment, but a genuine *understanding* of war as a broad political, social, and cultural phenomenon, from the Late Bronze Age to the end of the Hellenistic period. I also hope to convey some of the major scholarly controversies surrounding this vast topic, which get to the heart of *how* we know what we know, or at least what we think we know, about ancient Greek warfare. Finally, throughout I have attempted to highlight the broader questions the subject of Greek warfare should force us to ask; questions that I think continue to have bearing on our world today.

Any one book aiming to cover more than 1,200 years of history is going to be selective and leave out many important events, themes, and topics. I do try, however, to focus on the larger themes and issues in the study of Greek warfare, and to show the links between topics and between chapters. Rather than offer a narrative of Greek military history, each chapter draws out major trends and questions about a specific period, including the ancient sources and nature of the evidence, modern scholarly approaches and debates, and brief case studies of specific battles and campaigns, all while going beyond the mere "drums and trumpets" of war. Each topic is illustrated by representative selections from ancient literature, including some inscriptions on stone, and images of topography, landscape, and various material and art-historical objects from archaeological excavations and museums. Rather than detailed scholarly footnotes, each chapter ends with an annotated list of suggestions for further reading (mostly restricted to works in English), which should provide a good starting point for student essays and further research. Unless otherwise stated, all translations are my own.

This book is the product of teaching ancient Greek warfare courses to undergraduate students, for which there was until now no comprehensive scholarly textbook. I hope I have helped to remedy that situation. I could not have written this book without the enthusiastic and challenging conversations I have had with many students, both at Wabash College and at the University of New Brunswick. I owe these students a great debt. I would like to single out my UNB graduate students Emma McPhee and Jake Stoddard, both of whom have caused me to look at ancient warfare in new and productive ways. My colleagues at both institutions have provided wonderful academic homes, and Jim Murray especially has indulged my fascination with ancient warfare by graciously going along with my out-of-the-way forays onto battlefields while we co-led students in UNB's travel study programs to Greece.

I have been researching and writing about ancient warfare with Jake Butera now for several years, and he has read every word of this manuscript, and saved me from countless errors and pointed me in a better direction more times than I can count. Along with Jake, my wife, Jenny Denault, and my friend Kirk Ormand have walked over more Greek fields with me than they would care to mention. Many colleagues at the American School of Classical Studies at Athens have provided advice and feedback along the way. I thank in particular Lee Brice, Glenn Bugh Jack Davis, Denver Graninger, Peter Krentz, Maria Liston, John Oakley, Shari Stocker, and Georgia Tsouvala. Sally McGrath and Carolyn Willekes have taught me a lot about horses. Lee Brice and Jason Crowley graciously read the book proposal and helped to shape the project a great deal, and both offered feedback afterward. At Routledge, I thank Amy Davis-Poynter for reaching out to suggest this book in the first place, and for offering support during the writing process. Editorial Assistant Elizabeth Risch has been excellent to work with.

Barry Strauss taught me ancient Greek warfare, and so much more. I could not have asked for a better doctoral supervisor or scholarly friend in the years since finishing my PhD. I dedicate this book to him.

Matthew Sears
2018

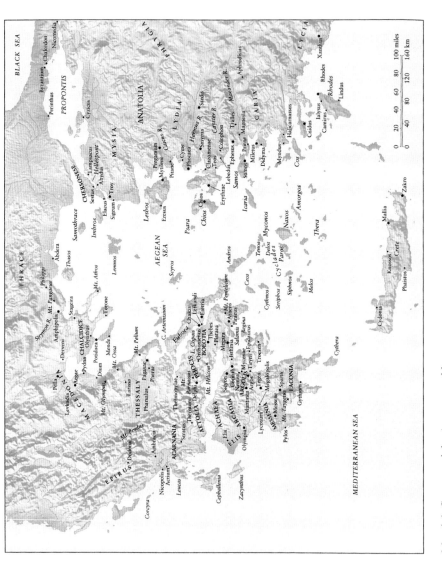

Map 0.1 Greece and the Aegean world.

Source: from *Ancient Greece* (3rd edition) by S. Pomeroy et al. (2012). From inside the front cover. By permission of Oxford University Press, USA.

1 Bronze Age and Homeric warfare
Achilles vs. Hector?

Introduction

The Greek literary canon begins with a single, evocative word: rage (*mēnis* in Greek). Homer, if he indeed was a real person (we will come back to this point later), carefully chose "rage" to start off the thousands of lines of poetry contained in the *Iliad*, the epic account of turmoil in the Greek ranks arrayed before Troy, in the final year of the ten-year-long conflict we call the Trojan War. In so doing, Homer also started, for all intents and purposes, Greek literature, and

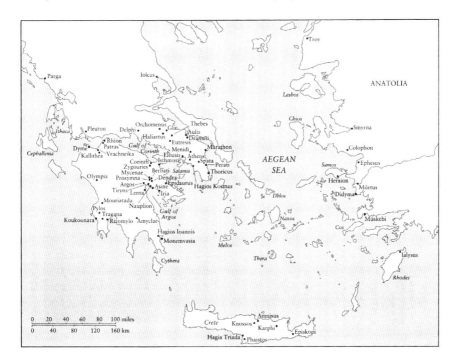

Map 1.1 Mycenaean sites in the thirteenth century BCE.

Source: from *Readings in Greek History* (2nd edition) by D. B. Nagle and S. Burstein (2014). Map 1.1, p. 3. By permission of Oxford University Press, USA.

composed a work that had an incalculable impact on every aspect of Greek life, including, perhaps most of all, war. The *Iliad*, and to a lesser extent the *Odyssey*, the other heroic epic attributed to Homer, tell of great warriors in battle, men of the front ranks, or *promachoi*, who single out worthy opponents from the other side and fight to the death. Though supposedly telling of the Late Bronze Age – the canonical date for the fall of Troy is 1184 BCE – the Homeric epics were mined as sources for moral instruction, as well as tactical maxims, by the ancient Greeks many hundreds of years later.

In this chapter, we will consider how the rage of Achilles, the *Iliad*'s preeminent hero, and the battlefield struggles surrounding it, can inform us about the Greeks at war. What drove Achilles to fight, and to refuse to fight after growing angry at his commander? What were the military values held by the Homeric heroes? And how did the regular soldiers, the masses in the shadows behind great leaders such as Agamemnon and Odysseus, experience war? Without understanding the world of Homeric epic, we simply cannot understand the Greeks, least of all in the sphere of warfare. Before turning to epic poetry, we will first consider what actual Late Bronze Age warfare was like in the Greek world and broader Mediterranean region, and to what extent the Bronze Age is reflected in the work of Homer, who composed some 500 years after the fall of Troy. We will then explore the figure of Homer himself, and the world of his heroes, before taking into account how Homeric poetry was received by later generations of Greeks. The chapter will end with a reconstruction – as far as is possible – of a duel and subsequent pitched battle in the *Iliad*, at least in terms of how later Greeks could reasonably interpret it.

The Mycenaeans and war

The world inhabited by the Homeric heroes had a real historical context, whether or not this context is accurately reflected in the *Iliad* and *Odyssey*. In the Late Bronze Age (*c.*1600–1100 BCE), central and southern mainland Greece, and other spots around the Aegean Sea, including Crete and parts of Asia Minor, were dominated by a palatial civilization scholars call Mycenaean. This civilization gets its name from the important archaeological site of Mycenae, which commands the Argolid plain in the northeastern Peloponnese. In literature, Mycenae was the city of Agamemnon, the most powerful Greek king and leader of the expedition against Troy. The location of Bronze Age Mycenae was never in doubt, since its imposing walls had always been visible. Accordingly, when the impressive site was excavated in the late nineteenth century by the controversial archaeologist-cum-treasure-hunter Heinrich Schliemann, it was proclaimed to be none other than Agamemnon's capital. Following this excavation, the entire Bronze Age civilization throughout Greece exhibiting the same or similar material culture as found at the site of Mycenae was dubbed "Mycenaean." It is important to remember that, even though there might well have been cultural, diplomatic, political, and military contact between several of the great Mycenaean sites in the Aegean, it is unlikely that these people called themselves

Mycenaeans, let alone were ruled by the literary Agamemnon and his peers. Nevertheless, the impressive remains of Mycenaean palaces, citadels, and tombs likely inspired the Heroic tradition in Greek culture, meaning that the Mycenaeans are significant for the study of Greek warfare. Moreover, we now know that the historical Mycenaeans spoke an early form of the Greek language (recorded in a script called Linear B), meaning that they were by definition Greeks. We thus begin our study with the Mycenaeans and their way of waging war.

One of the most striking things about the Mycenaeans is just how warlike they were. The civilization that inhabited the Aegean islands during the Middle Bronze Age in the centuries preceding the construction of Mycenaean palaces was comparatively peaceful, at least in terms of what material culture can reveal. The Minoans, as this earlier people was named by scholars after the mythological king Minos of Crete, ruled from large and lavish palaces in cities like Knossos on Crete, and decorated their walls with glorious frescoes, as can be seen most spectacularly at Akrotiri on the island of Thera, now called Santorini. The Minoans, who were not Greek, had wealth and culture to spare, but while there are suggestions that they might have engaged in some violent practices, including most disturbingly human sacrifice, military imagery is relatively lacking in their iconography.[1] To be sure, the Minoans forged swords, portrayed warriors on some of their objects, and even, in the case of the frescoes preserved at Akrotiri, represented fearsome naval flotillas on their walls.[2] But the sheer prevalence of weaponry and military imagery seen in the Mycenaean period simply was not there for the Minoans. Most tellingly, the great Minoan palatial centers were as a rule un-walled, meaning that the Minoans did not fear violent assaults from political rivals or marauders eager for plunder. These un-walled sites, particularly Knossos on Crete, might be due to the maritime dominance of the Minoans rather than an inherently peaceful nature, but whatever the case may be, the world of the Minoans does not seem to have been as violent and unstable as later periods in the Aegean would be. The Minoans were eventually replaced – defeated? – by the Mycenaeans, who were based on the Greek mainland rather than the Aegean islands. By contrast to their predecessors, the Mycenaeans were fixated on the image of the warrior, and their centers were eventually walled in the most impressive way possible.

In the 1600s–1500s BCE, the rulers of Mycenae were buried in lavish style in two "grave circles," respectively called Grave Circle A, the later series of graves found within the fortification walls of a subsequent building phase, and Grave Circle B, somewhat earlier than Grave Circle A and now located outside of the walls. Schliemann's discovery of Grave Circle A was an epochal moment in Mediterranean archaeology. Contained within these burials was a nearly unbelievable level of wealth, including the famous gold funerary masks of which Schliemann dubbed one the "Mask of Agamemnon" (despite being several hundred years too early for Homer's Agamemnon). In addition to luxury goods, these rulers were buried with the status markers of great warriors, including swords, daggers, and even gold seals depicting scenes of combat and the hunt. Some of the stone *stelai*, or slabs, placed atop these graves depict images

Figure 1.1 The Mycenaean Warrior Vase, thirteenth century BCE.

Source: National Archaeological Museum, Athens (no. 1426). Photo credit: Scala/Art Resource, NY.

including riders atop chariots, the ultimate military status symbol in the ancient world. In addition to their wealth and status, those buried in the Mycenaean grave circles clearly wanted to identify with and advertise their participation in the warrior ethos. Later phases of settlement at Mycenae, roughly contemporary with the Trojan War, furnish examples of frescoes and other artistic media that demonstrate the continued importance of martial imagery. Several frescoes depict "figure-eight" type shields, while the celebrated "Warrior Vase," found near Grave Circle A, portrays several warriors marching in a line, equipped with round shields and thrusting spears. Such imagery is virtually absent from Minoan contexts, indicating that the Mycenaeans were a decidedly more militaristic people.

In 2015, Jack Davis and Sharon Stocker, the directors of the University of Cincinnati excavations at Pylos, another prominent Mycenaean site in the Peloponnese, dominated by the "Palace of Nestor," named after one of Homer's heroes, discovered a remarkable tomb roughly contemporaneous with the Mycenaean grave circles. This so-called Griffin Warrior Tomb, named because of the stunning ivory plaque decorated with a griffin found within, might represent one of the earliest material examples of the Mycenaean eclipse of the Minoans. This tomb was the final resting-place of a single male warrior, who

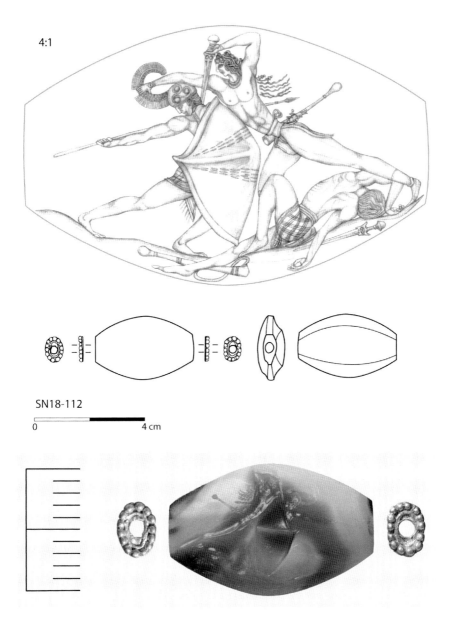

4:1

SN18-112

0   4 cm

Figure 1.2a–b The Combat Agate from the Grave of the Griffin Warrior at Pylos, fifteenth century BCE.

Source: courtesy of the Department of Classics, University of Cincinnati.

was buried with a plethora of weapons and armor, including a meter-long sword with a gold hilt and boar's tusks for the type of helmet described in the Homeric poems, and a handsome collection of jewelry, metal vessels, and other luxury items. Most spectacular of the finds in the grave is an agate sealstone depicting a scene of combat in such remarkable detail that the sealstone and its imagery must have been especially significant for the warrior and those who buried him. Many of these items were of Cretan origin and design, suggesting that this warrior, who was most likely a prominent leader at early Mycenaean Pylos, took full advantage of the wealth of Minoan Crete, demonstrating that what the Minoans had once enjoyed without the need for fortifications or the promotion of an overt warrior culture were now the prerogatives of the type of warrior-kings that so impressed Homer and his Greek audience centuries later.[3]

In later, historical periods, we know that Mycenaean tombs were frequently used as centers of cult, the natural place to venerate the heroes who were buried in such lavish and militaristic style. Homer and his audience, therefore, could well have been aware of the Mycenaean funerary culture only revealed to the modern world by archaeologists not even a century-and-a-half ago. What must have impressed Homer's audience most of all, however, were the remains of the walls of Mycenaean citadels that would have been still visible in the Archaic and Classical periods. Modern visitors to Mycenae are struck first by the sheer scale of the site's walls, and the impossible size of their stones. The walls at Mycenae and other Mycenaean fortified sites, including nearby Tiryns, and Gla to the north in Boeotia, were built first in the 1300s BCE – a couple of centuries after the Grave Circles and the Griffin Warrior Tomb – suggesting that by that time the level of violence in the Aegean world had increased markedly. Today we call the type of masonry seen in the walls of Mycenaean citadels, characterized by large undressed stones arrayed in rough courses with small stones used to fill in gaps, "cyclopean," since only mythical creatures like the Cyclops, made famous by Homer's *Odyssey*, could possibly have worked with stones of such heft. The Roman author Pliny the Elder, citing Aristotle as his source, attributed such structures to the cyclopes even in antiquity (*Natural History* 7.56.195). These citadels were impossible obstacles for any potential enemies, since not until the late Classical and Hellenistic periods did ancient Greek armies develop effective siege tactics (though other ancient cultures, such as the Assyrians, did develop such tactics in earlier periods). Mycenaean walls can fairly be said to have been overbuilt, constructed taller and thicker than dictated by any purely tactical considerations. In addition to providing protection from enemies, Mycenaean walls would have been another demonstration of the superhuman power and wealth of Mycenaean rulers, a message directed at rivals and perhaps also at the rulers' own people, living in far humbler dwellings outside and in the shadows of the citadel. Surely those who built such things, as Homer and his listeners might have reckoned, were far beyond the normal men and women of everyday experience. The common Mycenaeans too probably thought their rulers to be supermen.

In discussing the warfare of the Mycenaean world, it is crucial to keep in mind that the Mycenaeans existed in a broader eastern Mediterranean context.

Figure 1.3 The Walls of Tiryns, thirteenth century BCE.
Source: author's photograph.

Elite Mycenaeans were influenced by the rulers of other, more powerful and wealthy, Late Bronze Age civilizations, including New Kingdom Egypt and the Hittite Empire based in what is now Turkey. Extensive networks of material and cultural exchange crisscrossed the eastern Mediterranean during the Mycenaean period, as they had done for centuries before the Mycenaeans even arrived on the scene. The Egyptian pharaohs and the Hittite kings commanded vast armies of infantry and chariots, and advertised their military exploits in official correspondence and on monumental inscriptions and relief sculptures. Even though the most powerful Mycenaean rulers commanded far less territory and far fewer soldiers than their Near Eastern counterparts, they adopted the martial iconography and ethos of their more powerful neighbors. As the study of Mycenaean art and archaeology has revealed, Mycenaean kings and nobles rode into battle on chariots – even though Mycenaean topography is much less suited to chariot warfare than the broad plains of the Near East. They also brandished ornate bronze weapons, and celebrated their heroic prowess with martial artistic motifs and status objects. In light of the Mycenaean elite's desire to advertise themselves as similar to their neighbors, let us consider briefly how the great powers of the Late Bronze Age waged war, and to what extent the Mycenaeans fought in similar ways.[4]

New Kingdom Egypt, the wealthy and powerful state along the fertile land watered by the Nile River, still looms large in the modern imagination. The pharaohs were experts at self-promotion, most famously by building the pyramids, but also by advertising themselves and their military exploits on the walls of their temples in both text and image. Ramesses II, better known as Ramesses the Great, praised his own valor to the skies on the temple at Abu Simbel and other sites throughout the country, memorializing Egypt's battle against the Hittite Empire at Kadesh in 1274 BCE. The Hittites, Egypt's sparring partner in this first battle for which we have anything close to a complete picture, are much less well-known. Controlling most of what is now Turkey and a good portion of Syria and the Levant, the Hittites ruled a vast empire and left a copious record of diplomatic correspondence and other texts in an Indo-European language related to Greek. The Battle of Kadesh between the Egyptians and the Hittites will serve as a useful case study in how these neighbors of the Mycenaeans fought.

The armies of Ramesses II and the Hittite King Muwatalli II met in 1274 BCE at the city of Kadesh, lying on the Orontes River in what is today Syria and what was then disputed territory between the two great powers. Our main source for the battle is from the Egyptian side, since Ramesses inscribed an official account on several temples, accompanied by vivid visual representations of the fighting, with a larger-than-life Ramesses taking center-stage. We have, unfortunately, little from the Hittite side except the text of the peace treaty between the Egyptians and the Hittites signed in the years following the battle. Because of the Egyptian written account and because of known events of history preceding and following the battle, scholars have been able to piece together the strategic and tactical situation of Kadesh to a remarkable degree. The picture that emerges is of a great clash of arms that ended in a slight tactical victory for the Egyptians but perhaps a long-term strategic victory for the Hittites. The fighting itself involved two of the largest armies ever fielded by ancient powers – in the realm of 40,000 soldiers on each side – and a melee dominated by grand formations of chariots. In terms of the battle's scale, Kadesh was unique; but in the predominance of chariots as the primary offense arm of both sides, the battle was typical of its time.

Near Eastern rulers like Ramesses II described their armies simply as their infantry and chariotry, the two main branches of armed forces in the Late Bronze Age. Cavalry is conspicuously absent from Late Bronze Age warfare. While horses played a large role, in combat they were used primarily to pull chariots rather than be ridden by cavalrymen. At Kadesh there were thousands of chariots on both sides, and they were responsible for most of the action. The Egyptians and the Hittites had different approaches to chariot warfare. The Egyptians had light and fast chariots capable of supporting two passengers, including one driver and one soldier armed with ranged weapons such as arrows or javelins. Ramesses II depicts himself as driving a chariot by himself, with the reins tied around his waist to allow him the freedom to fire his bow. Such virtuosic skill was surely a rarity, if not a self-indulgent fabrication on the part of the pharaoh. The Hittites, on the other hand, by the time of Kadesh had adopted heavier chariots capable of carrying three soldiers, which included one driver, one soldier equipped with a short-range weapon such as a thrusting spear, and another soldier wielding a shield to protect the entire crew. The heavier chariots of the Hittites would have been less mobile and less quick than the forces of their Egyptian foes, but the Hittites made up for their lack of speed with pure striking power. The broad plains of the Near East, such as that abutting the Orontes River near Kadesh, were well-suited to chariot warfare, and these glitzy weapons pulled by horses were just the sort of armament a king should favor as a way to highlight his power and wealth. The sight and sound of thousands of chariots thundering across the plain must have been terrifying.

At Abu Simbel, Ramesses describes his activities at Kadesh in terms appropriate for Homeric warriors:

> Then His Majesty started forth at a gallop, and entered into the host of the fallen ones of Hatti, being alone by himself and none other with him … And found 2,500 chariots hemming him in on his outer side, consisting of all the fallen ones of Hatti with the many foreign countries which were with them … I called to you, My Father Amun, when I was in the midst of multitudes I knew not. All foreign countries were combined against me, I being alone by myself, none other with me, my numerous infantry having abandoned me, not one looking at me of my chariotry. I kept on shouting to them, but none of them hearkened to me as I called. … I found Amun come when I called him; he gave me his hand and I rejoiced … All that I did came to pass. I was like Mont. I shot on my right and captured with my left … I found the 2,500 chariots, in whose midst I was, sprawling before my horse. Not one of them found his hand to fight … I caused them to plunge into the water even as crocodiles plunge, fallen upon their faces one upon the other. I killed among them according as I willed.[5]

Bronze Age infantry were generally equipped with spears and swords for hand-to-hand combat. As for how these infantry fought, we are at the mercy of material evidence and artistic representations, since no written accounts provide any tactical details. We can be sure that massive armies like those deployed at Kadesh would have consisted largely of conscripted troops since no ancient kingdom could afford to have so many men in a standing army while still meeting the basic agricultural and other needs of the state. While raw recruits would have been limited in terms of the tactics they could employ in battle, Near Eastern kings in the Bronze Age would have relied on elite and professional corps of infantry soldiers as a bodyguard and to anchor their armies. We can reconstruct some of the equipment and tactics of Bronze Age infantry, especially these professional standing troops, who tend to be featured prominently in art.

One of our most fascinating pieces of evidence comes in fact from the Early Bronze Age. Yigael Yadin, in his classic *The Art of Warfare in Biblical Lands*, provides an illustration and discussion of the famous Stele of the Vultures, sculpted in the third millennium BCE in Mesopotamia.[6] Yadin argues that this

Figure 1.4 Ramesses II in a chariot with bow and arrow at the Battle of Kadesh, Great
Temple of Ramesses II at Abu Simbel, thirteenth century BCE.

Source: photo credit: Album/Art Resource, NY.

very ancient monument depicts a dense infantry formation of spearmen in a
column of six files with each file being eleven men deep. Upon examination of
the relief, the spearmen also look to be uniformly equipped in both armor and
weapons, which points to some sort of regular contingent with a degree of professionalism. Jumping ahead to Kadesh, the reliefs of the battle depict an elite
contingent of troops in the Egyptian army as advancing in an ordered phalanx of
ten deep, while the bodyguard of the Hittite king are likewise arrayed in close
formation. Whether or not the Greek hoplite phalanx introduced a new type of
dense infantry formation many centuries later (which we will explore in the next
chapter), during the Bronze Age, soldiers appear to have been quite capable of
fighting in close order.

We know some details about the permanent contingents relied upon by
Bronze Age rulers to maintain a high-quality war machine, which can reveal
important details about how these kingdoms waged war. Elite units in the Egyptian army, complete with their own special commanders, are explicitly mentioned in the sources as *nfrw* and were deployed in special arrangements. The
pharaoh Thutmose IV, for example, made it a point to marshal these elite troops
on both flanks, a vulnerable and therefore tactically crucial position. Foreign
troops were also employed to great effect as both auxiliaries and supplements to
the regular Egyptian forces. These contingents included, among others, skilled
Anatolians, Shardana, and Nubian soldiers. Often these foreign troops were

originally prisoners captured by Egypt, later admitted into the kingdom, given small fiefs of land, and employed as the pharaoh's own elite bodyguard and specially trained mercenary army. The phenomenon of POWs serving as the king's bodyguard and as special troops in the national army was widespread throughout the ancient Near East. These forces were used to great effect by the pharaoh in foreign wars and were also kept at home to control the local population.

In the fifteenth century BCE, Thutmose III attacked the city of Megiddo in the Levant. Leading the assault and breaching the walls was a unit known as the *Kenyt-Nesu*, or "King's Braves," who were ordinary soldiers promoted to the prestigious unit for demonstrated valor. Instances of select foreign auxiliary troops can be seen at Kadesh, where Ramesses made use of Shardana warriors in the regular army and apparently as a special bodyguard for himself. The Shardana, or Sherden, had been captured by the Egyptians when they came as raiders into the Nile delta in the early thirteenth century BCE. As can be seen in the Abydos reliefs depicting Kadesh, the Shardana were equipped differently than the rest of the force, employing small round shields, horned helmets, and swords as well as spears, and played a key role in the battle. They are seen acting as the pharaoh's special guard, marching in ordered formation, and performing crucial acts such as killing plundering Hittite soldiers and cutting off the hands of slain enemies. The military skill of these troops is brought out in an inscription from Tanis, describing them as warriors "whom no one had ever known how to combat."[7] Shardana became a regular special unit in the Egyptian army, listed along with Nubians as separate from the regular infantry and chariotry by Ramesses III. They were also identified with skilled foot-soldiers not only in Egypt, but in other Near Eastern centers such as Ugarit.

Also at Kadesh was a force called the *Na'arun*. In the initial stages of the battle, the Hittite forces had surprised and ambushed a large section of the Egyptian army while they were crossing the Orontes, triumphing over and routing much of Ramesses' force while the pharaoh himself was across the river and unable to bring aid. Instead of pressing home the assault, the Hittites began looting the Egyptian camp. It was at this moment that the *Na'arun*, whom Yigael Yadin describes as a crack unit of Canaanite troops in the Egyptian army who had been held in reserve, attacked the Hittites plundering the baggage, slaughtering them all. The *Na'arun*, depicted in the Kadesh reliefs as attacking in a disciplined phalanx of ten ranks, turned the tide of the battle by driving back the Hittites and paved the way for the Egyptians to come back from near defeat and prevent a crippling strategic loss.

The Hittites had their own crack infantry forces, in addition to an elite chariot corps. In the Kadesh reliefs, Muwatalli II is depicted employing a bodyguard of crack *Teher* warriors marshaled in close formation. Furthermore, the Hittite king had brought with him to this crucial battle an extensive host comprised of forces from several nationalities, listed by Ramesses II in his descriptions of the battle, many of whom were likely serving in a mercenary capacity. Such a force must be reminiscent to the modern reader of the Achaean confederacy arrayed at Troy in Homer's *Iliad*. Incorporated into this force along with the regular standing army was the Hittites' conquered enemy, the Kaška. Before they were conquered, these people had enjoyed quite a bit of military success against the Hittites for several years, proving to be a constant thorn in the king's side. It is conceivable that once they were made a part of the Hittite army, they were allowed to use their own unique weapons and fighting style just as the analogous Shardana in Egypt.

This discussion of elite foreign troops brings us back to our consideration of Mycenaean warfare, since the Mycenaeans themselves seem to have served regularly as mercenaries in the employ of other Bronze Age powers, as Robert Drews extensively argues. Recently, it has been plausibly suggested that Mycenaean warriors clad in boar's tusk helmets are depicted fighting other peoples in a fragmentary papyrus found in el-Amarna, implying their presence in Egypt as mercenaries. Also, two heavily armed Mycenaeans and a mercenary soldier from further north in the Balkans are believed to have been part of the crew of the late fourteenth century BCE Levantine merchantman found near Uluburun off the southern coast of Turkey. The presence of these three warriors could have been a deterrent for possible pirates and looters desirous of the valuable wares aboard the ship.[8]

The Mycenaeans seem to have employed their own foreign professional soldiers. Some of the Linear B tablets found at the important Mycenaean center of Pylos in Messenia list what appear to be groups of soldiers under different ethnic designations, which suggests that foreign professional soldiers of non-Messenian origin were employed by the palace at Pylos. These soldiers may have been originally POWs or foreigners admitted into the kingdom and given small parcels of land in exchange for military service, a situation analogous to that in many Bronze Age societies. Similar troop lists appear in Linear B tablets found at Mycenaean-occupied Knossos on Crete. It has been argued that these foreign troops would have made up the mainstay of Mycenaean infantries and would have been used by the rulers to, among other things, maintain the kingdom's security. Like other Bronze Age powers, the Mycenaeans could not afford to maintain large standing armies, and therefore would have relied upon elite units to supplement conscript forces.[9]

While chariots were not appropriate for most of the landscape in the Mycenaean world, the Mycenaean infantry probably fought in battle in much the same way as their neighbors did. As in the case of the Stele of the Vultures and the reliefs from Kadesh, at least some Mycenaean soldiers employed well-ordered infantry formations. Both the Warrior Vase and the Warrior Stele from Mycenae portray troops in uniform equipment marching in what appears to be disciplined battle order. In both pieces, the troops are carrying spears and round shields not totally unlike the equipment of later hoplite armies.

What is perhaps most interesting for our discussion, however, are the reasons the Mycenaeans went to war. Hittite texts, which Gary Beckman has usefully gathered in his indispensable *Hittite Diplomatic Texts*, indicate that peoples living in the vicinity of Mycenaean Greece, whom the Hittites called the Ahhiyawans, regularly engaged in sea-borne raiding against Hittite territory, particularly in the part of Turkey where ancient Troy was located. In addition to fighting

Figure 1.5 Mycenaean dagger inlaid with a scene of a lion hunt, from Grave Circle A at Mycenae, sixteenth century BCE.

Source: National Archaeological Museum, Athens. © Vanni Archive/Art Resource, NY.

in what might have been a historical "Trojan War," or maybe a series of "Trojan Wars," these Ahhiyawans might have been threatened by or even numbered among the fabled "Sea Peoples" who have frequently been blamed for destabilizing the eastern Mediterranean at the time of the Late Bronze Age collapse of civilizations. Many have pointed out – though not all scholars agree – that the Ahhiyawans look very similar in name, location, and military activities to the Achaeans, Homer's favorite term for the Greeks. It is possible, therefore, that the Mycenaeans might have provided some actual historical material for the later Greek epic tradition, in addition to the clear impact they had on the Greek imagination.

Homer and his "heroes"

Before we examine the warfare depicted in the *Iliad* and *Odyssey*, which purport to tell of heroes from what we call the Late Bronze Age, it is important to consider first the "Homeric Question." Even though the ancient Greeks agreed that someone named Homer wrote both the *Iliad* and the *Odyssey*, and the manuscript tradition ascribes several smaller works to Homer too, scholars now virtually agree that the same poet did not write both major epics. Furthermore, it is impossible to tell whether either of the poems was written by anyone named Homer, let alone the Homer described in later biographical traditions. The composition and internal coherence of both poems also present numerous problems. For example, even though most scholars now think that the *Iliad* and *Odyssey* were first composed around 700 BCE, with the *Iliad* likely being the earlier of the two, the poems were originally composed orally, perhaps by illiterate bards, and might have had many variations. The epics were probably not written down in any formal way until at least a century-and-a-half later, and even then many additions and changes might have been made in the subsequent centuries. The entirety of Book 10 of the *Iliad*, which describes a night raid led by Odysseus and Diomedes against Troy's allies outside of the city's walls, is regularly considered to be a later interpolation, as is much of the last book of the *Odyssey*. Perhaps most vexing of all, it was for a long time reckoned impossible that someone composing an oral epic in 700 BCE could have recalled anything from a Trojan War that took place 500 years earlier, especially since during those 500 years the Greek world was without writing.

Students would be well within their rights, therefore, to consider, as the great historian M. I. Finley did, that the Homeric poems depict the world of the poet's own day. Moreover, Finley was decidedly pessimistic about Homeric descriptions of warfare, considering them to be purely literary creations, unintelligible in terms of any real tactics, strategy, or equipment, and as such essentially useless for military historians. Instead, for Finley, as he argues in *The World of Odysseus*, Homeric poetry was useful for understanding Greek society at the end of the "Dark Age" and beginning of the Archaic period, when the polis and other crucial Greek institutions were just emerging. Why, then, include Homeric warfare in the history of Greek warfare at all, let alone in a chapter on the warfare of the Late Bronze Age? I suggest two reasons. First, the warfare depicted in the *Iliad* and *Odyssey*, and the heroes who went into battle, served as the foremost model for all later Greeks, well into the Hellenistic period. Therefore, Homeric poetry is an essential source for how all ancient Greeks thought about war. Second, in recent decades a great deal of scholarly work, including the scientific excavation of Troy itself, has demonstrated that there is a whole lot of material in Homeric poetry that befits the Late Bronze Age and that something like the Trojan War might have actually happened. As Barry Strauss argues in *The Trojan War: A New History*, there might be a lot more continuity, in terms of both tactics and ways of thinking about war, between the Mycenaean world of the Late Bronze Age, the world of Homer, and the world of the later Greeks than earlier generations of scholars recognized.

The *Iliad* and *Odyssey* tell of the Trojan War and the famous soldiers who fought in it. Or, more accurately, the poems focus on select themes derived from events and personalities surrounding the Trojan War, rather than offering a full narrative account of the war itself. In Greek mythology, the Trojan War was a ten-year-long conflict between a coalition of Greek states led by the Mycenaean king Agamemnon and the city of Troy and its allies in what is now northwestern Turkey. The war began because Paris, son of the Trojan king Priam, absconded to Troy with Helen, the legendarily beautiful wife of the Spartan king Menelaus, brother of Agamemnon. The war ended when the Greeks were able to penetrate the walls of Troy inside the Trojan Horse, at which point the city of Troy was utterly destroyed and its people killed or enslaved. The *Iliad* centers on a brief period of around two months in the final year of the war. Achilles, the greatest of the Greeks at Troy, is usually seen as the epic's main character, since the very first word evokes Achilles' rage at Agamemnon, and the poem describes Achilles' withdrawal from battle after Agamemnon deprived Achilles of his war-prize, a girl named Briseis. Agamemnon took Briseis in order to save face after having to return his own prize, Chriseis, who happened to be the daughter of a priest of Apollo and thus the cause of divine wrath against the Greeks. Achilles only returns to the fighting to slay the Trojan prince Hector, after Hector kills Achilles' friend Patroclus. The *Iliad* ends with the funeral of Hector, and the haunting sense that Hector's city will soon be destroyed too. Within the *Iliad*'s twenty-four books are many lengthy descriptions of pitched battle beneath Troy's walls. The *Odyssey* focuses on the harrowing ten-year return journey of the Greek hero Odysseus from Troy to Ithaca, and his reestablishment as the rightful head of his household, and husband to Penelope and father to Telemachus. Though the *Odyssey* has far fewer battle descriptions than the *Iliad*, it is still invaluable for what it tells about the nature of heroism and what sorts of attributes an ideal warrior should possess.

So how did Homer's warriors fight on the plain before Troy? The traditional view is that Homeric battle represents an era of warfare before the hoplite phalanx. Instead of massed formations of citizen-soldiers, Homer's armies were led by aristocratic warriors who ranged freely across the battlefield, calling each other out for one-on-one duels. In essence, according to this traditional view, Homeric battle amounted to little more than a series of duels between aristocratic heroes, even though each army deployed thousands of soldiers. In such a scheme, there was a clear and decisive change with the advent of hoplite weapons and armor in the early Archaic period, a true "Hoplite Revolution" that sparked the change from chaotic aristocratic fighting to massed phalanx warfare. As we will see in the next chapter, the very notion of a Hoplite Revolution is far more complicated than it once was, and there are many scholars who think they can pick out dense formations on the plains of Troy, whether or not those formations represent Bronze Age or Early Iron/Archaic Age battle.

The chief exponents of the view that Homeric battle represents clashes of dense phalanxes are Joachim Latacz, whose 1977 book argued that the *Iliad* represents the same sort of battle as that depicted in the early Archaic lyric poets Kallinos and Tyrtaios, and W. K. Pritchett, who in a 1985 study claimed that while the *Iliad* represents the warfare of many different periods, massed fighting is paramount. For both Latacz and Pritchett, Homer's very vocabulary, which includes *phalanx* (though only in the plural) and other words and phrases indicating well-ordered ranks and dense formations, evinces phalanx warfare. Furthermore, many times throughout the *Iliad*, armies are represented as being arranged "like stones in a wall" and so close together that shields overlap and horsehair plumes touch when the men nod their heads. Two passages describing the Myrmidons of Achilles and the soldiers rallying behind Ajax particularly stand out as evincing dense formations:

> The dense ranks stood behind the two Ajaxes, ranks which neither Ajax nor Athena, leader of the host, would scorn should they have come upon them. For the picked best men awaited godlike Hector and the Trojans, a hedge with spear intertwined with spear, shield with sloping shield. Shield leaned upon shield, helmet upon helmet, man upon man; their horse-hair crests with resplendent plumes met when the men moved their heads, so densely did they stand with each other.
>
> (13.126–13.133)

They drew closer in dense ranks when they heard their king. As a builder makes a wall with densely packed stones for a lofty house, keeping out the violence of the wind, so were packed their helmets and bossed shields. Shield leaned upon shield, helmet upon helmet, man upon man; their horse-hair crests with resplendent plumes met when the men moved their heads, so densely did they stand with each other.

(16.211–16.217)

Where Homer does focus on individual duels between great heroes, typically called the "front-fighters" or *promachoi*, he employs the poetic exaggeration of a storyteller. The overemphasis on the leading heroes, in other words those who captivated Homer's audience, should not detract from the larger picture of massed infantry.

In addition to arguing for the predominance of dense phalanxes, Latacz offers a clear and comprehensive reconstruction of a typical *Iliadic* battle. First, two armies in dense ranks, called phalanxes in the text, approach to within missile range, at which time a missile bombardment of throwing spears and arrows takes place. The leading soldiers in the front line, the *promachoi*, then venture forward in an attempt to open gaps in the opposing army's formation. Once the *promachoi* have demonstrated their prowess, the dense ranks on both sides close and press against each other until one side breaks and retreats. This phase looks very much like the traditional scholarly picture of hoplite warfare. Latacz's final stage consists of the victorious army pursuing the fleeing enemy, while officers in the retreating force urge their own soldiers to stop the retreat and form fresh lines. If these officers do succeed in halting the retreat, the entire process can start over again. Latacz's reconstruction, while seeming to make sense of many passages in Homer's poem, has not convinced all readers.

Hans van Wees offers a different interpretation of Homeric battle, one emphasizing loose and fluid formations rather than dense phalanxes. For van Wees, readers of Homer cannot remove or deemphasize all references to one-on-one combat and the mobility of soldiers on the battlefield without doing violence to the text as a whole. Homer's warriors, beyond singling each other out for the sort of single combat sure to have been exciting for Homer's audience, also range freely from one end of the battlefield to the other and return to and from the camp at will, all while in the thick of heated battle. A representative passage describes the Trojan hero Aeneas ranging across the field to find and speak to a particular comrade, all in the thick of a melee:

When Aeneas saw Diomedes wearing down the ranks of Trojans, he went right through the tumult of spears searching for godlike Pandarus, in case he should find him somewhere. He found the good and brave son of Lycaon, approached him, and addressed him with a speech: "Pandarus, what are you doing with your bow and winged arrows, your glory?"

(5.166–5.172)

Rather than ignore these many passages, or treat them as literary embellishments as Latacz and Pritchett do, van Wees claims that the strange type of warfare found in the *Iliad* has a real-world parallel, namely the tribal warfare modern anthropologists have observed in the highlands of Papua New Guinea. Like Homer's heroes, fighters in Papua New Guinea are known to have employed nebulous formations – if indeed they can be called formations at all – in battle. Instead of rushing headlong into combat *en masse*, these warriors take the time to single out opponents from the other side, and spend a great deal of their effort on rattling their weapons and making belligerent displays rather than killing and dying. Warriors in the front line regularly trade places with those in the rear ranks, and also often withdraw from battle altogether to rest and chew tobacco, demonstrating the same sort of mobility during combat as Homer's heroes do. For van Wees, therefore, Homeric battle is both coherent and realistic, and probably represents the sort of tactics employed by the phalanxes of the early Archaic period in Greece, that is, Homer's own day. Thus, van Wees challenges not only the notion that phalanxes are predominant in Homer, but also the traditional understanding of the hoplite phalanx itself, a topic to which we will return in the next chapter.

Perhaps the stalemate between the Latacz/Pritchett interpretation of Homeric battle on the one hand and that of van Wees on the other cannot be resolved. Both sides, after all, have strong support in the text, which might turn out to be mutually contradictory. Earlier scholars who saw in Homer's description of battle a literary jumble and smorgasbord might have had a point. In an article responding to this debate, I argued that both sides were in fact right, that there are phalanxes depicted on the plain before Troy, and there are also looser formations which allow Homeric warriors a great deal of mobility and opportunities for single combat. The discrepancy between the different descriptions of battle can be explained by the fact that tactics in the *Iliad* are variegated rather than uniform. Homer's Greek force is in fact a coalition made up of dozens of different states, from many different regions of the Greek world. It is reasonable to suppose that these different contingents might have employed different ways of war – which would parallel the real armies of the Late Bronze Age, in which ethnic divisions within larger forces, such as the Shardana in Egypt, often retained their own particular equipment and tactics. Most of the fighters on the plain of Troy might have fought as best they could, in dense formations where possible but more often than not in a loosely organized melee. The Greek force would have been buttressed, however, by elite units, especially those troops under great champions like Ajax and Achilles. In many respects, Achilles' force, called the Myrmidons, are clearly distinct from the rest of the Greek army, including in their level of battlefield skill. Where phalanxes predominate in the text, it is usually these elite forces that are being portrayed.

Aside from the soldiers themselves, chariots present an interesting challenge for students of military history. Chariots are prominent in both the *Iliad* and the *Odyssey*, as they were also in the material culture of the Late Bronze Age. The centuries between the collapse of the Mycenaean palaces and the composition of

Homeric poetry, however, show virtually no evidence of chariots at all, a likely reflection of the relative poverty of this period. Because of this long gap, some have suggested that Homer simply did not understand how chariots were used in battle, but includes them anyway to give his story some Bronze Age flair. All prominent warriors in the epics ride chariots, and chariots along with their teams of horses represent the pinnacle of battlefield prizes. The actual role of chariots in battle, though, is sometimes unclear. Where the armies of the Egyptians and the Hittites were dominated by large chariot formations that regularly played decisive parts in battle, Homer's chariots appear to be little more than taxis for elite champions. There are some scenes in the *Iliad* depicting soldiers fighting and dying from chariots, yet for the most part heroes go to and from combat on chariot but dismount before fighting their opponents. In the *Iliad*, chariots serve few functions beyond that of the chariot used to convey Odysseus' son Telemachus between Greek cities in the *Odyssey*. Maybe chariots are a clumsy literary intrusion into a picture warfare that reflects Homer's own day more than the Bronze Age. Then again, it is unlikely that the Mycenaeans used chariots in the same way as their contemporaries, given the unsuitability of the Greek terrain for large chariot formations in battle. But Mycenaean rulers used chariots in any case, probably, as we have already discussed, to emulate their peers in Egypt, the Hittite Empire, and other Near Eastern kingdoms. The historical Mycenaean approach to chariots might not have been much different than Homer's literary portrayal.

While the *Iliad* is in many ways a poem about raging battles, we must remember that pitched battle between infantry soldiers is but a fraction of the warfare represented in the Homeric epics. The *Odyssey*'s protagonist is the shrewd unconventional fighter who masterminded the Trojan Horse, but the *Iliad* also alludes to plenty of other military activities, including raiding, sieges, and instances of trickery aside from the fabled Trojan Horse. Book 10 of the *Iliad* describes a night raid undertaken by Odysseus and Diomedes, in which these stalwart warriors slaughter a contingent of Troy's Thracian allies in their sleep, before making off with a prize chariot team. This book is frequently labeled a later addition to the text, for reasons of language and vocabulary, but also because of its seemingly incongruent subject matter. However, this night raid is not unlike other operations described in uncontroversially authentic passages. Before the Trojan Horse, an episode of crafty deceit if there ever was one, Odysseus had infiltrated the walls of Troy in disguise, only to be recognized by Helen. The women-as-war-prizes Chryseis and Briseis, who sparked the conflict between Agamemnon and Achilles, were both taken in small raiding operations far from the main theater of action. On their way home from Troy, Odysseus and his men conduct a murderous plundering raid against the Kikones, a Thracian people in the north Aegean. The Trojan Horse itself, if likely a literary invention, bespeaks the kind of subterfuge common in siege warfare in the time before effective siege engines and tactics had been developed by the Greeks. Homer, just like the historiographical sources that followed him, might have focused his creative energies on describing great battles, but war is rarely only a matter of open confrontation between armies.

All things considered, I think warfare in general, and infantry battle in particular, in the *Iliad* is intelligible, if clearly subject to literary embroidery, and reveals a variety of equipment and tactics that cannot be neatly situated into one scholarly box or another. As we will see throughout the course of this book, I think the scholarly boxes themselves are a little too neat and tidy, and that no warfare of any period can be as cleanly schematized as has been the custom among ancient historians for generations. It is unlikely that scholars will ever resolve the debates swirling around Homeric warfare. What is far more certain and concrete is the effect Homer's poems had on later generations of Greeks. It is this reception of Homeric descriptions of warfare and warriors that represents epic poetry's most important contribution to Greek military history.

Homeric receptions

What drove Homer's heroes to fight? What made Homer's heroes "heroic" and worthy of emulation? Most importantly, how did Homer's heroes influence Greeks in the Archaic, Classical, and Hellenistic periods? First of all, we must define what a Homeric hero is. In later periods, the Greek word "hero" became a religious term denoting a certain class of demigod that received cultic veneration at designated hero-shrines. Often these heroes were identified with figures from Homeric epics. For example, near Sparta, the mythological home of Menelaus, there was a prominent shrine to Menelaus, still visible today overlooking the Eurotas valley. Other areas in Greece were replete with similar shrines, frequently emphasizing figures tied to a particular location. For Homer and other early Archaic authors, however, "hero" did not have such a clear religious meaning. Homer, and especially Hesiod, who likely composed his poems not long after the *Iliad* and *Odyssey*, conceived of warriors like Achilles and Hector as members of a different race, standing as intermediaries between even earlier and more god-like beings and present-day humans. Famous warriors of the "Heroic Age" were quite literally different from normal men and women: closer to the gods (in fact, sometimes directly related to gods as family members), stronger, more beautiful, and possessed of a wider range of passions. As Michael Clarke points out, in the *Iliad* and *Odyssey*, "hero" is nearly a synonym for "man," such were those who roamed the earth in the time of the Trojan War. Homer's heroes, therefore, are not the "main characters" of the epics, but virtually all the individuals Homer names and for whom he usually provides at least some genealogical details, regardless of whether or not these individuals appear in hundreds of lines or only a single verse.

Homer's heroes were preoccupied with fame and honor, respectively *kleos* and *timē* in Greek. Nearly without exception, the afterlife in Greek thought was a grim affair, an eternal existence as a ghostly shade in the gloomy halls of Hades. As Nathan Arrington argues, we cannot understand the sacrifice of Greek soldiers in the same way as that of modern soldiers, such as those who fought and died in the two World Wars of the twentieth century. For many modern warriors in the West, the promise of a richly rewarded afterlife in a Christian heaven compensated for the mortal sacrifices made in battle against the enemy. The Greeks looked forward to no such eternal reward, and therefore strove to be remembered and honored after death by their family and other members of the community.[10] Because of their view of death, a famous and remembered name was of paramount importance for Homer's characters, as it was for Greeks of later periods too.

Homer's heroes were also fiercely competitive. It was not enough to be famous. One strove to be *more* famous than others. One Homeric warrior is famously encouraged to "be the best, better than all the rest" (*Iliad* 6.208). In the nineteenth century, scholars such as Friedrich Nietzsche and Jacob Burckhardt identified this competitiveness, centered on the *agōn*, or "struggle," as the animating spirit of ancient Greek life. It is in the context of constant competition that Achilles' rage at Agamemnon for stealing his war-prize can be understood. A hero earned the right to *kleos* and *timē* by demonstrating superior *aretē*, the Greek word for excellence. Although the term eventually came to mean something close to "virtue," it originally had far less ethical significance. Rather, Homeric heroes conceived of *aretē* as simply being good – or better than others – at any particular thing, primarily fighting on the battlefield and speaking in the assembly. If a hero demonstrated ample *aretē* by, for example, killing a great number of the most valiant enemy soldiers, he would be rewarded with an outward sign of his *aretē*, such as a valuable status-object or even a human prize like the beautiful Briseis. This outward symbol of *aretē* is called in Greek *geras*, and it was the public removal of his *geras* that sparked Achilles' deadly wrath.

The "heroic code" operative in Homeric and other Archaic poetry can be summed up thus: a hero strives with others in *aretē* in order to receive *geras*, which then translates to *kleos* and *timē* that ideally persist long after the hero has died – as indeed it did with figures like Achilles. This competition for fame and honor was a zero-sum game, that is, a hero typically received recognition as being better than others, who in turn enjoyed less recognition. There really was not enough room in the Greek camp for both Agamemnon, who enjoyed his status based on his command of the greatest number of men, and Achilles, who was honored because he was the best at killing. A central theme of the *Iliad* is the tension between different responses to the heroic code, namely that which represents the surest sign of true *aretē*, and the limits of the heroic code. Achilles explicitly rejects the code, only to return to fight because of grief and a desire for revenge rather than to obtain *kleos* and *timē* (though he did gain these distinctions in any case).

Every educated Greek of later generations knew the *Iliad* and *Odyssey*, and often memorized large sections. Even those many Greeks who were not elite enough to receive a thorough literary education were steeped in a culture that embraced the Homeric warriors as moral and military examples, and as suitable objects of actual worship and cult. Not that emulating Homer's heroes was unproblematic. First of all, as we have seen, within the poems themselves there are competing views on what constitutes *aretē*. Is Agamemnon the most excellent of Greeks because he commands the most men? Or is Achilles the greatest

Figure 1.6 Achilles and Ajax playing dice on an Attic black-figure amphora by Exekias, *c.*540–530 BCE.

because he kills the most men? Is Achilles' refusal to fight a fitting response to a slight against his honor, and is his return to battle to slaughter countless Trojans out of grief appropriate behavior for a hero? Or are Hector's selfless efforts to protect his city and family to be preferred? The *Iliad* begins with the wrath of Achilles, but it ends with the stirring burial of Hector. Is the open warfare of the *Iliad*'s great battles the best forum for demonstrating *aretē*, or do the clever words and devious tricks of Odysseus also reveal an excellent warrior? This very debate was apparently the subject of a lecture given at Athens by Hippias of Elis, a famous teacher who is portrayed as conversing with Socrates in Plato's *Hippias Minor*. And finally, as Michael Clarke asks, can and should Greek war-riors emulate Homer's heroes, who were from a different race of humans and therefore capable of greater feats in battle but also subject to dangerous extremes of passion ill-suited to regular human soldiers?

Yet emulate them they did. Whether or not the hoplite phalanx was reflective of how Homer's heroes fought, it was regular practice for painters of both black- and red-figure pottery to represent Homeric warriors as hoplites contemporary with the vases themselves. Greek vase painters were in this way no different from Renaissance artists who depicted Jesus and the Apostles in the garb of fifteenth-century Florentines. Still, the message was probably clear: figures like Achilles and Ajax fought like hoplites, and therefore hoplites should fight like Achilles and Ajax. J. E. Lendon, in his brilliant survey of Greek and Roman Warfare, *Soldiers and Ghosts*, argues that many tactical developments of Archaic, Classical, and Hellenistic Greece were based on the desire to copy Homer. For example, the rigid formations and stand-your-ground passive courage required in the phalanx might have been a way to demonstrate excel-lence in a context without glorious single combat. After the clash of phalanxes, those soldiers who stood firm would be revealed to possess the most *aretē*. By the same token, the light-armed fighting of the fourth century BCE, notably that of so-called peltasts, who hurled javelins, could have been an attempt to fight in ways similar to the *Iliad*'s spear-throwing soldiers. The very fact that Greek generals led from the front, and tended to die in high numbers, is at least partly rooted in the example set by the *Iliad*'s *promachoi*, the front-fighters who took the lion's share of the glory. When Alexander's soldiers mutinied on their march back west, he appealed to their conscience by offering to reveal all the wounds he had sustained in battle (Arrian *Anabasis* 7.10.1), wounds that Troy's king Priam said were noble and beautiful for a warrior in his prime to possess (*Iliad* 22.71–22.73).

Later authors regularly depict real historical battles and soldiers in Homeric terms. Herodotus, for example, lists by name the most valiant soldiers on both sides after a major engagement (in, for example, 9.71–9.75) just like Homer singles out the leading troops among the Greeks and Trojans at the end of his catalogue of the forces in Book 2 of the *Iliad*. Before the Battle of Plataea in 479 BCE, as recounted by Herodotus, the Persian commander Mardonius insults the Spartans and called their courage into question (Herodotus 9.48), in much the same way that Agamemnon chides his own soldiers for much of *Iliad*

Book 4, demonstrating that the same appeals to courage or the lack thereof resonated with Homeric and historical Greek soldiers. Herodotus also depicts the struggle over the body of the fallen Spartan king Leonidas at Thermopylae (7.225) in such a way as to recall the Homeric struggle over the body of Achilles' slain friend, Patroclus (*Iliad* 17). Thucydides, too, has been recognized as depicting the Spartan general Brasidas as a new Homeric hero. In the struggle between the Athenians and Spartans for control of Pylos in 425 BCE, Brasidas valiantly encourages his men before fainting from his wounds (4.12), just like Homer's heroes do on several occasions. At Amphipolis three years later, Brasidas rouses his men by claiming to practice the same courage he expects from others, before dashing off to his death against the Athenians (5.9). The entirety of the treatment of Brasidas in Thucydides has been labeled an *aristeia*, the literary term applied to extended passages of individual heroism in epic poetry.[11] Even the great philosopher Socrates, pleading his case before an Athenian jury in Plato's *Apology*, appeals to the *Iliadic* Achilles as a moral example of preferring death to disgrace and dishonor (Plato *Apology* 28c–d). Socrates is best known as the founder of Western ethical philosophy, but he also served as an Athenian hoplite in several battles during the Peloponnesian War.

Aside from tactics and a soldier's general attitude to battle, in the Classical period Homer's Trojan War became a cultural rallying cry for the Greeks to unite in order to crush the Persians, widely represented in art and thought as the new Trojans. In the fourth century BCE, some Greeks tired of the constant warfare between the Greek poleis, and instead appealed to ideas of pan-Hellenism. Agesilaus, an energetic Spartan king, launched an invasion of Asia and presented himself as a new Agamemnon by trying to offer sacrifice on behalf of the campaign at Aulis in Boeotia, like Agamemnon did before the Trojan War (Xenophon *Hellenica* 3.4.3–3.4.4). Alexander the Great, succeeding where Agesilaus had failed, reportedly slept with a copy of the *Iliad* under his pillow (Plutarch *Alexander* 8), and stopped at Troy after he crossed over to Asia, where he and his companion Hephaestion paid homage to Achilles and Patroclus respectively (Arrian *Anabasis* 1.11–1.12). Agesilaus and Alexander were only expressing more overtly an idea that had long been simmering. In the fifth century BCE, for example, Herodotus begins his monumental history by presenting the Persian Wars as just the latest in a long series of conflicts between monolithic and largely contrived cultures of "Europe" and "Asia." Herodotus' sources claim that the Trojan War was among these conflicts (1.1–1.5).

The Trojan War, either as presented in the Homeric epics or in other works of the so-called "Epic Cycle," provided the later Greeks – especially the Athenians – with material with which to reflect on war in general and on particular wars and military questions. As a general rule, mythology served as the base upon which Attic tragic playwrights built their commentaries on contemporary questions, and the Trojan War looms large in the tragedies that have survived to the present day and is featured in many of the titles of now-lost plays. An especially poignant example is Euripides' *Trojan Women*, which treats in horrifying detail the wretched lot of the surviving women of Troy at the hands of their Greek conquerors. Euripides produced his play in 415 BCE, a year after the Athenians sacked the tiny island of Melos, killing its men and enslaving its women and children. The indignities inflicted upon the royal women of Troy, who had lost their husbands in bloody battle only to be taken as the sex-slaves of their husbands' very killers, mirror the sufferings of the victims of Athens' imperialistic democracy in the Peloponnesian War.

Though Euripides is perhaps harsher towards his fellow Athenians than other tragedians, he is no innovator in dramatizing war as an ugly stain on humanity. The *Iliad* itself, while demonstrating that the greatest heroes are those who possess *aretē* in the realm of killing, contains plenty of passages that can be read as anti-war, or at least aware that war is a true horror. The foreboding of Andromache, Hector's wife, at the imminent death of her husband in Book 6, and the terror of Priam in Book 22 at the prospect that his aged body will be left as pathetic fodder for wild beasts, provided plenty of inspiration for Euripides and others as they wrestled with portraying war in all its grim elements. The feast of the gods at the end of *Iliad* Book 1, in which the Olympians, all of whom have taken one side or another in the Trojan War, resolve their divine disputes in order to feast and be merry stands as a painful contrast to the life of mortal humans, for whom deadly war seems inevitable, even necessary. As Achilles pursues Hector around the walls of Troy in Book 22, Homer points out the landmarks that the people enjoyed during peace, including the washbasins where the Trojan women would gather and converse as they did their households' laundry in the time of peace before the Greeks came (22.151–22.156). I detect a similar sentiment in the words of the Lydian king Croesus in Herodotus (1.87): "No one is foolish enough to choose war over peace. In peace, sons bury fathers; but in war, fathers bury sons."

Homeric battle: the Duel of Paris and Menelaus, and its aftermath

Since Homeric warfare is most valuable for our purposes in how it was interpreted by later Greeks – and applied to historical Greek warfare – let us take a closer look at one of the most striking scenes of combat in the *Iliad*: the duel between Paris and Menelaus in Book 3 and the pitched battle that breaks out in Book 4. These passages give us an idea of the equipment and tactics Homer envisioned, even if they represent primarily his literary imagination. The duel and its aftermath also reveal some of the most important cultural aspects of Homeric warfare that continued to hold sway many centuries later.

As the Greek and Trojan armies approached each other on the plain in front of Troy, Homer employs striking similes to form an image of the action. The Trojan side, made up of many peoples speaking many languages, is said to fill the air with a chaotic clamor, just like the racket made by flocks of cranes as they swoop over Africa. The Greeks, on the other hand, move forward in silence, bravely resolving to stand firm by one another. Perhaps not too much should be made of this literary contrast between the two sides, but the idea of the better trained and more fearsome army advancing in silence is one happily adopted by the historical Spartans. In the same way, non-Greeks, who are often depicted as the successors of the Trojans, are frequently stereotyped in historical periods as multi-lingual mobs generally lacking in composure, a stark comparison with the unilingual and calm Greeks. Such unflattering portraits of non-Greeks become especially common after the Persian Wars of the early fifth century BCE, when this Iliadic passage probably resonated deeply.

Proudly stepping out in front of his lines, Paris vaunted his prowess in front of the Greek troops and looked for a challenger in single combat. These duels, fought often in the midst of pitched battle, are what cause many readers to dismiss Homeric battle as nothing more than artistic fiction. How, after all, could two soldiers deliberately single each other out amid the throng and din of pitched battle? However, duels were a common feature of warfare across many cultures and in many periods. The eminent scholar of Greek warfare, W. K. Pritchett, has gathered all the examples of real historical duels in Greek history, and there are many. While it might strain credulity to portray warriors having as much freedom of movement and choice of combat partner as Homer's warriors seem to have, the duel itself is an important historical phenomenon, and was revered in Greek culture as a particularly manly and impressive activity. Alexander the Great himself, one of history's biggest fans of Homer, conceived of his huge battles as duels between himself and Darius, Great King of the Persian Empire. At both Issus and Gaugamela, Alexander even spied out Darius himself, and rushed towards him in an attempt to kill him personally, all in the thick of massed combat.

When Menelaus saw Paris, he was filled with delight; now he finally had the chance to kill the one who stole Helen. Paris, however, recoiled in terror at seeing Menelaus, at which no one who knows the story of the Trojan War and the character of its most notorious prince – handsome yet hardly a strapping warrior – should be surprised. But after being chided by his brother, Hector, Paris agreed to a duel between himself and Menelaus to settle the war once and for all. To the victor will go Helen and the treasures she brought with her to Troy, while the rest of the soldiers on both sides will go home to live in peace. Aside from such duels really happening several times in the historical period, the way the duel is described suggests several important cultural aspects of warfare, even if the combat itself betrays unrealistic, stylized elements.

As the two heroes prepare for battle, the poet describes in loving detail each element of Paris' armor and weaponry while the Trojan prince equips himself. Vivid literary portraits of the instruments of war are common in Homer's poetry – none more famous than the long description of Achilles' shield, which encapsulates many of the *Iliad*'s central themes – and this trend continues well into the Classical period, especially in visual art. Many examples of painted pottery, for example, show warriors arming for battle. Even more artistic pieces focus on dazzlingly rendered shields and weapons, a vehicle by which the artist could show his skill, to be sure, but also a reflection of the continued importance of a soldier's arms and armor for the Greeks.

Since a duel is a highly ritualized form of combat, the two combatants drew lots to determine who could first hurl his spear. In historical periods, Greek heavy infantry used spears only for thrusting, while more lightly armed troops used javelins, a much smaller weapon, for throwing. Homer's warriors, on the other hand, seem to use the same weapon for both throwing and thrusting, a form of combat unattested in other Greek sources. Perhaps this hybrid spear is a poetic fiction, or perhaps Homer's warriors carried two different spears – though Homer describes even the thrown spears as "long-shadowing," indicating a sizeable weapon. After marking out the space for the duel, Paris threw his spear at Menelaus, which just glanced off Menelaus' shield without inflicting any damage. Menelaus then took his turn, hurling his own spear with such force that it broke through Paris' shield and armor, but failed to wound the Trojan. Enraged, Menelaus closed on Paris, striking him with his sword on the crest of the helmet, only to have the sword shatter in his hands. Menelaus then seized the helmet of Paris, who was stunned by the sword blow, and began to drag him towards the Greek lines. The Trojan prince could only pull at his helmet strap helplessly as he approached certain death. By any measure, Menelaus had won the duel, and would soon have his fill of glory by killing his nemesis, stripping him of his armor, and ending the war in one fell swoop. Paris' divine champion, Aphrodite, however, had other plans. Shifting from a fairly realistic portrayal of single combat, Homer describes the goddess shrouding Paris in mist and spiriting him away to his bedroom before Menelaus could finish the job. Outraged to find himself holding only an empty helmet, Menelaus tossed it into the crowd of his comrades. The duel had solved nothing, despite Agamemnon's protests that his brother had won and the Trojans should yield.

Pitched battle broke out between the two sides after the Trojan Pandarus, supposedly spurred on by Athena, who wanted the fighting to continue, shot Menelaus with an arrow. Before he did so, his bow is lovingly described, just as Paris' arms and armor had been. While drawing back his arrow, Pandarus was protected by the shields of his companions, just the sort of tactic used by the Greek archer Teucer, who frequently fought from behind the shield of the mighty Ajax. Light-armed troops making use of the shields of their more heavily armed allies is a technique advocated by the Spartan poet Tyrtaeus in the seventh century BCE, suggesting that Homer's description here is a realistic one. Prior to the "canonical" hoplite warfare of the fifth century BCE, light-armed troops and ranged weapons seem to have been a regular part of Greek warfare, and they were not nearly as despised as is sometimes assumed. Sure, the cowardly Paris was an archer, but so were many braver fighters on both sides in the Trojan War. After Pandarus loosed his arrow and struck Menelaus, he was reviled not because of his archery, but because of his treacherous violation of the truce that had been in force for the duel.

After the wounded Menelaus withdrew from the field temporarily to receive medical attention, the Greeks prepared to engage en masse with the Trojans, who had already decided on battle and were closing in. Before the two sides came to blows, Agamemnon ranged up and down his ranks to harangue his men, singling out individual heroes for specific encouragement, and sometimes chastisement as befitting military "reverse psychology." While it is difficult to imagine an effective speech being given to an entire army, especially as the enemy quickly approaches in full gear, our sources from historical periods nearly always include a pre-battle speech from the commander. Alexander the Great, before the Battle of Gaugamela, ranged up and down the ranks of his men as he steeled them for battle against a far larger force. Like Agamemnon, Alexander called out individual soldiers by name and celebrated them for their exploits earlier in the campaign. Homer's leaders had set the example for all Greek generals.

Homer describes the Greeks marching into battle silently, heeding the commands of their leaders. The Trojans, by contrast, are once again derided as a multi-lingual mob, bleating like sheep according to Homer's simile. As the two sides met one another, shield pressed against shield in an image of massed warfare that resembles the hoplite phalanx. Soon after, however, the battle devolved into a series of one-on-one duels, either due to poetic embellishment, or because Homer's warriors do not fight in phalanx-like dense formations for long. As the battle stretches over the next several books, one of the most notable sections is the *aristeia* – a sort of epic set-piece that shows off a hero's accomplishments – of the Greek leader Diomedes, who killed many great Trojans before turning to fight the gods themselves, who regularly participate in Homeric battle. Diomedes wounded the hand of Aphrodite, before turning to fight the war-god himself, Ares, and wounding him too. While real Greek soldiers were unlikely to have fought the gods of Olympus, anyone who had participated in a pitched battle would have seen episodes of berserker rage of the type displayed by Homer's Diomedes. And sources like Herodotus do often include stories of gods or heroes taking part in battles, indicating that the Greeks of the historical period did not see divine intervention in war as something beyond belief.

The stripping of arms from slain enemies, for the personal glory of their killers, is a key feature of battle in the *Iliad*, often to comic effect since many warriors are killed while they are busy hauling off a dead man's breastplate. Though stripping a fallen opponent is unlikely to have happened in the midst of a melee, displaying an enemy's weapons was an important way for later Greeks to commemorate victories. A battlefield trophy, set up at the point where the enemy was turned to flight, typically consisted of an ad hoc monument decorated with the weapons and armor of the vanquished. On the parapet below the Temple of Athena Nike on the Athenian Acropolis, the Athenians displayed the shields taken from nearly 300 Lacedaemonians who were captured in 425 BCE. One of these shields, inscribed with the message "taken from the Lacedaimonians at Pylos," can still be viewed in the Agora museum. Later Greeks followed in the Homeric heroes' footsteps by viewing a battlefield victory as worth much more if one could show off afterwards.

As a final note on the battle that raged following the duel between Paris and Menelaus, let us consider the curious exchange between the Greek Diomedes and the Trojan Glaucus in Book 6.119–6.236. As the two are about to fight to the death in the midst of the raging battle, they pause in order to recite to one another their respective lineages. When they discover that their families have ties stretching back generations, rather than fight they exchange armor (Diomedes gets by far the better end of the bargain) before turning aside to fight other opponents. Leaving aside the absurdity of two soldiers engaging in a lengthy conversation on the battlefield, that family ties would bring enemies together is quite in keeping with later practice. Alexander I, the king of Macedonia in the early fifth century BCE, was sent by the Persians to negotiate terms with the Athenians, since Alexander's family had ties to Athens (Herodotus 8.136). The Homeric idea of guest-friendship between individuals and families continued in the Archaic and Classical periods, especially among the elite, while individuals could also represent in their home city the interests of entire cities with whom they had historic ties.

In terms of the history of Greek warfare, the extent to which the duel between Paris and Menelaus and the subsequent battle is an accurate representation of the combat of any period is perhaps less important than the cultural impact it had on all later Greeks. Whether or not Greeks fighting in Archaic, Classical, and Hellenistic battles knew such passages by heart – the elite certainly did – Homeric battle was simply part of the Greek understanding of war. Just as Homer's poetry formed a foundation for the Greek view of themselves and the world, let it inform our own study of Greek warfare.

Notes

1 As a topic, Minoan human sacrifice obviously attracts great popular interest, though the evidence is not conclusive: https://archaeologynewsnetwork.blogspot.com/2014/01/possible-evidence-of-human-sacrifice-at.html#sWLHDtXbpGFcdfLK.97.
2 The standard work on these frescoes is Doumas (1992).
3 Davis and Stocker (2016, 2017) and their team continue to analyze the finds from this spectacular tomb.
4 A terrific example and microcosm of the interconnectedness of the eastern Mediterranean in the Late Bronze Age is the Uluburn Shipwreck, a vessel of the fourteenth century BCE found off the coast of Turkey. An up-to-date account of this ship and its contents can be found in Pulak (2010).
5 As translated by Trevor Bryce (after Gardiner) (2005, 237–238).
6 For this stele, see Yadin (1963, vol. 1. 134–135). Throughout this section, I rely heavily on Yadin and also Beal (1992), Bryce (2005), Drews (1993), and Spalinger (2005).
7 Translated by Kitchen (1982, 40–41).
8 For the Mycenaeans represented at Amarna, see Parkinson and Schofield (1994); for Mycenaeans on the Uluburun wreck, see Pulak (2005).
9 For mercenaries in the Pylos Linear B tablets, see Driessen and MacDonald (1984); see also Chadwick (1976, 175–176), who argues that these foreign tribesmen were simply used in lesser positions such as lookouts, and were probably not trusted in the regular army. For the importance of foreign troops for Mycenaean armies, see Drews (1993, 155–156) and Driessen and MacDonald (1984, 52–56).
10 Arrington (2015, 7–8). Arrington's book is essential reading for understanding how the Classical Athenians understood death in battle, and how the Classical practice differed but also drew from traditions such as Homeric epic.
11 For a discussion of Brasidas as a Homeric figure in Thucydides, see Hornblower (1991–2008, vol. 2, 38–61).

Further reading

Beckman, Gary. 1999. *Hittite Diplomatic Texts*. Atlanta.

A useful collection of Hittite documents in English translation, providing insight into diplomacy in the Late Bronze Age, including the reasons states went to war. Several texts highlight the interactions between the Hittites and the Ahhiyawans, who might be Homer's Achaeans.

Burckhardt, Jacob. 1963. *History of Greek Culture*. New York.

An abridged English translation of this Swiss historian's seminal work highlighting the competitive spirit among the ancient Greeks.

Chadwick, John. 1976. *The Mycenaean World*. Cambridge.

A standard reference work written by one of the scholars who deciphered Linear B.

Clarke, Michael. 2004. "Manhood and Heroism." In Robert Fowler (ed.), *The Cambridge Companion to Homer*. Cambridge. 74–90.

A concise treatment of manhood and heroism in Homer's poetry, including a discussion of how later Greeks viewed Homer's heroes.

Cline, Eric H. (ed.). 2010. *The Oxford Handbook of the Bronze Age Aegean*. Oxford.

A collection of chapters on various topics pertaining to the Aegean Bronze Age, including warfare, trade, and cultural interaction.

Cline, Eric H. (ed.). 2014. *1177 B.C.: The Year Civilization Collapsed*. Princeton.

This book is essential reading for understanding the interconnected world of the Late Bronze Age and the collapse of major kingdoms throughout the eastern Mediterranean at the end of the thirteenth century BCE.

Drews, Robert. 1993. *The End of the Bronze Age: Changes in Warfare and the Catastrophe ca. 1200 B.C.* Princeton.

A survey of Late Bronze Age warfare and an explanation of the Bronze Age collapse of kingdoms as due to the introduction of a new type of sword.

Finley, M. I. 1954. *The World of Odysseus*. New York.

This classic study treats the Homeric poems as providing insight into Early Iron Age and early Archaic Greek society rather than the Late Bronze Age.

Fowler, Robert (ed.). 2004. *The Cambridge Companion to Homer*. Cambridge.

An accessible and interesting collection of essays, written by leading scholars, on a variety of scholarly issues pertaining to Homer.

Kirk, G. S. (ed.). 1985–1993. *The Iliad: A Commentary*. Cambridge.

This multi-volume commentary on Homer's *Iliad* is the standard reference work for anyone wanting to study the text in depth.

Latacz, Joachim. 1977. *Kampfparänese, Kampfdarstellung und Kampfwirklichkeit in der Ilias, bei Kallinos und Tyrtaios*. München.

Though in German, this book was groundbreaking in its attempt to present a coherent account of battle in the *Iliad*, which Latacz argues is reflected in the Archaic poetry of Callinus and Tyrtaeus.

Latacz, Joachim. 2005. *Troy and Homer: Towards a Solution of an Old Mystery*. Oxford.

A thorough discussion of the historicity of the Trojan War and the archaeological excavations at Troy.

Lendon, J. E. 2005. *Soldiers and Ghosts: A History of Battle in Classical Antiquity.* New Haven.

Argues that successive developments in Greek warfare were due to a desire to emulate the fighting styles and ethics of Homer's warriors.

Morris, Ian and Barry Powell (eds.). 1997. *A New Companion to Homer.* Leiden.

Although more than twenty years old, this edited collection provides a comprehensive overview of the main areas of Homeric studies.

Pritchett, W. K. 1985. *The Greek State at War, Vol. 4.* Berkeley.

While arguing that battle in the *Iliad* likely represents a mixture of time periods, Pritchett says dense phalanxes appear to be the norm in the poem. He also provides a list of duels in Greek antiquity, showing that ritualized one-on-one combat is not out of the ordinary even in historical periods.

Raaflaub, Kurt. 2008. "Homeric Warriors and Battles: Trying to Resolve Old Problems." *Classical World* 101: 469–483.

Explains the mixture of fantastic and realistic elements of battle in the *Iliad* by reference to Homer's alteration between broad panoramic and narrow scenic perspectives.

Sears, Matthew A. 2010. "Warrior Ants: Elite Troops in the *Iliad*." *Classical World* 103: 139–155.

Resolves the inconsistencies in Homeric battles by suggesting that there were many types of units and tactics at Troy, and that the troops with Achilles and Ajax represented elite units that fought in denser formations than the other soldiers.

Strauss, Barry. 2007. *The Trojan War: A New History.* New York.

Bringing together literary and archaeological evidence, Strauss writes a compelling "what if?" history of the Trojan War, analyzing the conflict as if it were a real military event in the Late Bronze Age.

van Wees, Hans. 1992. *Status Warriors: War, Violence, and Society in Homer and History.* Amsterdam.

In this volume, van Wees offers his views not only on Homeric warfare, but on Homeric society in general.

van Wees, Hans. 2004. *Greek Warfare: Myths and Realities.* London.

A broad study of Greek warfare distilling many of van Wees' most important scholarly contributions, including his ideas on loose formations in the *Iliad.*

Yadin, Yigael. 1963. *The Art of Warfare in Biblical Lands.* New York.

A standard resource, complete with detailed illustrations and images.

2 The hoplite phalanx

The rise of the polis

Introduction

Perhaps the single most important subject in the study of ancient Greek warfare is the hoplite phalanx, the dense formation of heavy-armed infantrymen that dominated Greek battle for centuries. Perhaps unsurprisingly, the hoplite phalanx is also among the most controversial and contentious of scholarly topics. As well it should be, given that the stakes for ancient history could not be higher. As a tactical development and way of battle, understanding the phalanx is necessary for any picture of warfare between Greek states, and between Greeks and various non-Greek peoples. The outcome of the Persian invasion of Greece, for example, was largely due to the superiority of hoplites to less heavily armed troops. The phalanx, however, is important well beyond the battlefield. A standard line on Greek history is that the polis itself, along with its attendant values such as egalitarianism and mass political participation, went hand-in-hand with the hoplite phalanx, and that the polis might in fact be the natural and inevitable result of phalanx warfare. The hoplite phalanx, therefore, has long been held to be essential for understanding the ancient Greeks, and why they are a people worth studying even in the twenty-first century.

In this chapter, we will discuss the evidence for the rise of the hoplite phalanx in the early Archaic period, along with the equipment and tactics that defined this supposedly new way of war. We will also explore the various questions surrounding the phalanx's role in the rise of the polis, such as the socio-political leveling effect that standing side-by-side in a dense infantry formation had on the polis' first citizens. We will take a close look at several battles involving hoplites, including conflicts between Greek poleis and between the Greeks and the Persian Empire. Finally, we will consider the cultural preeminence of the hoplite in Greek society, particularly as demonstrated in dramatic literature and the visual arts. In important ways, this chapter will lay the foundation for the rest of the book, since hoplites and their heavy-armed successors were a fixture throughout ancient Greek military history, and the standard against which other ways of combat were judged.

The phalanx: its rise, equipment, and tactics

"Phalanx," a word meaning an infantry rank or formation, appears in the *Iliad*, though only in the plural. As we saw in the preceding chapter, some scholars take the presence of "phalanx" and words like it in descriptions of the battles on the plains of Troy to indicate that Homer means to convey massed infantry combat, rather than loose formations or no formations at all. "Hoplite" – a Greek term meaning a fully armed infantrymen, or a soldier equipped with a type of shield called a *hoplon* – does not appear in the Homeric epic, and for decades a majority of scholars believed that the hoplite and his specific type of equipment was a new phenomenon of the early Archaic period, that is, sometime around the late eighth and early seventh centuries BCE. Whether or not the *Iliad* represents the combat of the Late Bronze Age, the Early Iron Age, the early Archaic period, or a mixture of all three, the emergence of hoplite arms and armor and phalanx in which they were used were long thought to have revolutionized Archaic Greek warfare. But as we first touched on in our discussion of Homeric battle, it is far from certain that the Archaic period gave rise to a unique infantry formation such as had never before existed. Let us, then, first consider how the idea of a "hoplite revolution" first arose, and how the current scholarly debate stands.

As is implied by the very term "revolution," the hoplite phalanx is supposed to have emerged suddenly and decisively at a specific moment in history. This idea was widely popularized in 1947 by H. L. Lorimer in an article arguing that the emergence of the hoplite shield at some point in the seventh century BCE gave rise to a new type of dense formation, that is, the hoplite phalanx. This round shield, about 1 meter in diameter, concave, and held with the left arm via a unique double-grip, first appears in the archaeological record as dedications at sacred sites such as Olympia in the early 600s BCE. The round shield and dense formations also appear in vase-painting at about the same time, especially on the famous Chigi Vase, a Proto-Corinthian pitcher from the mid-600s BCE. The material record, according to Lorimer's thinking, thus provides a relatively certain *terminus post quem*, or earliest possible date, for the type of warfare such a shield would necessitate. In the more than seventy years since Lorimer's publication, no shields of this type have been found of markedly earlier date, meaning that if she was right about the link between the shield and the rise of the phalanx, her argument still stands. But what is so special about this shield in the first place?

The hoplite shield, sometimes called the *hoplon* but more regularly the *aspis*, is not special because of its size, shape, or even its concavity. Its material, namely wood, sometimes embellished with a bronze boss and rim, makes the hoplite shield heavier than some other ancient shields, such as the wickerwork shields favored among the soldiers of the Persian Empire. A shield's weight has a great effect on how it can be wielded. As a general rule, the heavier the shield the more protection its bearer would have, but at the expense of mobility. But many cultures favored large and heavy shields – like Ajax's fabled "tower shield" in the *Iliad* – over lighter and more maneuverable ones. Rather, it is the

Figure 2.1 The Chigi Vase, a Proto-Corinthian oenochoe depicting hoplites, mid-seventh century BCE.

Source: Museo Nazionale di Villa Giulia. Photo credit: Scala/Art Resource, NY.

double-grip that makes the hoplite shield a different sort of defensive arm. In the center of the concave shield was affixed a loop through which the hoplite put his arm up to the elbow, while on the shield's rim was a hand-grip, usually represented in art as a cord. Thus, the hoplite held his shield with his entire left forearm, providing for a remarkably stable and firm grip and allowing for a heavier shield to be wielded for longer periods of time. But, as scholars such as Lorimer point out, the hoplite shield's double-grip was the ultimate surrender of mobility in favor of greater security. In fact, according to the orthodox reconstruction of hoplite battle, a dense phalanx is the only possible formation appropriate to such shields.

When facing straight ahead, with feet planted shoulder-width apart – which is how most envision a hoplite standing in the ranks – a soldier can only cover the left half of his body with the shield. Being round and held by the forearm, the shield's center will line up with the left shoulder, leaving the right side of the soldier exposed. The only hope the soldier has for protecting himself on the right, given that his right arm is engaged in holding a spear or sword, is to find cover in the protruding half of the shield of the soldier to his right.

Therefore, not only did this new type of shield afford the soldier less freedom of movement to engage in skilled one-on-one combat, it also necessitated as dense a formation as possible, with each man depending for his very life on the man next to him. Later literary sources attest to this situation, especially Thucydides, who says that a hoplite phalanx tends to veer to the right as it advances into battle, since every soldier moves ever rightward in an attempt to cover his own unshielded side (5.71). The right wing, being by nature the most vulnerable position since there would be no protection for the soldiers' unshielded side, was understandably the traditional place of honor for those brave Greeks looking to demonstrate their superior courage and *aretē*. Spartan kings, for example, frequently went into battle on the extreme right lest anyone else appear to be braver, despite the danger to the army should the king himself fall.

The double-grip shield was an absolutely necessary piece of equipment for a hoplite. In addition to the many examples of shields dedicated at Olympia and other shrines, the shield and shield-imagery feature prominently in Greek military culture. A Spartan mother famously enjoined her son as he was going off to war to return either with his shield or on it, meaning he must either come home carrying his shield after standing firm in battle or being carried as a corpse on his shield (Plutarch *Moralia* 241f). A soldier without a shield was likely a coward who fled from the enemy, since the heavy shield would be the first thing to go in a panicked retreat. The Archaic lyric poet Archilochus mocks this military maxim by saying that he could not care less if an enemy laughs at him for abandoning his shield, since a new shield can be found without any trouble: "Some Saian delights in my shield, a faultless item, which I unwillingly left in a bush. But I saved myself. What do I care about the shield? To hell with it. I'll get another one just as good" (F 5). Archilochus' irreverence is only biting if the Spartan woman's sentiment was widely shared among the Greeks. In the same vein, shields were among the most prized spoils taken from a defeated enemy, frequently displayed on the battlefield itself as an ad hoc victory trophy. The archaeology museum in the Athenian Agora displays a shield taken from the Spartans from the Battle of Pylos in 425 BCE. This shield and hundreds like it were displayed in one of the most prominent public places in Athens, on the wall of the Acropolis beneath the Temple of Athena Nike.

Hoplites in the Archaic period were often protected by other pieces of defensive gear too, examples of which are also found as dedications and depicted in art. Early hoplites preferred the bronze helmet of the so-called Corinthian type, the iconic helmet that totally covered the head except for a small t-shaped gap for the eyes and mouth, interrupted by a protrusion to protect the nose. Like the shield, the Corinthian helmet afforded protection at the expense of mobility since it would have strictly limited what a soldier could see or hear, leaving few options other than to face ahead at a small fraction of the battlefield. Wealthier soldiers – hoplites, unlike many conscript or standing armies, had to supply their own equipment – supplemented the shield and helmet with other pieces of armor, including metal breastplates, shin guards called grieves, and even arm

Figure 2.2 Relief from the north frieze of the Siphnian Treasury at Delphi, depicting the battle of the giants against the gods, *c.*525 BCE.

Source: Archaeological Museum of Delphi. Photo credit: Erich Lessing/Art Resource, NY.

guards for the unshielded right side. A hoplite's offensive weapon was primarily the thrusting spear, with a wooden shaft about 2.5 meters long and a flat leaf-shaped iron blade. As a secondary blade and tool for finishing off fallen enemies, the spear usually had a bronze butt-spike with a square cross-section. Vase-painting and sculpture virtually without exception depict hoplites holding their spears in their right hands with an overhand grip. A hoplite's secondary weapon was an iron sword, either of a straighter thrusting type or a curved slashing type. The indelible image of a hoplite is a heavily armed and armored infantryman protected and burdened by a great deal of sturdy defensive and offensive equipment. Together in a phalanx, hoplites presented the enemy with a wall of shields and hedge of spears.

Traditional reconstructions of the hoplite phalanx envision a dense formation of soldiers with a broad front and a depth of eight ranks. Each hoplite would require approximately a square meter of space, meaning that a phalanx of 5,000 men – a rather large army for the Archaic period – would have a front of 650 meters but a depth of only 8. It is difficult to imagine such a broad yet shallow formation. Artistic representations of hoplites are of little help since they usually only show a few hoplites together, if they depict any sort of phalanx at all (as opposed to an idealized duel between two epic heroes clad as hoplites). Hollywood movies, too, tend to show great crowds of soldiers arranged in depth, if they are indeed arranged in a recognizable formation. The Roman legion, portrayed so memorably in plenty of sword-and-sandals films like 1960's *Spartacus*, was arrayed in a deep formation, since it kept about two-thirds of its soldiers in reserve at any given time instead of in direct contact with the enemy. The traditional hoplite phalanx, on the other hand, had no reserves. Instead, every available soldier was deployed against the enemy, and the success or failure of the army depended on the integrity of this single shallow battle line.

There are good tactical reasons for the shallowness of the typical phalanx. Since hoplite soldiers were apparently encumbered with much armor and awkward shields, and a heavy thrusting spear they wielded with an overhand grip, they could only really fight against an enemy positioned straight ahead of them. The flanks, or sides, of a phalanx were thus extremely vulnerable and were best kept as thin as possible, while the front was made as wide as possible. At the Battle of Marathon in 490 BCE, for example, the Athenians made the center of their phalanx even shallower than usual in order to stretch the front as far as they could to match the greater number of Persians arrayed against them (Herodotus 6.111). The main reason that the Spartans and their allies were so successful during the first two days of fighting the Persians at Thermopylae in 480 BCE was that the narrow terrain forced the Persians to attack the heavy-armed Greeks head-on rather than use their superior numbers to surround and overwhelm them (Herodotus 7.175–176).

Given the importance of providing a broad front, why have a depth of even eight ranks? The one-handed spears of hoplites were only long enough for the first two or maybe three ranks to project their points against the enemy, leaving the five or six rearmost ranks unable to kill their opponents directly. What, then, did these rear ranks do in battle? I can think of three perhaps complementary possibilities. The rear ranks either served as a reserve, to move up when needed to replace soldiers who were killed or wounded in the front ranks; or they provided moral support for the front-fighters while simultaneously preventing the front-fighters from shying away from the enemy; or they added literal weight to the push of the phalanx against its opponents. The first possibility is attractive because the nature of hoplite battle meant that if any gaps formed in the line – that is, the wall of shields and hedge of spears – the formation would be in danger of complete collapse and defeat. Replacing any fallen soldiers as quickly and seamlessly as possible would therefore be of great importance. The second possibility makes sense too, since soldiers might well fight more confidently knowing that a great crowd of their comrades stands behind them. At the same time, the terror of facing the spears of the enemy would be somewhat offset by the very impossibility of retreat or even withdrawal through the dense ranks of soldiers behind the front. Even Homer's leaders sometimes arranged their contingents with the best and bravest fighters in the exterior ranks, with the cowardly riff-raff sandwiched in the middle. The third possibility, however, has been the favorite of scholars, though it is today highly contentious and cuts to the heart of the debate about how hoplites actually fought.

The Greek noun *othismos*, which means a "push," and its related verb *otheō*, "to push," are often seen as central to understanding how the phalanx worked. An idea championed most famously in recent years by the scholar Victor Davis Hanson, the *othismos* has become the crucial element of hoplite battle, a mass shove through which the combined weight of one phalanx broke the formation of the other and thus won the day. Hanson and others vividly describe the operation of the *othismos* as the men in the front rank of one phalanx pressing their shields with all their might against the shields of the other phalanx's front rank, all the while trying to kill or wound enough opponents so that the enemy's shield wall buckles and collapses under constant pressure. This picture of battle evokes the line of scrimmage in an American football match, in which the players in the offensive line shove against the defensive line of the other team, at once trying to prevent the defenders from penetrating the offensive line to sack the quarterback and at the same time forcing gaps in the defensive line through which a running back can carry the ball. This activity of the front-fighters of both sides makes a lot of sense and is fairly intuitive. What is more difficult to picture is the role Hanson and others of his school posit for the ranks behind the front-fighters, namely physically shoving against their comrades in front by pressing their own shields into the backs of the front ranks to add weight to the *othismos*. Aside from American football, this mass shove in depth has been likened to a "rugby scrum from Hell," referencing a formation in sports that relies on the combined weight and shoving power of three rows of players rather than a single line. In this reconstructing of hoplite tactics, the eight rows of the phalanx would be important primarily for the weight and force they provide to the *othismos*, not merely for their roles as a reserve and source of moral support. The standard depth of eight ranks, therefore, would seem to be the ideal compromise between the competing needs for weight in the mass shove and a broad front to prevent being outflanked.

Is the mass shove as described by Hanson practical or even possible? From my perspective, writing this chapter seated at a comfortable desk in my office, I cannot imagine how the front-fighters would be able to sustain their own relentless pressure against the enemy as they attempt to fell opponents with spears and prevent their opponents' spears from hitting their mark – all while being unceasingly pushed from behind by seven ranks of men. Even I leave my desk from time to time, and have found that physical experiments with the phalanx formation do not make the *othismos* seem more plausible. When I taught at Wabash College, an all-male liberal arts college in Indiana, I held a mock battle as part of my course on ancient Greek and Roman warfare, for which several enterprising students in the class had constructed wooden shields and long metal poles tipped with foam to stand in for spears. For one of our experiments, we arranged both sides in the mock battle three or four rows deep (we did not have enough students for a full eight ranks) and instructed the rear ranks – mostly comprised of NCAA football and basketball players – to shove against those in front of them.

Standing in one of the front ranks myself, it was all I could do to maintain my footing while pressing my shield against the student arrayed against me, and after a few seconds of this mass shove, we called for a halt before any injuries resulted from the great pressure of bodies. Granted I was not wearing a Corinthian helmet (instead I donned a fencing mask) or a metal breastplate, but I came away from this experience amazed that any ancient soldier, especially one in the front ranks, made it through a pitched battle without serious injury. What also struck my students and me was just how exhausting wielding large shields became after only a few minutes, keeping in mind that most of the students were much larger than the typical ancient Greek, were not fighting in terror for their lives, and were enjoying a mild spring day rather than the oppressive heat of a Greek summer.

Because of the apparent implausibility of a literal mass shove, many scholars now dissent from the Hanson-led orthodoxy on the hoplite *othismos*, particularly Peter Krentz and Hans van Wees. Krentz argues, based on an analysis of actual material remains, that hoplite equipment, usually thought to have been in the order of 50–70 pounds, was in fact much less, closer to 30 pounds. For Krentz, the less cumbersome the equipment, the more flexible and maneuverable the soldiers and the less necessary a dense phalanx and its mass shove would have been. Van Wees similarly argues for a looser formation than usually believed, especially for the Archaic phalanx. He thinks that the shield could be wielded most effectively with a sideways stance, the left foot out front and the right behind, the shield extended in such a way as to protect the hoplite's whole body instead of just his left side. This stance would also allow for greater balance in combat and more force for the spear thrust, and most importantly would cut down on the need for a dense formation in which soldiers stood shoulder to shoulder. For Krentz and van Wees, and others who challenge the prevailing view of the mass shove, hoplites would have been far more capable of single combat than usually believed, and would have enjoyed much more freedom and mobility on the battlefield. The *othismos*, according to this revisionist view, was figurative rather than literal. Indeed it is common to describe armies of any historical period pushing their opponents from the field, even when no actual pushing takes place.

In Hanson's defense, the course of several historical hoplite battles suggests that depth really did make a decisive difference in ways that are difficult to explain by reference to the need for reserves or moral support. As already noted, the Athenians at Marathon made the center of their line shallower in order to offer a broader front against the Persians. During the battle, the Athenian center gave way, while the full-strength wings were victorious. No explanation is given for the center's defeat other than that it was disadvantaged by being shallower than the wings. At the Battle of Delium in 424 BCE, the Thebans stacked their right wing twenty-five deep, which was able to push back their Athenian opponents, as described in a passage of Thucydides that strongly suggests a literal push. Again at Leuctra in 371 BCE, the Thebans stacked one of their wings to a much greater depth than usual, only this time it was their left wing and it was stacked with an unprecedented fifty ranks. This unique formation proved decisive in crushing the Spartan phalanx, long thought to be invincible in a fair fight. While it is difficult to imagine what the soldiers in the fiftieth rank of this formation were doing during the fight, that extra depth was tactically effective is undeniable, especially when the deeper phalanx was able to deploy in this unique way without exposing itself to a flank attack despite its narrower front.[1]

The *othismos* is but one of many points of contention in this "hoplite debate." Another major factor in the traditional understanding of hoplite warfare, and one that has faced many recent challenges, is the exclusivity of the hoplite soldier on the Greek battlefield. The phalanx, or so the standard line goes, is not only suited to dense formations that employ the mass shove, it was also employed at the exclusion of all other types of arms, such as archers and cavalry. More than that, hoplite phalanxes were supposed to clash in the open, on level terrain, in a ritualized fair fight without either side resorting to trickery, or indeed any type of clever tactics or strategy. A standard literary passage underlying this view of hoplite warfare comes from Herodotus, who puts the following words in the mouth of the Persian general Mardonius giving advice to the king, Xerxes (despite there being very little chance Herodotus could have known what was said at the Persian court):

> I have learned that the Greeks are accustomed to waging war in the most foolish way possible, because of senselessness and stupidity. When they declare war on each other, they find the most level and smoothest piece of ground, and go there to fight, so that even the victors depart after suffering heavy losses. I can't even begin to speak of the losers; they're destroyed completely. Since the Greeks speak the same language, they should instead send heralds and other messengers to discuss their differences, and do anything rather than fight. But if they need to wage war against each other, each side should discover how they will have most advantage, and fight in that way.
>
> (7.9b)

Such people, Mardonius argues, will be easy for Xerxes to conquer. Not only is this passage held up as proof of the uncomplicated and ritualistic nature of hoplite battle, it is also taken as an editorial comment on the part of Herodotus extolling the upright and noble way of war among the Greeks as opposed to the ignoble and cowardly trickery and ranged weapons used by non-Greeks like the Persians. Herodotus' character Mardonius gets to the heart of what Hanson calls the "Western way of war," that is, a preference for decisive battles, which, while undeniably violent and brutal, produce clear winners and losers. The non-Western tradition of other peoples has favored protracted campaigns, which usually entail far greater and longer lasting suffering.

Archilochus, the poet mentioned above who mocked the hoplite reverence for the shield, also provides a key piece of literary evidence for the ritualized nature of the phalanx. Discussing the Lelantine War, a protracted struggle on the island of Euboea between the cities of Chalcis and Eretria that supposedly took place between the late eighth and early seventh centuries BCE, Archilochus says:

> Not many bows will be drawn, nor will there be many slings, whenever Ares gathers toil in the plain. But the much-groaning work will be of swords. For the lords of Euboea, famous for their spears, are skilled in this kind of warfare.
>
> (F 3d)

Historians have taken these lines to mean not only that hand-to-hand combat was the predominant mode of battle in this conflict, but that missile weapons were actually banned from the field to ensure the purity of the infantry clash. Literary depictions of Archaic warfare before the Persian Wars are few and far between, so Archilochus' verses have been seized on by students of ancient warfare as providing a precious contemporary account of the earliest period of the phalanx.

We can now offer a general description of the orthodox view of hoplite warfare when it emerged in the Archaic period. Two phalanxes met on a level plain and fought one another in a ritualized fashion, without making use of missile weapons or cavalry and without resorting to trickery, ambush, or clever formations. These two phalanxes were densely packed with hoplite soldiers standing shoulder to shoulder and all equipped with at least the double-grip shield and thrusting spear, and often with even more defensive armament.

Figure 2.3 The permanent trophy monument from the Battle of Leuctra, 371 BCE
(or possibly later).

Source: author's photograph.

Where possible – that is, if there was little danger of being outflanked by a broader formation – these hoplites were arrayed in eight ranks. When the phalanxes clashed, the two sides pushed against one another, shield pressed against shield. Soldiers in the front two or three ranks tried to kill or wound with their spears soldiers in the other phalanx in order to weaken the solidarity of the enemy line. Once too many had fallen and too many gaps had formed, a phalanx would lose cohesion and thus the battle, the surviving soldiers having little choice but to flee from the victorious phalanx lest they be cut down without the protection of a solid wall of shields. The victorious side would then set up a trophy, *tropē* in Greek, a word meaning "turning point," at the spot where the enemy was first turned to rout. This trophy was usually an ad hoc assemblage of arms and armor taken from the enemy. After exceptional battles, permanent trophy monuments were sometimes set up at a later time. The losing side would typically sue for the right to collect their dead from the field, an open acknowledgment of defeat. Hoplite battle left little room for ambiguous results, and the field would go to whichever phalanx was able to sustain the *othismos* and maintain cohesion the longest. Such is the picture of hoplite warfare mocked by Mardonius and described by Archilochus. And such is the type of massed combat, free of maneuver or any real tactical sophistication, necessitated by the development of the double-grip round shield, as Lorimer argued so influentially.

As with the *othismos* and the density of the phalanx, however, the uniformity of hoplite battle has also been called into question. First of all, the sources cited above are far from clear descriptions of the orthodox phalanx battle. Archilochus, for example, says that swords will be the primary offensive weapon in the Lelantine War, not spears as one might expect. Furthermore, while he stresses the use of swords and says that missile weapons were not a major factor in the war, he does not say that ranged attacks were outright banned in order to preserve the ritualistic integrity of the phalanx. Mardonius' comment might seem to provide an iron-clad case for how the Greeks understood their own peculiar way of war but for one important point: during the actual Persian invasion of Greece, it was the Persians, especially Mardonius, who wanted to fight out in the open, while the Greeks managed to lure the Persians into disadvantageous terrain on both land and sea. The Greeks showed a great deal of strategic and tactical awareness by trying to block the Persian advance at Thermopylae and Artemisium in a coordinated land and sea effort, which very nearly worked had the Greeks at Thermopylae not been betrayed and the Persians shown a hidden path to the rear of the defenders' position. At Salamis, the Athenian Themistocles managed to lure the Persians into a naval battle in narrow straits, neutralizing Persia's superior numbers. And at Plataea, Mardonius tried to lure the Greeks into a battle in the plain, while for several days the Greeks were careful to camp on hills to prevent the Persians from surrounding them. As Roel Konijnendijk has recently pointed out, Herodotus' own narrative strongly suggests that Mardonius is in fact the butt of his own mockery.[2]

Two seventh-century BCE poets beside Archilochus, the Ephesian Callinus and the Spartan Tyrtaeus (yes, Sparta did produce a poet or two), also provide poetic descriptions of infantry battles during their time, and the image they convey is not one of hoplites alone with no supporting arms. Both poets encourage their listeners to march resolutely into battle, and to make good use of stout shields and well-ordered formations. However, both also speak of javelins and arrows, sometimes wielded by the same soldiers who have thrusting spears and large shields, and sometimes used by light-armed troops who work in conjunction with the more heavily armed. Tyrtaeus urges the light-armed to work within the ranks of the heavy-armed hoplites, to use the hoplite shields for defense between hurling volleys of missiles at the enemy. Both poets can be usefully quoted at length:

> …It is pleasant to pierce the guts of a fleeing man in deadly war, and a dead man is shamed lying in the dust with the point of a spear having pierced his back. But let everyone remain in place well astride with both feet planted on the ground, biting his lips with his teeth, covering with the broad belly of his shield his thighs and legs below, and breast and shoulders above. Let him shake a sturdy spear in his right hand, and let him move a terrible crest upon his head. Let him learn how to wage war by doing mighty deeds, and do not let him stand holding his shield out of the range of missiles. Let him instead drawing close with a long spear, or with a sword, wound and take his enemy. Setting foot beside foot and resting shield beside shield, crest beside crest and helmet beside helmet, let him fight with a man breast to breast, taking the grip of a sword or a long spear. And you, O light-armed troops, crouching on either side beneath the shield, pelt the enemy with great stones and hurl smooth javelins against them, standing close to the heavy-armed soldiers.
>
> (Tyrtaeus F 8)

> How long will you lie about? When will you have a stout heart, young men? Aren't you ashamed to be slacking off in front of those that live near you? Do you think you can sit in peace while war has taken hold of the whole land? … let every man hurl a javelin one more time while he is dying. For it is an honorable and glorious thing for a man to fight his enemies on behalf of his land and children and wedded wife. Death will only come when the Fates allot it. Let a man go straightaway brandishing spear and stout heart beneath his shield, when war first breaks out. A man cannot escape his allotted death, not even if he is descended from the race of immortals. Often, if he returns after escaping battle and the strike of javelins, the doom of death catches a man at home. And this death is not precious or a cause of regret to the people, but both small and great lament a man who dies in battle, if anything at all should happen to him. When a mighty man dies, grief affects the whole people, and he lives a life worthy of a demigod before he dies. They look upon him with their eyes as if he were a tower, for though alone he does things worthy of many men.
>
> (Callinus F 1)

The infantry battle described by these poets bears a striking resemblance to the warfare described in the *Iliad*, as many scholars, most notably Joachim Latacz, have noticed. The archer Teucer, for instance, hides behind Ajax's famous tower shield as he fires arrows at the Trojans (*Iliad* 8.266–8.334). So close are the parallels that Latacz makes a compelling case that Tyrtaeus and Callinus describe the exact same warfare as Homer does, and from the same period. Whether or not Homer portrays the early Archaic phalanx – we addressed this topic in the previous chapter – Tyrtaeus and Callinus claim to encourage soldiers of their own day, that is, during the very period in which the phalanx and its shield are supposed to have emerged. The tactics and equipment they describe are variegated rather than uniform.

Like in Homeric poetry, warfare in Archaic Greece was not only a matter of pitched battles between phalanxes. Raids, ambushes, trickery, and even sieges were also a regular part of conflict, as Peter Krentz emphasizes.[3] As we will discuss below, the hoplite and his phalanx might loom largest in Greek culture, particularly in literary and artistic representations of warfare and warriors, but there were plenty of other ways to fight wars and plenty of different types of soldiers. Even slaves sometimes took part in battles – including perhaps the iconic Battle of Marathon – though their participation is often overlooked or ignored in the sources because of authorial and artistic bias, as Peter Hunt has persuasively argued.[4]

To end this section, let us return to the question with which we started this chapter, namely whether or not the hoplite phalanx emerged suddenly in the Archaic period with the development of the double-grip shield. The notion of a hoplite revolution forces us to confront a classic "chicken and egg" problem. That is, did the phalanx arise as a battlefield formation in response to the invention of this new shield, or was the shield invented to complement an already-existing battlefield formation? Even if the adherents to the orthodox view of the phalanx's density and immobility are right, and that this shield is uniquely suited to such a dense and immobile formation, did dense phalanxes not exist in earlier times? Simply put, did the shield mark a decisive boundary between pre-hoplite and hoplite warfare? In the last chapter, we considered whether or not dense phalanxes are present in the *Iliad*, often held up as a literary example of aristocratic warfare in an age before the hoplite. Our discussion was inconclusive, but I did try to show that it is difficult to argue that there are not at least some cases of dense formations in the epic.

The orthodox view of hoplite warfare, including its equipment, tactics, and centrality to the Greek way of war, is evocative and compelling, and described in especially vivid and stirring detail by Hanson. Ultimately, though, the orthodox view seems to provide a reconstruction that is too uncomplicated to account for the full range of military thought and experience in Archaic Greece. Even van Wees, however, agrees that hoplite battles did in fact take place in much the way that Hanson describes them, with densely packed formations and few if any non-hoplite soldiers such as archers. But these "canonical" hoplite clashes took place centuries later than the supposed emergence of the phalanx, specifically in the Classical period after hoplites had demonstrated their effectiveness against the Persians during Xerxes' invasion of Greece in 480–479 BCE. Literary sources such as Thucydides and Xenophon describe great clashes of phalanxes. Thucydides provides one of the most famous and important comments on the phalanx formation and the density of its soldiers:

> All armies do this same thing: as the troops are marching into battle, the right wing is pushed out, with the result that the right wings of both sides overlap the enemy's left. This happens because each man out of fear tries to protect his unarmed side behind the shield of the man stationed to his right, thinking that the closer the shields are packed, the safer he will be.
>
> (Thucydides 5.71)

The clash that elicited this comment from Thucydides was the Battle of Mantinea in 418 BCE, a struggle between many thousands of Greek hoplites more than ten years into the Peloponnesian War. Xenophon offers a more pithy description of the Battle of Coronea, fought in 394 BCE: "They pushed, fought, killed, and died" (Xenophon *Hellenica* 4.3.19).

The accounts of Mantinea and Coronea, along with Nemea, fought earlier in the same year as Coronea, are frequently employed by scholars to paint a picture of hoplite warfare as it emerged centuries earlier. But as van Wees argues, these fifth- and fourth-century BCE sources cannot be used as evidence for the battles fought by those wearing the type of equipment dedicated at Olympia and other sites that inspired Lorimer's idea of a hoplite revolution. Instead, once the hoplite had proven his value at Thermopylae and Plataea, other troop types were increasingly marginalized while the phalanx itself was made denser and denser in the following decades, becoming the staple of Greek warfare that captures the imagination today. At these later battles, light-armed and other troops really do not play a major role, while the right wing of each phalanx tends to extend beyond the enemy left, because of the rightward drift described by Thucydides. In such battles, the left wings of both sides are usually defeated easily before the two right wings take each other on in a great push to determine the final outcome. These battles were fought on open plains without too much advantage being sought in high ground or other topographical features, just as Mardonius described, perhaps ironically, in Herodotus' account of a war fought decades earlier and in a much different way. This way of fighting also dominated the Greek way of war in the Classical period, so much so that the Greek poleis were unable to adapt to face the new military machine of Philip of Macedonia in the second half of the fourth century BCE.

In defense of the orthodox view, however, and to add one final point to demonstrate that the debate over the development of hoplite tactics is far from settled, Hanson points out that it makes little sense to argue that Classical phalanxes were more densely packed than Archaic ones given that Archaic equipment was in fact much heavier and more cumbersome than later kit.

Why, Hanson asks, would fifth- and fourth-century BCE soldiers, who tended to wear helmets with much less facial coverage than the famous Corinthian type and had taken on linen cuirasses instead of the old bronze ones, employ less mobility and maneuverability on the battlefield than their Archaic forebears, whose equipment would have encouraged (or forced) them to rely on dense and straightforward formations?

Hoplites: the world's first citizens

As I said in the introduction to this chapter, there is much more at stake in the "hoplite debate" than just the development of tactics. The hoplite phalanx has generated so much attention in large part because it has long been thought to have contributed to the rise of the polis, the quintessentially Greek form of political organization that gave rise to notions of egalitarianism and vigorous and open debate, and eventually the world's first democracy. To understand how a tactical formation could be so influential socially and politically, we must look not only at how hoplites fought, but at who the hoplite soldiers were. In short, hoplites are thought to have been among the world's first citizen-soldiers, fighting as free men for their own homes, instead of professional or conscript troops that fought for a king or the interests of a narrow elite.

As many first-year university students learn, the Greeks treasured the mean, or middle ground between two extremes, as most famously captured by Aristotle's doctrine of the "Golden Mean." On the Temple of Apollo at Delphi, one of the most important sacred precincts in the Greek world, was inscribed two slogans that defined the Greek intellectual experience: "know thyself" and "nothing in excess." The Greek preference for the mean did not only lead to choosing an ethical or behavioral middle ground, such as the virtue of courage between the two vices of recklessness and cowardice, it also theoretically privileged a middle social class, between haughty aristocrats and the lowly poor. Hoplites are often seen as being drawn from this middle class, or *hoi mesoi*, the "middling ones." They are neither the horse-riding aristocrats that supposedly dominated the warfare of the Early Iron Age and remained at least a minor fixture in Greek states in later periods, nor the landless poor who could not afford a shield and spear and who later found military service primarily as light-armed skirmishers and rowers in ships.

More than merely occupying a middle class, the earliest hoplites importantly owned their own property, usually farms that produced more than the basic needs for subsistence. There were of course richer private farmers and poorer private farmers, but none of the members of the hoplite class were so rich as to dominate their neighbors or so poor as to eke out an existence only with great difficulty. Many reasons are given for why this class of independent farmers should have taken hold in Early Iron Age Greece, when in other parts of the ancient world things returned to more natural forms of government, most predominantly monarchy in which all of the land is technically owned by the king or a very narrow nobility. Kings tend to hold onto power because they can claim a monopoly in several important areas, especially wealth, access to the gods, and military power. After the collapse of the Bronze Age Mycenaean kingdoms, elites in the Greek world were relatively wealthy without being over-whelmingly wealthy in the way Near Eastern kings were in comparison to their subjects. Greek shrines and temples tended to be built in the Early Iron and Archaic Ages to serve as centers of community worship, rather than sanctuaries controlled by rulers or an exclusive priestly caste. And finally, military power tended to be in the hands of private land-owners banding together for the common defense, rather than at the beck and call of a king or lord. The hoplites represent this third prong of the unique historical circumstances that prevented monarchy from re-emerging in Greece as it did in most other parts of the eastern Mediterranean.

In addition to authoring influential studies on hoplite tactics, Victor Davis Hanson has in many ways shaped the conversation about these middle-class Greek farmers who are thought to have banded together in the first phalanxes. Hanson subtitled his first book *The Agrarian Roots of Western Civilization* because he thought that not only did these modest land-owners participate in an important new infantry formation, but they also formed the backbone of the world's first citizenry, to which they brought the values of self-sufficiency and equality. These farmers have a literary representative, or so Hanson argues, in the person of the farmer-poet Hesiod, who in his *Works and Days* extols the nobility and utility of sensible farm work and providing for oneself. Hesiod, writing just a short time after the *Iliad* and the *Odyssey* were first composed, seems a very different sort than Homer's heroes. In fact, Hesiod seems to dis-parage the rulers of his day as "bribe-eating lords" that are prone to corrupt judgments.[5]

In the military sphere, no matter how wealthy a farmer was, if he had enough to provide for a shield and spear – and this would require an estate of some size – he fought in the phalanx alongside his fellow farmers. The military equality arising from fighting in a formation in which each man was dependent on the man beside him for his very life led naturally to social and political equality in the community. The hoplite phalanx in which these farmers fought together for their own land was both a result of these new ideals and a catalyst for them. The society in which these farmers organized themselves came to be known as the polis. The Greek word "polis" – from which we get the word "politics," literally meaning "things having to do with the polis" – is usually translated as "city-state." Perhaps, though, a better translation would be "citizen-state," since the polis was identified less with the urban core and surrounding countryside that defined its physical characteristics, but rather with those men who participated in its government (and it was always only men, since the Greeks fostered a male-dominated society). As the lyric poet Alcaeus says: "Neither finely roofed houses, nor the stones of well-built walls, nor even canals and dockyards make up the polis; but men do." Ian Morris, a leading scholar of the rise of the polis, who attributes both the phalanx and the polis to a newly ascendant "middling ideology," puts it in more modern terms:

The Greeks invented politics, and made political relationships the core of the form of state which they called the polis. The essence of the polis ideal was the identity of the citizens with the state itself … The citizens *were* the state.[6]

The orthodox view of the hoplite phalanx, therefore, holds that the phalanx and the polis were complementary. This notion makes a great deal of sense considering that the polis is generally accepted to have emerged in the early Archaic period at just about the same time that hoplite equipment begins showing up in the material record. Thus, if the phalanx emerged as a result of the new double-grip shield, the chronological coincidence of the phalanx and polis is difficult to miss. The two developments might very well have had much to do with each other. There is more going for this argument than simple correlation. For example, the material of hoplite weapons, namely iron, was amenable to larger armies populated with private soldiers. After the collapse of the Bronze Age and the intricate trade networks that were a part of that world, bronze as a material became nearly impossible to acquire. Bronze is made from both copper and tin, neither of which are abundantly available in Greece and had to be brought in from great distances abroad. The Bronze Age was replaced by the Iron Age, named for the much harder metal that could be found and refined in Greece relatively easily and inexpensively. Where only the very richest could afford bronze weapons and armor, meaning that warfare in the Bronze Age was the province of kings and the armies they supplied, in the Iron Age many more individuals could afford to be soldiers on their own accord, leading to an emerging hoplite class. Also, given that the phalanx was vulnerable most of all to being outflanked, it was in a state's best interest to field as many soldiers as possible in order to ensure a broad front, meaning that a larger share of the population was needed in warfare.

Perhaps the piece of evidence that casts the longest shadow over the hoplite debate is a passage from Aristotle's *Politics*, written towards the end of the fourth century BCE:

The earliest form of government among the Greeks after the monarchies were overthrown was a government of the warriors, especially of the horsemen … But when the cities increased and the hoplites grew in strength, more people had a share in government. This is why those states which we call polities were earlier called democracies.

(Aristotle, *Politics* 1297b15–1297b25)

As is his wont for virtually every subject conceivable, Aristotle tries to make sense of the long history of Greek political development by constructing a neat schema: monarchies gave way to aristocracies led by horsemen, which in turn gave way to more representative forms of government, made possible largely because more had a share in warfare as heavy-armed hoplites.

As in the case of tactics, the correlation between phalanx and polis has come under scrutiny. Van Wees says that the notion of a broad middle class in Archaic

Greece is no more than a myth. He calculates, based on an accounting of the territory of various poleis and the size of a farm required to allow its owner to live beyond the subsistence level, that only about 10–15 percent of Greeks would have qualified to be one of Hanson's independent farmers. Instead of a dominant middle class, Greek society was instead made up of a small number of "gentlemen farmers," a term that far more accurately describes Hesiod, as van Wees argues, and a much greater number of people who had to work for a living. While there were certainly various levels of wealth among the leisured classes, and various degrees of poverty among everyone else, there were really only two social classes in Archaic Greece.

Furthermore, the phalanx, despite all its inherent solidarity and camaraderie, does not necessarily lead to a polis-type social and political organization. The Etruscans, Rome's neighbors to the north in what is today called Tuscany, used hoplite equipment, which they probably adapted after having contact with the Greeks. The Etruscans, however, never developed anything resembling the polis. The Romans themselves, before the development of the legions for which they are most famous, fought in phalanx formations and with equipment similar to the kit of hoplites, but they had vastly different political traditions and institutions than the Greeks. The early Romans even fought as citizen-soldiers, that is, amateur warriors stepping away from their farms for brief campaigns, just like the Archaic Greeks, without developing a polis of their own. As we have already seen, there is good evidence that phalanx formations were used in the Bronze Age, well before the supposed "hoplite revolution," indicating the dense formations of heavy infantry can be tactically effective without being socially and politically revolutionary.

Hoplite battles: Thermopylae and the Nemea River

In order to understand the hoplite phalanx more fully, let us consider in detail two historical battles, one in which hoplites squared off against more lightly armed non-Greek troops, and another in which two Greek phalanxes clashed. Even though the canonical age of hoplite warfare was in the Archaic period, due to a lack of sources we must relegate those early battles to the realm of speculation. The first author to write intentionally as a historian was Herodotus, who describes the conflict between the Greeks and the Persian Empire, especially Xerxes' invasion of Greece in 480–479 BCE. This war consisted not of short campaigns between rival poleis, but rather a protracted struggle for the future of the Greek world between the heavy-armed phalanx and the light-armed soldiers of the Persian army. No battle encapsulates the tactical advantages of the phalanx against light-armed troops better than the Battle of Thermopylae in 480 BCE, that famous contest of few against many. Thermopylae proves that the phalanx could be a devastatingly effective formation rather than just a ritualistic expression of polis values. The second battle we will consider was fought near the Nemea River in 394 BCE, nearly a century after the Persian invasion of Greece. Despite taking place long after the supposed rise of the phalanx, and despite the fact that

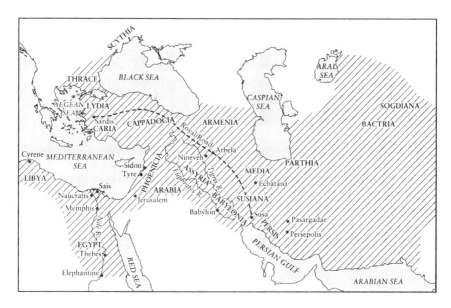

Map 2.1 The Persian Empire in the reign of Darius.

Source: from *Readings in Greek History* (2nd edition) by D. B. Nagle and S. Burstein (2014). Map 3.1, p. 81. By permission of Oxford University Press, USA.

the utility of non-hoplite arms had been demonstrated on several occasions in the intervening decades, Nemea was a straight-ahead clash between Greek hoplites, showcasing several of the tactical principles thought to be inherent to hoplite battle.

One of the impressions left by studying the traditional accounts of the rise of the phalanx is that hoplites were designed to fight against other hoplites. Every aspect of hoplite battle, including the focus on heavy infantry at the expense of other arms, the preference for level ground, and the mutual agreement on both sides regarding who won and who lost, smacks of ritualism. Hoplites were well-suited to fighting duels between two equally matched poleis, analogous to the duels between individual heroes in epic poetry, and the phalanx reflected and established the polis virtues of egalitarianism and mass participation. Yet, when a few thousand hoplites managed to hold off tens of thousands of Persians for more than two days at the narrow pass of Thermopylae, the phalanx was shown to be tactically effective far beyond any ritual significance. Beginning with Herodotus (7.173–7.239), who wrote his stirring and epic-influenced account of Thermopylae around fifty years after the battle, students of the Persian invasion have credited the heavy armor, long spears, and dense formations of the Greeks as the main reason the Persians lost the war on land.

When Xerxes invaded Greece by land and sea, he expected his unprecedented numbers to overawe the few remaining Greek holdouts. If the Greeks

really had chosen to fight in open plains, as Xerxes' advisor Mardonius supposedly said they would, then the Persians would have overwhelmed them easily.
The hoplite phalanx is vulnerable most of all to being outflanked, so out in the
open the Persian infantry, which might have numbered in the neighborhood of
150,000 light- or un-armored spearmen and archers, could have surrounded
even the largest army the Greeks ever fielded. The Persians also had a large
cavalry force, the pride and joy of Xerxes' army. Persian horsemen were primarily mounted archers, exploiting the speed and mobility of horses to swarm
around an enemy and loose arrows, before falling back out of range to regroup
for another attack. Cavalry were particularly effective at killing large numbers
of retreating soldiers who, outside of the protection of organized ranks, were
easy targets for mobile horsemen who could attack at will. Out in an open plain,
Greek hoplites would have been sitting ducks. The Persians were not offering
the Greek defenders the sort of fair fight to which Archaic hoplite phalanxes
supposedly agreed.

But, as I have said above, the Greeks did not fight as Mardonius predicted.
Instead, facing an invasion on an unprecedented scale, the Greeks forged an alliance under the nominal leadership of Sparta, traditionally Greece's greatest
power and the state with the deadliest hoplite soldiers, in order to decide upon
the most strategically viable spot for a smaller force to ward off one much larger.
The patriotic Greeks – who, by the way, were outnumbered by fellow Greeks
from Ionia and elsewhere who were actually fighting on the side of the Persians
– decided to make a stand at the Vale of Tempe, the narrow pass between Mt.
Olympus and Mt. Ossa, forming the border between Thessaly and Macedonia.
The choice of this pass reflects the Greeks' awareness of an important tactical
principle: for a phalanx fighting a larger and more mobile foe, a narrow pass is
an effective force-multiplier. The Vale of Tempe offered a confined space in
which the Greeks could fight with a relatively narrow front while having their
flanks protected by rugged mountainous terrain, nullifying the Persians' numerical advantage. The Greeks later used the same principle in deciding to fight the
Persians at sea in the straits between the island of Salamis and the mainland near
Athens, with the result that the much larger Persian fleet suffered a stunning
defeat. Tempe, though, proved to be a bust. Despite sending 10,000 hoplites to
defend the pass, the Greeks learned that there were alternate inland routes into
Thessaly which threatened the hoplites with encirclement. Dispirited, the Greeks
withdrew south to regroup and look for another option.

The next best option was decided to be the pass of Thermopylae, literally
named the "hot gates" for the sulfur springs in the area that still flow today. This
pass runs in an east–west direction between Thessaly to the north and Boeotia to
the south, and at some points offered barely enough room for two carts to pass
each other on a narrow road between the steep slopes of Mt. Kallidromos and
bluffs overhanging the sea. The pass was made even more defensible by a series
of "gates" and a defensive wall that the Greeks set about reinforcing. Thermopylae was both narrower than the Vale of Tempe and offered the additional
advantage of lying near straits between the mainland and the promontory of

Artemisium on the island of Euboea where the Greek navy could hold off the Persian fleet at sea. Far from the strategically and tactically simplistic warfare suggested by the traditional understanding of the Archaic phalanx, at Thermopylae the Greek defenders decided on a sensible plan of defense, taking advantage of the geography on both land and sea. While the Battle of Thermopylae is most famous for the final and fatal stand of 300 Spartans against insuperable odds, at first the Greek defenders numbered as many as 8,000. The Persian army was still impossibly larger, but in the confines of a pass that prevented any outflanking maneuvers and offered no space for cavalry to operate, the hoplite phalanx had the advantage in terms of equipment and tactics.

Many poleis were represented on the Greek side at Thermopylae, but the Greek army was anchored on the 300 Spartans. Though a very small number, due, as the Spartans themselves claimed, to a religious festival that prevented a larger army from taking the field until several days later, 300 Spartans would have punched well above their weight. Unlike the citizen-soldiers of most other Greek poleis, who fought as amateur hoplites before returning to their real jobs as (usually) farmers, full Spartan citizens trained continually for war since the agricultural and other needs of the society were seen to by the helots, essentially state-owned serfs. The Spartans were conditioned to show remarkable courage in battle, especially in their adherence to the principle of never yielding to the enemy one's spot in the battle line. Herodotus touches on this point through the mouth of his character Demaratus, an exiled Spartan king who served as an advisor to Xerxes. When his master was incredulous that so few would stand against so many, Demaratus said that the Spartans fear their own principle of standing firm in battle much more than the Persian soldiers fear Xerxes. As such, the Persian king could expect a grueling fight. Coupled with heavy armor and stout spears that outclassed the Persians' equipment in a fair fight, this Spartan resolve proved formidable. The other Greeks at Thermopylae too showed the tactical worth of their equipment and the phalanx formation.

For two days, the Greeks, led by the Spartans, dealt death to Xerxes' army. The Persians, more lightly armored than the Greeks, equipped with shorter spears, and not making use of dense formations, charged against the Greeks in wave after wave. The soldiers of the hoplite phalanx stood firm, cutting down countless Persians and apparently suffering few losses themselves, heavily armored as they were. Xerxes even sent his elite unit against the Greeks, but with no effect. The Immortals, a contingent 10,000-strong and so named because each casualty was immediately replaced in order to keep the numbers at full strength, fared no better against the hoplites. Although the narrow battlefield at Thermopylae was enough of a force-multiplier to give the Greeks a decisive advantage over their opponents, the well-trained Spartans still demonstrated some impressive tactical feats. As Herodotus describes it:

> The Lacedaemonians fought in a way worthy of renown, and among other things demonstrated what it is like for experienced warriors to fight the inexperienced.

They would turn their backs and retreat as if in a disordered mass, upon seeing which the barbarians would set upon them with a shout and crash. But as soon as the barbarians had overtaken them, the Lacedaemonians would turn around to face them and would cut down numberless Persians.

(Hdt. 7.211)

Feigned retreats are among the most difficult maneuvers for any army to execute, and it is likely that only the Spartans, who trained continually for war, were able to pull them off. Their Greek allies, however, probably learned a thing or two about hoplite warfare after fighting for two days alongside the Spartans.

On the third day of the battle, Xerxes finally prevailed, but only because a Greek traitor had shown the Persians a hidden mountain path that allowed the Immortals to appear behind the Greeks and surround them. When Leonidas, the Spartan king, learned that the Immortals were making their way around the mountain and that the Greek defenders would soon be surrounded, he ordered the majority of the Greek force to depart and live to fight another day. Only Leonidas and the 300 Spartans, along with 700 allies from the small Boeotian city of Thespiae, stayed to act as a rearguard, and every last one of them was killed as they stood firm. Had the mountain path not been revealed to Xerxes, it is not inconceivable that the Greek defenders could have held the pass long enough to kill so many Persians that Xerxes thought better of his invasion. Given the right terrain, the heavy-armed hoplite fighting in a dense phalanx proved remarkably effective against even much greater numbers of more lightly armed soldiers.

Figure 2.4 Modern monument to Leonidas and the Spartans at Thermopylae.
Source: author's photograph.

A year later, after the Battle of Plataea, Herodotus says explicitly that the heavy armor, long spears, and phalanx formations of the Greeks were a decisive factor in defeating the Persians, who, although they fought valiantly enough, simply could not contend with the hoplite phalanx.

The Persian Wars, especially the Battle of Thermopylae, demonstrated that the hoplite was an effective and deadly soldier in the right conditions – namely, in an environment in which more mobile troops such as light infantry and cavalry could not threaten to outflank the phalanx – regardless of any socio-cultural factors that might have led to the emergence of the phalanx in the first place. Far from simply being the vehicle for ritualized duels between rival poleis, the hoplite phalanx had humbled the world's greatest power. In the decades after Xerxes' invasion, hoplites became even more celebrated in Greek culture, and Greek hoplites came to be sought, especially by the Persians themselves, as valuable mercenaries to supplement light-armed troops.[7]

Unlike Thermopylae, the Battle of the Nemea River, fought in 394 BCE between the Spartans and a large coalition arrayed against them during the Corinthian War (395–387 BCE), is not a household word. The glamorous and odds-defying struggle for freedom against the Persians has proven much more satisfying as a historical topic than the much drearier – yet more common – clashes among the Greeks themselves. When battles between Greeks are studied, they tend to be from the Peloponnesian War (431–404 BCE), which did indeed feature two (and only two!) pitched hoplite battles. The Battle of the Nemea River, however, represents perhaps the largest pure hoplite battle that ever took place. For the battle itself, the ancient sources make no mention whatsoever of light-armed and other non-hoplite soldiers, despite their participation in the broader Nemea campaign and their importance to several Peloponnesian War operations. In order to understand the mechanics of the phalanx and the typical course of hoplite battles, therefore, Nemea is as important a battle as any. Our main source for the battle is Xenophon the Athenian (*Hellenica* 4.2–4.3), who, although he often omits the fine details that modern military historians want to know, was an experienced soldier and friend of the Spartans and therefore placed as well as anyone to understand the Spartan phalanx and how it performed in combat.

Unlike Thermopylae, the Battle of the Nemea River was fought in an open plain, along the broad strip of agricultural land stretching between Corinth and Sicyon on the northern coast of the Peloponnese. The Spartans and their Peloponnesian allies, amounting in total to around 18,000–19,000 hoplites, entered the plain to the west, near Sicyon, and suffered as they marched eastwards by continual attacks from enemy light-armed troops positioned on the escarpment that forms the southern boundary of the plain. Though the Spartan side is said to have had its own light troops and cavalry, we are not told how they were used. Indeed, throughout Xenophon's descriptions of the warfare of the early fourth century BCE, the Spartans appear uniquely inept at exploiting non-hoplite arms, even though they realized that a combined-arms approach was rapidly becoming a necessity. Once the Spartans reached the spot for their camp near the Nemea River, the enemy light-armed troops broke off their attacks. The anti-Spartan coalition amounted to some 24,000 hoplites drawn from several of Greece's most powerful states, including Athens, Thebes, Argos, and Corinth. This larger force was encamped in the plain to the east of the Spartans, closer to Corinth.

Typically, the best troops in a hoplite phalanx were given a position on the right wing, theoretically the most dangerous position – and therefore the position of honor – given that a hoplite's right side was unshielded. In practice, however, a phalanx's right wing tended to be victorious since it was matched against the weaker troops of the enemy phalanx's left wing. Many hoplite battles in the Classical period bear this out, and the Nemea River is no exception. The elite Spartan soldiers took the right wing in their own army, and in the anti-Spartan coalition the tough hoplites from Thebes ended up fighting on their own right, stacked probably twenty-five hoplites deep in an effort to lend extra weight to their push. Once the battle commenced, the Thebans veered ever rightward in an attempt to outflank their opponents, leaving their allies in the lurch as they were forced to drift rightward themselves to prevent gaps from opening in the phalanx. When the armies collided, the Athenians, manning the left wing of the coalition, found themselves dangerously outflanked by the Spartans. While the Thebans made short work of the Spartans' allies arrayed against them, the Athenians had a hard time of it. Those Spartan soldiers that found themselves extended beyond the leftmost of the Athenians simply wheeled to the left and began to march across the field in a direction perpendicular to the main lines, rolling up the enemy formation as they went. In addition to the great numbers of Athenians who died as they were hopelessly surrounded and outflanked by superior Spartan troops, the Thebans and others making their way back after driving off the Spartans' allies found themselves hit on the flank by the well-ordered Spartan phalanx. Though both right wings had been victorious, the Spartans carried the day because they kept formation and executed a brilliant turning movement to drive across the entire enemy line.

The Battle of the Nemea River showed that the Spartans were still masters of hoplite warfare. It also showed that the phalanx's greatest vulnerability was in being outflanked, and that the army with the most disciplined and cohesive right wing would usually win in the end, no matter how the battle went in the rest of the field. This was a lesson that was taught time and again during the age of the hoplite phalanx, and it is rather astonishing that Greek armies fought for as long as they did without making adjustments to seize advantages from the tactical realities of phalanx warfare. At least three pure hoplite clashes in the late fifth and early fourth centuries BCE – Mantinea, the Nemea River, and Coronea – ended with the Spartan right taking the field, despite impressive tactical gains made by their enemies in other parts of the line. It was not until Epameinondas, a visionary leader of the Thebans, decided in the late 370s BCE to stack his left wing with his best soldiers and at a great depth that hoplite tactics changed and the Spartan monopoly was ended. At the Battle of Leuctra in 371 BCE, Epameinondas led the Theban phalanx, stacked an unprecedented fifty deep on the left wing, to victory against the Spartans, after the Spartan right was crushed and a Spartan king was killed.

The iconography of the citizen-soldier

Scholars, both those who study warfare and those who focus on art and material culture, are quick to point out that the Greeks were captive to the "hoplite ethos," the notion that not only were hoplites the most effective and important – if not, the only – soldiers in battle, but they also represented the ideal of Greek citizenship, indeed of Greekness itself. The hold the hoplite ethos had on the Greeks is used to explain why the hoplite phalanx remained the predominant form of warfare among the Greeks well into the latter half of the fourth century BCE, even after combined-arms armies had demonstrated their effectiveness time and time again. At Chaeronea in 338 BCE, Philip of Macedonia employed his own combined-arms army, which included a reformed and more deadly phalanx, to devastating effect against the greatest hoplite army the Greek poleis could muster. But beyond the field of battle, the hoplite ethos is thought to have informed artistic and material representations of Greeks and Greek warfare to an inordinately high degree, even to the visual exclusion of non-hoplite soldiers and ways of war. In the final section of this chapter, let's explore the iconography of the hoplite in the surviving material record, and explore the degree to which the hoplite did represent the ideal citizen-soldier.

At the Battle of Marathon – in which the Athenians and their allies from Plataea heroically drove a much larger Persian force from Athenian territory in 490 BCE, and long held up as the hoplite's finest hour – a later source writing in the Roman period says that slaves fought alongside their Greek masters. If these slaves, who were probably equipped as light-armed troops, do not show up in the account of Herodotus, the fault lies with Herodotus' bias towards citizen hoplites, or so Peter Hunt argues in an influential study on slaves and warfare in ancient Greece. Herodotus, though, does to a certain extent acknowledge the diversity of arms in the Greek armies fighting against the Persians. He tells us, for instance, that at the Battle of Plataea the Athenians employed a corps of citizen archers and the Spartans equipped the helots – Sparta's state-owned serfs – as light-armed troops. And one of the greatest victories of the war, acknowledged by Herodotus himself to have saved Greece, was the Battle of Salamis in which Greek sailors, predominantly those who could not afford to serve as hoplites, bested the Persian navy. Nevertheless, after the Persian Wars the hoplite became more and more the image of the ideal Greek citizen-soldier, especially and perhaps surprisingly at Athens, which was growing into a predominantly naval power. Aeschylus, the first of the three great Athenian tragic playwrights, in his play *The Persians*, dramatizing the Battle of Salamis and performed just over a decade after the battle itself, highlights a relatively minor hoplite skirmish that took place during the naval encounter, and suggests that the loss of a few Persian soldiers at the hands of Greek hoplites was as decisive as the much larger struggle taking place among the ships. Even the navy's great achievement, it seems, was eclipsed by the emerging hoplite ethos.

While hoplites had been present in Greek art before the Persian Wars, in the fifth century BCE they came to dominate military imagery. Red-figure vases from

Athens regularly depict heroes from the Trojan War, such as Achilles and Hector, fighting duels while dressed as fifth-century BCE hoplites. A common artistic motif on vases became the departure scene, in which a young hoplite soldier is depicted saying farewell to his family as he departs to fulfill his civic duty in the phalanx. On the greatest public monuments erected in the fifth century BCE, including the Acropolis temples constructed as part of Pericles' famous building program, Greek hoplites are depicted in pediments and friezes as fighting against the non-hoplite armies of exotic forces such as Amazons or Trojans. Such scenes are commonly interpreted as standing in for the Persian Wars themselves, which the Greeks came to see as a struggle between Hellenism and barbarism, or hoplites against light-armed infantry and cavalry. The artistic contrast is great between, say, the Parthenon, which was built in the 430s BCE and depicts the Greeks or the Greek gods fighting a variety of strangely clad and monstrous enemies such as centaurs and giants, and the Siphnian treasury at Delphi, which was built in the 520s BCE before the Persian Wars and depicts the "good guys" (such as the gods) and the "bad guys" (such as giants) equipped in much the same way, predominantly as hoplites. After Xerxes invaded Greece and his foreign soldiers were defeated by Greek hoplites, hoplites came to represent not only the ideal Greek citizen-soldier, but Greeks in general, while non-hoplites came to represent the "other."

The most influential work on this topic was written nearly thirty years ago by the French scholar François Lissarrague, called *L'autre guerrier*, or, "The Other Warrior." In this important book, Lissarrague argues that the hoplite came to be deliberately contrasted in art, especially vase-painting, with other, especially non-Greek, soldiers such as Thracian peltasts and Scythian archers. Iconographically, the hoplite represented Greekness, while non-hoplites represented the "other," a contrast that became especially pronounced after the Greeks encountered the other in the Persian Wars. David M. Pritchard has in many places expanded upon these ideas, pointing out that in Athens the hoplite dominated the image of warfare, and also what he calls "the military performance of citizenship." To be a citizen simply meant being a hoplite, at least conceptually. Even if non-hoplite soldiers continued to fight in Greek armies, artistically and culturally the Greek way of war was represented by the hoplite. But, as Hans van Wees argues, after the Persian Wars non-hoplite arms came to be excluded from Greek armies more than ever before. Rather than the Archaic Age representing the period of the hoplite phalanx, as was the orthodox view, van Wees argues that the Persian Wars changed the reality of Greek warfare just as it changed the artistic representation of Greek soldiers. As the hoplite dominated art, he also dominated the field of battle and made it culturally taboo to fight in other ways. After all, it is the barbarian other that fights as an archer or a peltast.

As always, things were not quite so simple. The Parthenon, for example, also highlights Athenian horsemen as ideal representatives of their polis, and eventually there was some iconographic pushback against hoplite imagery, as is provocatively demonstrated by the Dexileos Monument (see Chapter 5, Figure 5.4), a funerary monument from the early 300s BCE that depicts an Athenian cavalryman riding down an enemy hoplite.[8] The navy also had a prominent place in the Athenian landscape, perhaps more in the form of monumental buildings and large harbors tied to ships than in the visual arts, which we will explore in the next chapter. In general, though, the Greeks, and especially the Athenians from whom we have the most artistic evidence, privileged the hoplite above all other types of soldier, a trend that became most pronounced after Xerxes' invasion. Whatever the origins of the hoplite phalanx, and whatever relationship it had with the emergence of the polis in the Archaic period, the hoplite ethos gripped the Classical Greeks to such an extent that other ways of war were not explored as much as they could have been, even when it eventually became obvious that other ways of war were necessary.

Notes

1 For a detailed discussion of the *othismos* and how scholars have interpreted it, see Matthew (2009).
2 Konijnendijk (2016).
3 See especially Krentz (2000).
4 Hunt (1998).
5 But see Barry (2016), who argues that Hesiod was a lonely crank who did not reflect the views of his contemporaries.
6 Morris (1987, 3).
7 In their classic commentary on Herodotus, How and Wells argue that the heavy equipment and dense formation of the Greek hoplites was one of the decisive factors in the Greek victory over the Persians. See How and Wells (1912, vol. 2, 397–414). Both the Greeks and Persians seemed to take this lesson to heart after the Persian Wars.
8 See Ober's (2005, 237–247) influential, but controversial, discussion of this monument and how it can be read as an anti-democratic and anti-hoplite image.

Further reading

Cartledge, Paul. 2007. *Thermopylae: The Battle that Changed the World*. New York.

A lively treatment of Thermopylae, its context, the tactics involved, and its significance.

Hall, Jonathan M. 2006. *A History of the Archaic Greek World: ca. 1200–479 BCE*. Malden, MA.

This introductory survey demonstrates just how shaky our evidence is for Archaic Greece, and how uncertain our understanding of that period, including the rise of the hoplite phalanx, must be.

Hanson, Victor Davis. 1999. *The Other Greeks: The Family Farm and the Agrarian Roots of Western Civilization* (second edition). Berkeley.

A passionate argument in favor of the thesis that small, independent land-owners formed the hoplite class and drove the rise of the polis.

Hanson, Victor Davis. 2009. *The Western Way of War* (second edition). Berkeley.

Hanson applies a "face of battle" approach to analyzing hoplite battle, arguing that hoplites fought in dense formations and that the hoplite phalanx established the bloody decisive battle as the primary way of solving disputes in the West.

Kagan, Donald and Gregory F. Viggiano (eds.). 2013. *Men of Bronze: Hoplite Warfare in Ancient Greece*. Princeton.

An up-to-date edited collection of chapters from leading scholars in the debate about the nature of hoplite warfare, featuring new work from Hanson, Krentz, van Wees, and others.

Krentz, Peter. 2010. *The Battle of Marathon*. New Haven.

A thorough and readable book on the famous battle that also lays out Krentz's critique of the standard interpretation of the hoplite phalanx, based on many of Krentz's earlier publications. Krentz argues that the phalanx was far more fluid than the standard view, and that the equipment was much lighter.

Latacz, Joachim. 1977. *Kampfparänese, Kampfdarstellung und Kampfwirklichkeit in der Ilias, bei Kallinos und Tyrtaios*. München.

Though in German, this book was groundbreaking in its attempt to present a coherent account of battle in the *Iliad*, which Latacz argues is reflected in the Archaic poetry of Callinus and Tyrtaeus and thus represents the early hoplite phalanx.

Lazenby, John F. 1985. *The Spartan Army*. Warminster.

A good treatment of the Spartan army and many of its key battles, including Thermopylae and the Nemea River.

Lissarrague, François. 1990. *L'autre guerrier: archers, peltastes, cavaliers dans l'imagerie attique*. Paris.

Though in French, this is essential reading for anyone who wants to understand the iconography of soldiers in Greek art, particularly the contrast between how hoplites are depicted versus other kinds of soldiers.

Lorimer, H. L. 1947. "The Hoplite Phalanx with Special Reference to the Poems of Archilochus and Tyrtaeus." *Annual of the British School at Athens* 62: 76–138.

A seminal work arguing that the adoption of the hoplite shield led to the hoplite revolution in tactics.

Morris, Ian. 1987. *Burial and Ancient Society: The Rise of the Greek City-State*. Cambridge.

An argument for the rise of egalitarian values in the Greek state based on a study of burial practices, particularly at Athens.

Morris, Ian. 1996. "The Strong Principle of Equality and the Archaic Origins of Greek Democracy." In J. Ober and C. Hedrick (eds.), *Demokratia: A Conversation on Democracies, Ancient and Modern*. Princeton. 19–48.

An important study about the development and nature of egalitarianism in the Greek polis.

Pritchard, David M. 1998. "The Fractured Imaginary: Popular Thinking on Military Matters in Fifth Century Athens." *Ancient History* 28: 38–61.

A good discussion of the place of the soldier in Athenian society, including the link between hoplites and citizens in iconography.

Pritchard, David M. (ed.). 2010. *War, Democracy and Culture in Classical Athens*. Cambridge.

A useful edited volume covering a wide range of topics on the interaction between war, politics, society, and culture in Classical Athens, including the relationship between hoplites and ideas of citizenship.

Pritchett, W. K. 1985. *The Greek State at War, Vol. 4*. Berkeley.

In discussing the development of Greek pitched battle, Pritchett says dense phalanxes appear to be the norm already in the *Iliad*. The hoplite phalanx was thus more or less operative in Homer.

Snodgrass, A. M. 1967. *Arms and Armour of the Greeks*. London.

A groundbreaking study of the material remains of Greek arms and armor, with clear implications for the development of hoplite equipment and tactics.

van Wees, Hans. 2001. "The Myth of the Middle-Class Army: Military and Social Status in Ancient Athens." In L. Hannestad and T. Bekker-Nielsen (eds.), *War as a Cultural and Social Force*. Copenhagen.

In this provocative article, van Wees argues that Athenian land use and demographics suggest that the hoplite phalanx did not represent the "middle class," but would have drawn on the lower classes too.

van Wees, Hans. 2004. *Greek Warfare: Myths and Realities*. London.

A broad treatment of Greek warfare, drawing from van Wees' earlier scholarly work. Van Wees argues that the hoplite phalanx was far less dense than generally thought, and only developed into its canonical form well in to the Classical period.

3   Greek naval warfare

Ruling the Aegean

Introduction

Few parts of the Greek world are far from the sea. Plato famously described the Greeks as "frogs around a pond" (*Phaedo* 109b), and the sea was indeed an integral part of Greek life and the Greek understanding of the world. Despite some words of warning from the Archaic poet Hesiod (*Works and Days* 619–694), who advised that journeys by sea should be undertaken only if absolutely necessary, the myth of the Trojan War demonstrates that the Greeks even as far back as Hesiod's time thought that seafaring, including sea-borne military expeditions, had always been a part of their history. Indeed, given the constraints of pre-industrialized travel and the mountainous nature of the Greek landscape, the sea acted as a source of relatively easy connection, rather than separation, between parts of the ancient world, not only commercially and militarily, but culturally too, as Horden and Purcell explore in their book *The Corrupting Sea*. While the hoplite might have dominated on land, at least in the Greek imagination, naval battles became an essential component of Greek warfare in the late Archaic period, and in many ways dominated Classical warfare, especially in terms of the numbers of men involved and the scale of the battles they fought.

The nature of ancient warships and their tactics, as well as the strategic considerations at play in powers vying for control of the sea, are essential topics for Greek warfare and will be treated as such by this chapter. Many of the conflicts of the ancient Greek world, including the Persian Wars and the Peloponnesian War, featured great naval battles that involved tens of thousands of sailors and altered the course of history and the map of the ancient world. But, as with the hoplite phalanx, Greek naval warfare both reflected and had a profound effect on Greek politics, society, and culture. In Athens, where as ever our evidence is strongest, the "naval mob" who manned the ships came to demand a share of political power commensurate with their military importance. Many scholars of Greek political history argue that true democracy did not take hold in Athens until the middle of the fifth century BCE, when champions of the rowing classes stripped away the last vestiges of elite political control and handed the state over to the masses. This chapter will examine the development and deployment of

Greek warships, especially the trireme, and will outline some representative naval battles. It will also consider the impact of the "naval mob" on broader developments in Greek history.

Greek navies

Unlike hoplites, whose bronze and iron armor and weapons have provided a great deal of evidence concerning the equipment of the phalanx (though there is still plenty of debate surrounding just how heavy the hoplite panoply was and at what periods various items of equipment were used), not much has survived of ancient warships. Except for extraordinary circumstances, the wooden hulls of ships have not survived in the archaeological record (and those that have tend to be merchant vessels), and only a scattered few remnants of other parts of ships have been found, including some bronze rams and even a marble eye that was affixed to a trireme's bow to lend the ship an intimidating appearance. Accordingly, there is much uncertainty concerning exactly how ancient warships were constructed and laid out, though several sources of evidence have given scholars a good idea about the fundamentals.

Vase-painting furnishes some examples of ancient warships, including highly stylized sixth-century BCE renditions of the legendary ship of Odysseus and of various types of combat-ready vessels, some even with sword-wielding marines visible on deck, particularly from the eighth century BCE, or the end of the Geometric period. A splendid relief sculpture carved into the living rock beneath the acropolis of Lindos on the island of Rhodes, from around 180 BCE, shows the stern portion of a trireme. The most important sculpture for reconstructing ancient ships, however, is the so-called Lenormant Relief from the Athenian Acropolis, dating to the end of the fifth century BCE. This relief depicts the inside of a trireme, and clearly shows three levels of oars, shedding light on one of the key questions concerning just how these ships worked. A few bronze rams have been found by underwater archaeologists, including a fourth-century BCE example from Greece, now in the Piraeus Museum, and the famous Athlit ram, of indeterminate date, found off the coast of Israel, which still had some of the ship's timbers inside. Recently several rams have been found off the Egadi Islands near Sicily, remnants of a battle between the Romans and Carthaginians in the First Punic War of the third century BCE, and are being analyzed by the RPM Nautical Foundation.[1] Rams are particularly useful finds since the angle at which the timbers joined the ram can help determine the size and shape of the ships themselves. By far the most valuable piece of evidence concerning the size of Classical Athenian ships is the discovery and excavation of several ship-sheds in the Piraeus, Athens' principal port. These monumental structures were built in the fourth century BCE to dry-dock the Athenian fleet, and their dimensions reveal fairly accurately just how big the Athenians' ships were at the time. Inscriptions from Athens also detail what kinds of rigging and other equipment ships needed, how much the ships and their tackle cost, and who was responsible for meeting the costs of construction, maintenance, and paying the crews.

Figure 3.1 Trireme relief from Lindos on Rhodes, *c*.180 BCE.
Source: author's photograph.

The greatest advance in our understanding of ancient warships came in the 1980s with the construction of the Olympias, a fully realized and working Classical trireme. A bold example of experimental archaeology, this ship was designed by naval architect J. F. Coates and ancient historian J. S. Morrison, and these two wrote about the project in their excellent and highly readable book, *The Athenian Trireme*, now in its second edition and updated by the rowing master N. B. Rankov. In general, since it is based on years of painstaking research, trial, and error, this book is essential reading for anyone wishing to understand ancient naval warfare. Undergoing a series of sea-trials with crews of volunteer rowers, the Olympias demonstrated what an ancient ship could do in terms of speed and maneuverability, reaching speeds of nine knots and executing remarkably sharp turns. The Olympias is officially commissioned as a ship in the modern Greek navy, and at the time of writing is on display in Faliro, an Athenian neighborhood close to the Piraeus port and identical to ancient Phaleron, the original port of Athens' navy before the Piraeus was developed.

The ancient Greeks – and the non-Greeks they fought at sea – used primarily two types of ships for combat. The *penteconter*, a narrow galley powered by oars, was usually just under 30 meters in length and had a rowing crew of fifty, twenty-five on each side. Its very name suggests the Greek word for "fifty."

Figure 3.2 The Lenormant Relief depicting the rowers in a trireme, *c*.410–400 BCE.

Source: Acropolis Museum, Athens (no. 1339). © Acropolis Museum. Photo credit: Socratis Mavrommatis.

Figure 3.3 The Olympias trireme, built in the 1980s.

Source: author's photograph.

The penteconter never really went out of use, but around the turn of the fifth century BCE it was largely superseded by its larger sibling, the *trireme*, which will be the prime focus of this chapter. "Trireme" literally means "three banks," and where the penteconter had only a single rank of rowers on each side, the trireme had three – though exactly how these ranks were arranged is not entirely clear. The Lenormant Relief suggests that the three ranks were arranged more or less vertically, with the lowest class of rowers relegated to the depths, while those of higher classes (though by no means the highest classes, who typically did not serve as rowers at all) sat on the higher benches. Triremes were about 10 meters longer than penteconters, but held much bigger crews: up to 200, including 170 rowers and 30 other crew members, consisting of a few marines on deck to protect the ship and board enemy ships, maintenance staff, a piper to keep time, the official commander of the vessel (called the trierarch), and, most importantly of all, the helmsman, who manned the large rudders at the stern and was the most experienced sailor on board. Both penteconters and triremes were outfitted with a sail, but this was only used while cruising from one destination to another. During battle, the sails were stowed and the rowers did all the work.

Triremes could be modified to serve special purposes, such as transporting troops and even horses, though other vessels could be used for those tasks too. While warships could travel great distances, they tended to stop each night to be hauled onto land to avoid becoming waterlogged, a limitation that shrank the number of usable routes and made control of sea-lanes, coastlines, and islands an important strategic consideration. More than anything, triremes were made for combat, usually against other triremes (there were of course differences between triremes of different Greek and non-Greek states, but the ships were fundamentally similar). The marines on deck, including archers and hoplites, could board an enemy trireme in an attempt to capture or disable the vessel. Many navies preferred this method of combat, namely fighting a land battle at sea, and consequently had larger decks and more marines. Most Greeks, however, and especially the Athenians, preferred to ram enemy vessels. For this purpose, triremes were equipped with a bronze ram at the waterline of the prow, protruding in three prongs that from the side looked like a trident, the weapon of Poseidon. These rams were designed not only to punch holes in the enemy's hull, but also to split the timbers, making a much larger gash than the footprint of the ram itself. As crews became more skilled, they learned to ram at just the right speed to cause significant damage while still being able to extract their own ship. Sometimes, though, a ship became hopelessly lodged in another, at which point the marines would take over.

Our sources pass on several Greek terms and some brief descriptions for trireme tactics, but scholars continue to debate just how some of these maneuvers were executed in practice. The *kuklos*, simply meaning "circle," is straightforward enough. Like a herd forming up to defend against predators, triremes could form a circle with their prows facing out, sometimes even placing slower or more vulnerable ships inside the circle. This tactic was useful for smaller numbers of ships to defend against a larger enemy force, since the enemy would be presented only with dangerous bronze rams instead of the more vulnerable midsections or sterns. The *diekplous*, which means "sailing out and through," is more difficult to reconstruct. Often the maneuver is said to be one of a single file of ships sailing through a gap in a much broader enemy formation, only to turn to ram the enemy amidships or in the stern. The *periplous*, or "sailing around," is usually understood to be employed by a broad front outflanking the enemy to attack the sides and rear of the ships at the edge of the enemy formation. Some scholars suggest that even more complicated maneuvers could be performed, including a ship sheering off an enemy's oars by having its own oars retracted at the last moment before the ram slammed into the enemy's oars as the two ships sailed past one another. The effect of this attack on the enemy rowers must have been most gruesome, as heavy oar handles were sent crashing through bones and teeth, all while those in the ship's hold were blind to the action unfolding around them.[2]

The tactical considerations of naval warfare were in many ways similar to land warfare. More numerous and more skilled fleets would seek to fight in open water, where they had space to overwhelm the enemy and execute their complex and carefully honed maneuvers. Just like cavalry on open plains, faster ships could literally sail circles around a less mobile enemy. As one would imagine, even the most talented fleets needed a great deal of space to maneuver. The Olympias needed at least two ship lengths, or 80 meters, to perform a full 360-degree turn at speed, meaning that a fleet of many ships would need many hundreds of meters to perform any feat of rowing. Smaller and less skilled fleets, accordingly, preferred to fight in confined waters, the narrow space nullifying both the numerical and nautical advantages of the enemy. As we will discuss below, the Persian Wars, in which the Greeks were outnumbered and outclassed, afford important lessons about advantageous formations and advantageous topography, particularly at Salamis in 480 BCE. Once the Athenians became masters of the sea, they took on the role of the Persian navy, preferring broad expanses of open water, as demonstrated at Naupactus in 429 BCE.

Strategically, however, particularly in terms of "grand strategy," naval warfare could not be more different than the hoplite phalanx, the backbone of Greek land warfare. Before the long-term conflicts of the fifth century BCE, hoplites by and large supplied their own equipment, and fought as amateur citizen-soldiers for short campaigns whenever the need arose. While a sizeable portion of a given polis could afford a shield and spear, no one but the ultra-rich could outfit a warship, let alone supply one with a crew. Naval warfare was by necessity the business of the state: a polis could only have a sizeable navy if it deliberately set out to do so. In addition to building, maintaining, and crewing ships, infrastructure such as large ports needed to be established, and sources of timber (precious little of which was available in mainland Greece) secured. Finally, the citizen-soldier model of hoplite warfare did not apply to navies. For the most part, phalanx battle is fairly simple, requiring little in the way of training or drill. The Spartans, who trained for hoplite battle constantly, were superior on the battlefield to virtually everyone else, but they were the exception rather than the rule. To achieve the kind of coordination required for 170 oarsmen to row in unison would have taken many hours of practice, let alone complicated battle maneuvers which would have taken years for a full naval culture to be established. As such, rowers could not be farmers most of the time, only taking their posts for intermittent campaigns. Rather, they would need to be at their oars for long stretches of time, and more often than not paid by the state in order to obtain a livelihood for the time they were at sea. Naval warfare, therefore, entailed a state-level scale of investment and foresight, making it an altogether different way of war than the phalanx. The best navies required a polis to adopt what can usefully be dubbed a "naval orientation."

Prior to the Persian Wars, some Greek poleis, including Corinth and the island poleis of Corcyra and Aegina, had developed formidable navies. But it was only in the years before Xerxes' invasion that one polis, Athens, began to develop into a true naval superpower. Around 483 BCE, a rich vein of silver was discovered at Laureum in eastern Attica. Rather than distribute this windfall to all Athenians, giving a modest amount of money to everybody, Themistocles, a wily and ambitious leader then prominent in the city, convinced the Athenians to give the money in trust to the hundred richest Athenians. Themistocles convinced these wealthy citizens to use the money to outfit a new fleet of triremes, ostensibly to use in the ongoing conflict with Athens' nearby rival Aegina, but really, or so Herodotus tells us (7.144), because he saw that the Persians would soon threaten Greece by land and sea to make up for the Athenian victory at Marathon in 490 BCE. Themistocles essentially inaugurated the "trierarchy," the public service (or "liturgy") enjoined upon wealthy Athenians for the maintenance and crewing of a trireme for a set amount of time. This new fleet provided the core of the Greek navy during Xerxes' invasion of Greece, which, as we will see below, culminated in the decisive Greek victory at Salamis, which Themistocles engineered. In addition to building the Athenian navy, after the Persian invasion Themistocles advised that the Piraeus, with its several natural harbors a few kilometers from the Athenian city center, be developed into a proper naval port and fortified with a great wall, just like the city itself was. Themistocles' vision was furthered by later leaders as two long walls were extended from the walled city to the walled Piraeus, and a third wall was stretched to Phaleron, Athens' older port. The large navy and impenetrable system of walls made Athens an "island on land," nearly invulnerable to assault by land forces – as Pericles described the city at the outbreak of the Peloponnesian War (Thucydides 1.143). In the fifth century BCE, exulting in its triumph at Salamis, the city put a great deal of its energy into becoming a peerless naval power, with profound consequences for all aspects of Greek history.

Thalassocracy: the naval mob and empire

Thucydides, the Athenian historian of the Peloponnesian War, was fascinated by sea-power, and considered the concept of *thalassocracy*, that is, "rule of the sea," to be essential for understanding the ebbs and flows of human history.

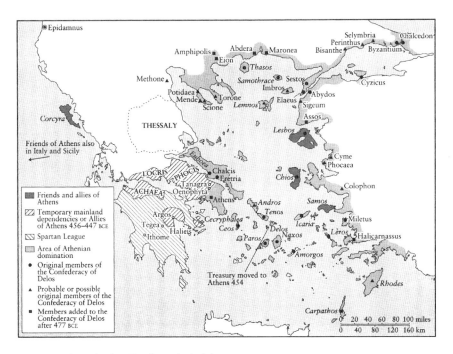

Map 3.1 The Athenian Empire at its height.

Source: from *Readings in Greek History* (2nd edition) by D. B. Nagle and S. Burstein (2014). Map 5.1, p. 163. By permission of Oxford University Press, USA.

Near the very beginning of his work, Thucydides looks back through the mists of time to Minos, the mythical king of Knossos in Crete, as the first Greek *thalassocrat* (1.8). In Thucydides' own day, the Peloponnesian War famously pitted the Aegean world's greatest sea-power, Athens, against the greatest land-power, Sparta, and he argued that the new imperial reach of Athens, made possible by its navy, had critically upended the traditional balance of power in the Greek world and led to the war in the first place. Though he did not live long enough to complete his history of it, Thucydides saw the end of the Peloponnesian War and surely would have had much to say about the simple fact that Sparta needed to build a world-class navy in order to defeat the Athenians, which in the end was possible only with Persian money. In many ways, the Peloponnesian War was a defining event for Classical Greek history, and sea-power was one of that war's central themes. Let us consider, therefore, the nature of Athenian sea-power, the empire it afforded, and the conflict it sparked.

The wily Themistocles was not only responsible for the Greek naval victory over the Persians at Salamis in 480 BCE. Because of his foresight in recognizing that Athens' future lay at sea, he was also the prime architect of the Athenian Empire, the first such political arrangement in the Aegean world whereby one

Greek polis effectively ruled other Greek poleis – and greatly enriched itself in the process. The prodigious resources needed to finance the building of the Parthenon, as well as the cultural flourishing that made Athens the center of art, literature, and learning in the fifth century BCE, was all due to the fleet and the "naval orientation" championed by Themistocles in his city. Because Athens had been most responsible for the victory at Salamis, and consequently the saving of Greece in Herodotus' estimation, the Athenians felt well within their rights to claim a new level of power and prestige. If the Greek agonistic ethos meant that those who demonstrated the most *aretē*, or excellence, in war received the most power and prestige, after Salamis no one had a better claim to *aretē* than the Athenians. Sparta, like Agamemnon in Homer's *Iliad*, had prestige because of its longstanding and traditional role as the leader of Greece. Athens, like Achilles, now demanded its share of prestige because of its chops. To boot, after the Persians were driven from mainland Greece, only the Athenians had the equipment, namely a large navy, to provide any meaningful support to the Greeks in Asia, who still lived in Persia's shadow, and only the Athenians had the stomach to continue military activities abroad to defend against future Persian incursions. The Athenian navy masterminded by Themistocles, therefore, was primed to gain for Athens unprecedented power.

Many factors account for the Archaic and Classical Greek world being divided up into hundreds of independent poleis rather than an ethnic nation-state or territorial empire. Foremost among these is the geography of Greece, which features large mountain ranges punctuated by narrow valleys suitable for habitation. As overland communication between different regions of Greece was made difficult by geography, so too was it daunting for any one power to dominate others given the constraints of pre-modern travel and communication. The Spartans managed the impressive feat of controlling the population of Messenia, despite the massif of Mt. Taygetus standing in the way. But the Spartans were only able to do so through developing a uniquely militarized society, brutal methods of oppression, and a pathological aversion to leaving their homeland, which would have provided the Messenians with room to revolt. Few other Greek powers even attempted the sort of control over others exercised by the Spartans. While the Greeks might have valued concepts such as freedom and political independence, in many ways they were forced to do so by geography. Sea-power, on the other hand, eliminated many of the constraints of geography and allowed the Athenians to subjugate many other Greeks, even those lying on the other side of the Aegean Sea, far more distant from Athens than Messenia was from Sparta.

It all began innocently enough. After the Persians were driven from mainland Greece, the Greeks living on the Aegean coast of what is now Turkey asked the Spartans and Athenians to help guarantee the freedom of the Greeks in Asia. Sparta had no stomach – or navy – for overseas adventure, and so declined, but not before absurdly suggesting that the Greeks of Asia move across the sea to the mainland. Athens all too happily picked up the slack. A great coalition of Greek states, including Athens, most of the Aegean islands, and the Greeks on the northern and eastern Aegean coasts, was formed and dubbed the Delian League since the alliance's treasury was based on the island of Delos. This coalition was to provide for the common defense against Persia, and member states, which were all supposedly equal, were required to supply either money or ships and men, with most opting for the former. Some of the most important inscriptions to survive from Classical Greece are the so-called "Athenian Tribute Lists," which detail the contributions of all league members. The result of this arrangement was that the Athenian navy grew ever larger, funded by league contributions, while the military forces of most league members dwindled.

When the Persians were driven from the Aegean for good in the middle of the fifth century BCE at the Battle of Eurymedon, every pretense for the league's existence had vanished. Athens, however, was in no way willing to give up its new position of power over so many fellow Greeks, and with no other navy capable of mounting a challenge to Athenian sea-power, Athens could seemingly do what it liked. The treasury was eventually moved from Delos to the Athenian Acropolis, ostensibly for security reasons, and states that stepped out of line by wanting to withdraw from the league were severely punished by Athenian military might. The island of Naxos was the first to try to opt out of the alliance, but it was quickly surrounded by Athenian ships, besieged, and brought back into the alliance in a humbled state and forced to pay an indemnity. Thucydides says that the conflict over Naxos was the first time one Greek state had subjugated another. The Delian League had morphed into an Athenian Empire.

Who was driving this newfound Athenian imperialism? Certainly there were military leaders, such as Cimon and his eventual arch-rival Pericles, who saw overseas expansion and power as a means to greater personal prestige, but at base it was the Athenian people that were most enthusiastic for empire. Their reason was simple: empire gave the Athenians, especially the lower classes, or *thetes*, not eligible for hoplite service, something important to do for their polis, something which also happened to offer regular pay. Those without land who could therefore afford to be away from home for long campaigns abroad found work on the Athenian triremes. The triremes and their crew were paid for by the richest Athenians, who were compelled by the state to take on a trierarchy and were given titular command of a vessel. In addition to a livelihood, the Athenian rowers gained a new measure of political power to go hand-in-hand with their military importance to the polis.

As the hoplite phalanx might have been instrumental in giving the hoplite class power over the state as the first oligarchies and proto-democracies began to spring up in the Archaic period, we know with much greater certainty that naval power led to the political power of even the lowest class of Athenian citizens. Pericles rose to power because, like Cleisthenes in the late sixth century BCE, he appealed to a broad share of the Athenian population – in this case, the *thetes* or rowing class – that had been underrepresented in government. Though Cleisthenes is generally thought to have founded democracy around 508 BCE, many scholars think the reforms of Pericles and his allies, which included stripping the last remaining aristocratic body, the Areopagus, of most of its powers and offering jury-pay so anyone could afford to participate in the judicial process, ushered in true democracy for the first time. On a more basic level, rowing in the fleet increased the *thetes'* political power because the very act of drilling at the oars day in and day out awakened the rowers' class-consciousness and taught them how to work together for a common purpose. Barry Strauss thus dubs the Athenian trireme the "School of Democracy."

An Athenian writer we call the "Old Oligarch" because of his anti-democratic bent, sums up the connection between naval power and democracy:

> First I will say this: it is right that the poor and the people have more than the rich and noble for the following reason, namely because the people are the ones who row the ships and thus affix power to the city. The helmsmen, the senior officers and the junior officers, the ruddermen, and the ship-wrights – these are the ones who give power to the city much more than the hoplites, the nobles, and the good and useful men. This being the case, it seems only right that there is a share for everyone in the magistracies, both those chosen by lot and by vote, and that any citizen who wants to can speak out.
>
> (Pseudo-Xenophon *Constitution of the Athenians* 1.2)

The words of the Old Oligarch notwithstanding, not everyone is convinced that the increased focus on naval power gave rise to greater democracy. While scholars like Kurt Raaflaub argue that the navy was instrumental in catalyzing the immense political changes of the fifth century BCE, whereby full political participation was opened up to even the poorest citizens, Josiah Ober counters that it was the democratic revolution that in fact made the Athenian navy possible in the first place. Since the construction, maintenance, and operation of a fleet of hundreds of ships would have required tremendous resources and cooperation across the entire spectrum of Athenian citizenry, Ober argues that a sudden change at the end of the sixth century BCE in Athenian political consciousness and solidarity paved the way for Cleisthenes' famous reforms and also the development of the Athenian fleet that stood up to Persia. On whichever side of this chicken-and-egg scenario you happen to fall – whether the navy and empire gave rise to democracy, or democracy gave rise to the navy and empire – the navy and the political power of the masses are closely linked in any case.[3]

In one of the great ironies of history, greater freedom and power for a greater number of Athenians was dependent on the oppression and exploitation of many non-Athenian Greeks across the Aegean. Not only did service in the fleet awaken the *thetes'* political ambitions, the revenues brought in by the Athenian Empire paid for democratizing measures like jury-pay, and also the famous temples on the Acropolis, including the Parthenon, that are supposed to have been monuments to Greek freedom and triumph over the despotic Persians. The Athens that has been for centuries the darling of Western culture – democratic, culturally vibrant, and richly decorated in gleaming marble – was in fact aggressively imperialistic, using its sea-power to enrich itself and elevate its status among fellow Greeks. The early architects of Athens' naval empire, especially Cimon, tried to expand Athenian power without competing directly with Sparta. The new generation of naval imperialists represented by Pericles, however, used Athens' control of the sea to challenge Sparta's traditional supremacy in Greece and ended up dangerously disrupting the balance of power. Pericles, both spurring on and backed by the "naval mob" (a term used by Thucydides) that now had great influence in Athens, refused to temper Athenian imperialism in order to avoid conflict with Sparta. The result, as Thucydides sees it, is that Sparta grew fearful of Athens' growing power, and egged on by those Greek states chafing under Athenian domination, decided to intervene militarily, sparking the Peloponnesian War, which would last twenty-seven years and end finally in Spartan victory – but only after Sparta built a world-class fleet of its own with Persian money.

The Peloponnesian War was the ultimate test of traditional Greek military power, namely the hoplite phalanx, against the new strategic policy of *thalassocracy*. Since they trained continually for warfare, no one could hope to match the Spartans on the field of battle, let alone the Spartans supplemented by their many allies in the Peloponnese. Pericles urged the Athenians to live as though they were islanders, to give up their extensive agricultural land in Attica if necessary and take shelter behind Athens' walls. Since the Athenians controlled the sea and had access to the vast resources possessed by their subject-allies, they could simply wait out annual invasions of the Spartan army while supplying themselves by sea to their heart's content. To make things even harder on the Spartans, the Athenians could launch raids against the Peloponnese by sea, wearing the Spartans down bit by bit. For their part, the Spartans thought that the sight of the enemy in Athenian territory and Athenian lands being ravaged would so offend the Athenians' pride that the Athenian hoplites would march out against the Spartans, for which many Athenians did in fact argue. In the end, though, Pericles' advice won out and the Athenians looked to the sea as their best chance for victory and for winning the sort of long-term prestige they so craved, even if in the short term they had to bear Spartans marching through their land with impunity – a situation lamented in Aristophanes' play *Acharnians*, produced in 425 BCE.

Despite some grievous setbacks, such as a devastating plague that struck Athens soon after the war began, Pericles' strategy seemed to work. For the first several years of the conflict, the Spartan invasions of Attica failed to bring the Athenians out to battle, while Athenian naval raids chipped away at the Peloponnese. The Athenian navy even managed to strand hundreds of Spartan soldiers on an island near Pylos in 425 BCE, 300 of whom were eventually taken prisoner. This devastating blow to Sparta might well have ended the war, with the result that Athens was recognized by their enemies as a legitimate great power among the Greeks. The war dragged on, however, in part because the successors of Pericles, who had died in 429 BCE, violated the original Athenian strategy by fighting pitched battles on land with disastrous results and overreaching in trying to expand their empire in war-time, most notoriously in Sicily. The Spartans, too, eventually changed their strategy by attacking Athens' possessions in the Aegean, especially Amphipolis, instead of simply trying to lure out the Athenian hoplites. But despite several crushing defeats for Athens, including the loss of thousands of men and hundreds of ships in Sicily, the Athenians hung on much longer than anyone might have expected.

Only a fleet of their own allowed the Spartans finally to defeat the Athenian navy and starve the city of Athens into submission. Navies are tremendously expensive. The Athenians only maintained their own navy because they could rely on regular contributions from their subject-allies. Having no empire of their own, the Spartans turned to Persia, Greece's supposed nemesis, for financial backing. In the last phase of the conflict, a period known as the "Ionian War" because most of the action took place at sea off the western coast of Turkey, the Athenians and Spartans fought several great naval battles, entailing the loss of thousands of men to compound the already significant losses sustained throughout the rest of the war. In 405 BCE, the Spartan fleet finally destroyed the Athenian navy in a battle at Aegospotami. Without control of the sea, Athens could no longer supply itself, and a Spartan naval blockade forced Athens' surrender in 404 BCE. In a groundbreaking study, Barry Strauss argues that the naval character of the final years of the war led to disproportionately high casualties among the Athenian *thetes*, so much so that the political character of Athens in the postwar years was changed dramatically.[4]

The fifth century BCE, long considered to have been Greece's Golden Age, had come full circle, largely because of sea-power. The Peloponnesian War broke out because Athens' new naval power, made possible by Athens' role in the war against Persia and supported by the newly enfranchised Athenian *thetes*, oppressed other Greeks and threatened Spartan supremacy. The war ended because the Persians were brought back into Greek affairs to fund a Spartan navy, and the Athenian *thetes* ended up bearing the brunt of the war's cost in lives. And while *thalassocracy* allowed Athens to flourish as few societies ever have, it also invited a conflict that nearly destroyed Athens completely. The following fourth century BCE certainly contained many cultural high points, including the careers of Plato and Aristotle and perhaps the most stable period of Athenian democracy, but constant warfare among the Greeks also became the norm, including many sea-borne expeditions across the Aegean Sea and attempts on the part of Athens to reestablish some semblance of their former naval supremacy.

Naval battles: Salamis and Naupactus

Let us consider two naval battles to get a better sense of what took place when fleets clashed in ancient Greece. We will first examine the Battle of Salamis, the great naval encounter of 480 BCE in which the patriotic Greeks, who were at that time relatively inexperienced in fighting at sea, decisively defeated a much larger Persian fleet, made up primarily of the Persians' Phoenician subjects, among the foremost mariners of the ancient world. With as many as 1,000 ships, the Battle of Salamis could have had as many as 200,000 men involved in the struggle, an extraordinarily large number. Salamis not only marked the beginning of the end of the Persian invasion of Greece, it also represented a turning point in the Greek engagement with sea-power, opening the door to the concept of *thalassocracy* and providing the impetus for Athens, which provided the lion's share of the fleet in the battle, to aspire to a naval empire. We will next look at the Battle of Naupactus in 429 BCE, representing two distinct naval engagements in the Corinthian Gulf in the early years of the Peloponnesian War, in which the Athenians were victorious. Although, with fewer than 100 ships involved, Naupactus was a much smaller affair than Salamis and did not result in such epoch-shaping consequences, the battle did demonstrate that Athens had become a naval power second to none, capable of remarkable tactical sophistication.

In the last chapter, we discussed the Battle of Thermopylae, the desperate stand led by the 300 Spartans at a narrow pass in central Greece. The Greeks were ultimately unsuccessful because their strong defensive position and the tactical advantages of the hoplite phalanx were overcome when a contingent of Persians was able to surround the defenders. Though Thermopylae was technically a defeat for the Greeks, it was in many ways a moral victory. Had the Persians not been informed by a Greek traitor of a hidden mountain path, the pass might not have fallen. Also, the Greeks demonstrated that a smaller number of hoplites could defeat a larger number of Persian troops provided the battle took place in a confined space in which the Persians could not make effective use of their numbers. Xerxes had taken the pass, but only after three days and terrible slaughter. The action at Thermopylae took place in concert with a naval engagement off the coast, in the narrow waters between the mainland and the northern coast of the island of Euboea, near a place called Artemisium. In the Battle of Artemisium, the Greek fleet, to which the Athenians were the largest contributors, fought the more numerous Persian ships to more or less a stalemate. The straits of Artemisium were only abandoned once Thermopylae had fallen, rendering the combined land and sea operation null. Just as the majority of the Greek infantry left Thermopylae once their position had been turned, leaving only the 300 Spartans and their 700 Thespian allies to fight to the death, the Greek fleet left Artemisium to gather at Salamis, an island off the coast of Attica and part of Athens' territory. Though there was no longer any talk of meeting the Persians on land, since no other place between Thermopylae and Athens offered suitable topographical advantages for the defenders, a naval stand at Salamis made a great deal of sense, precisely because the narrow straits between the island and the mainland offered the same benefits to the smaller Greek force as Thermopylae and Artemisium had.

Despite the advantages afforded by the Salamis straits, the battle almost did not happen. Xerxes and his army moved quickly south from Thermopylae and took the city of Athens, burning it to the ground along with its temples and shrines. Most of the population of Athens had evacuated in time, going to Salamis itself or across the Saronic Gulf to the Peloponnese. Since Athens had already fallen, the Greek fleet, which was led officially by Sparta (despite

Athenian ships making up the majority of the force), wanted to disband and instead fight the Persians on land at the recently fortified Isthmus of Corinth. Why waste ships and lives in a fight off the coast of Athens, to struggle for a city that had already been destroyed? It was Themistocles, the architect of the Athenian navy and in 480 BCE a leading statesman in Athens, that convinced – or rather tricked – the Greeks into fighting at sea.

As Themistocles reasoned, no amount of fortification at the Isthmus would make any difference if Xerxes still had control of the sea. With his fleet, the Persian king could sail around the Isthmus and land at will wherever in the Peloponnese he wished. Only the narrow waters at Salamis offered a chance to disrupt Xerxes' war effort, which had from the beginning relied on the fleet to support and supply his massive land army. In the end, Themistocles forced the issue. As the Greek fleet waited in the coves and harbors of the island, he sent a messenger in secret to the Persians, based a few kilometers away at the Athenian port of Phaleron. Themistocles' servant told the Persians that the Greeks planned to escape during the night, so the Persians would be well-advised to block the channels leading from the island in order to trap the smaller Greek force and crush it. According to Herodotus' gripping account, Xerxes leapt at the opportunity. When morning came, the Greeks, including those who had still planned to abandon Salamis, steeled themselves to fight the Persian fleet that they found blocking their way. The Persians, exhausted from spending a night at their oars, prepared to take on an unexpectedly spirited enemy.

The Greek fleet had between 310 and 370 ships, at least half of which were Athenian. The Persian fleet, anchored by skilled Phoenicians and filled by a host of other allies, including Greeks from Asia, doubled the force of the defenders, totaling between 600 and 700 ships. Herodotus tells us that the Persian fleet was arranged in three lines – exactly how, we do not know – and sailed into the straits in the morning to bring on the struggle, sticking to the coast of the Attic mainland. Since the waters were so confined, most of the Persian fleet remained outside of the straits, cut off from the rest of their force by a small island called Psyttaleia, which partially blocked the entrance to the battle site. Aside from being outnumbered, the Greeks were less practiced and manned less maneuverable vessels, so they would need all the help they could get from the narrow straits. Emerging from their various anchorages, the Greeks moved into battle formations along the island of Salamis, likely in a double line because of the small space. In order to encourage his men to fight as valiantly as possible, Xerxes perched on the hills overlooking the battle to view the fight in person. This did not have the desired effect.

Although Herodotus remains our fullest and most important source for the battle (8.49–8.100), the most vivid description of the outbreak of the naval clash comes from the tragedian Aeschylus, who was at Salamis:

> The trumpet call set them all ablaze; and at once, heeding the command, with the even pull of frothing oars they struck the briny sea. Quickly they were all in full view. The right wing, well marshalled, led the way in good

order. Next, the whole force set upon us, and at once a great shout could be heard: "O sons of the Greeks, go forth! Set free your fatherland, your children, your wives, the shines of your paternal gods, and the tombs of your ancestors! Now the contest is for all!"

(Aeschylus *Persians* 395–405)

This play, *The Persians*, an account of Salamis from the perspective of Xerxes and the Persian court, is widely considered to be the first work of Orientalist literature. That is, Aeschylus helps to define Greekness in opposition to the non-Greek, or the "other" – in this case, the supposedly decadent Persian Empire.[5] In Aeschylus' account, the Greeks sail out boldly against their perturbed foe, and the action begins in earnest when an unnamed Greek ship breaks off the entire stern of a Phoenician vessel. After this first encounter between ships, a general melee broke out at sea, with the Persian fleet being outdone by its very numbers. As Persian ships began to run afoul of each other in the confined space and their oars began to shatter, the Greeks took heart and pressed their victory, slaughtering numberless Persian sailors and soldiers. True to the Orientalist literature that would follow *The Persians*, Aeschylus portrays the Greeks as courageous and orderly, while the Persians lack heart and quickly fall into a state of disorder – even their language is described by Aeschylus as a cacophonous clamor.

Aeschylus' tragedy is a powerful work of art, and offers a stirring image of the battle. Herodotus' account, written half-a-century later, is still plenty exciting and a work of art itself, while presenting perhaps a more realistic version of what happened. According to Herodotus, the Greek fleet did attack the Persians, but not before backing water for quite some time, either because the Greeks were still nervous to fight their more numerous and experienced enemy or because they wanted to lure the Persians even further into the straits before springing a trap. Just as the Greek ships were about to run aground, one of the Greek ships darted out against a vessel of the foe. The Athenians claimed they were the first to attack, while the people of Aegina, Athens' longtime maritime rival, claimed it was one of their ships that struck first. Whatever the case may be, the Greek ship rammed its enemy, but then became lodged in the enemy's hull, unable to extract its bronze ram. Seeing these two ships locked together, the rest of the Greek fleet hurried into action to help their comrade, and the battle began to rage. Just as in Aeschylus' account, Herodotus tells us that the Persian ships began to run afoul of one another in the confined space, and the Greek fleet soon began to get the better of the Persian ships that had entered the straits. The greatest disaster befell Xerxes' force, however, when the first of his defeated ships began to flee to open waters. The large portion of the Persian fleet that had been stationed outside of the straits when the battle began, behind the island of Psyttaleia, tried to distinguish themselves in the eyes of their king. Persian ships thus began to pour into the straits just as other Persian ships were trying to leave, creating a deadly bottleneck that resulted in many more wrecks and countless dead. As Herodotus says, Xerxes' decision to watch the battle in person in fact harmed his fleet more than anything, inspiring misplaced zeal in his men. One captain in the Persian fleet managed to stand out despite the Greek victory: Artemisia, the queen of Herodotus' hometown of Halicarnassus, who rammed one of her own allies in the thick of the action in order to be mistaken for a friend of the Greeks and thus spared a ramming attack herself.

The Battle of Salamis reveals many important aspects of ancient naval warfare. First of all, just like the pass of Thermopylae was a force-multiplier for Greek hoplites, narrow waters were a force-multiplier for the Greek ships. The terrain was a benefit to the defenders for two reasons. Not only did the confined space nullify Xerxes' advantage in numbers, it also prevented the experienced Phoenicians in the Persian fleet from exercising their well-practiced naval man-euvers. Whereas the Spartan hoplites were the expert foot-soldiers at Thermopy-lae, the Greeks at Salamis were vastly outclassed in terms of nautical proficiency. The straits of Salamis made up for this deficiency. In the Great Harbor of Syra-cuse in 413 BCE, the Athenian fleet, which by then had taken on the Phoenician role as the Mediterranean's greatest sea-power, was similarly defeated because it was forced to fight in a confined space against a less skilled enemy. The Battle of Salamis also reveals one of the trickiest aspects of naval tactics, namely the difficulty in ramming an enemy ship with enough force to sink it but without getting one's own ship stuck in the process. Being made of wood and largely empty, triremes have positive buoyancy and thus do not sink. Rather, they can become disabled, but the soldiers on deck can still fight it out, which probably took place as the Greeks came to the aid of the Athenian of Aeginetan ship that had begun the battle by lodging its ram in the hull of an enemy. Salamis also demonstrated the importance of sea-power for both supplying an army and opening up new avenues for transport and invasion by bypassing geographical obstacles on land. Without his fleet, Xerxes' land invasion of Greece would have been far less feasible, and without combating his fleet, any Greek defense by land would have been largely ineffective, at best a stop-gap measure. Finally, both Aeschylus and Herodotus agree that Salamis entailed horrendous slaughter, with the waters churning red and bodies washing up on every shore. The sheer scale of many naval battles, involving hundreds of ships and tens of thousands of men, meant that naval warfare often involved far greater casualties than even the bloodiest land battles.

The Battle of Naupactus, fought fifty years after Salamis, was actually two separate naval encounters that took place some weeks apart in the waters of the Gulf of Corinth (Thucydides 2.80–2.94). In 429 BCE, the Peloponnesian War had only been raging for a couple of years, with the Peloponnesian army invading Attica every summer and the Athenians toughing it out behind their walls. In addition to waiting for the Spartans and their allies to grow tired of mounting expensive and largely pointless expeditions, Pericles wanted to hasten an end to the war by launching naval raids against the Peloponnese. Pericles' idea was to do some real damage to the territory of Athens' enemies, while pointing out the fact that Athenian ships could sail wherever they wanted with impunity. As long as Athens ruled the waves, and as long as the Athenian walls stood strong, the Peloponnesian League simply could not hope to defeat the Athenians.

Accordingly, the Athenians made use of the strong fortified site of Naupactus as a base. Possessing a fine harbor, and strengthened by imposing walls, Naupactus was located near the entrance to the Gulf of Corinth, on the southern coast of the Greek mainland looking across the waters to the northern Peloponnese. Not only could the Athenians use Naupactus to help them regularly circumnavigate the Peloponnese, they could also rely on the population of Naupactus to be unusually fierce and loyal allies. In the middle of the fifth century BCE, the site had been settled by ex-helots, that is, Spartan state-owned serfs that had been granted freedom from their cruel Spartan masters. Naupactus was therefore a strategically valuable site for the Athenians, and a constant source of annoyance for the Spartans and their allies.

In 429 BCE, the Spartans and their allies, including various local forces in western Greece, launched a campaign against Athens' allies in the vicinity of Naupactus, hoping to seize Naupactus itself if possible. This operation was supposed to take place on land and sea, with the Peloponnesians' western Greek allies beginning the campaign on land, supported by a Peloponnesian fleet that was to sail across the waters at the western edge of the Gulf of Corinth. This fleet, consisting of forty-seven ships, never made it over from the Peloponnese. An Athenian squadron of only twenty ships lay at anchor at Naupactus under the command of the admiral Phormio, and when it became clear that the Peloponnesians would try to sail to the aid of their land forces across about 10 kilometers of open water, Phormio launched his twenty ships to block the passage. By the time of the Peloponnesian War, Athens had been the dominant naval power in the Aegean for more than a generation, and Athenian crews had developed into experienced mariners capable of complex maneuvers, just as the Phoenicians had been. Even though Phormio was outnumbered, he knew that his crews' experience would be an insuperable advantage, especially in the open waters between the Peloponnese and the western mainland. To avoid their more proficient enemy, the Peloponnesians had set out well before dawn, hoping to make it across before the Athenians could oppose them. This plan did not work.

Even in the dark, the Athenian ships found their quarry. Phormio ordered the twenty triremes to approach in single file, while the Peloponnesian ships, many of which were slower and ill-equipped transport vessels, formed a circle, the *kuklos* formation, with their bronze rams facing outward and the slower vessels protected in the middle. A few of the best Peloponnesian warships were also placed in the center to look for opportunities to dart out and attack the Athenians. The *kuklos* had been adopted by the Greek fleet against the Persians at Artemisium in 480 BCE, and it was typically a formation employed by a smaller force to protect against a larger. At Naupactus, the larger force adopted the *kuklos* in an attempt to offset its lack of experience. According to Thucydides, Phormio was confident not only because of the skill of his crews, but also because he knew that each morning a strong breeze blew out of the gulf, which would throw the Peloponnesian fleet into disorder. This is exactly what came to pass. The Athenian ships in a single line began to circle the Peloponnesians, getting closer and closer with each pass and forcing the Peloponnesians into an ever tighter mass. When the expected breeze began to blow, the Peloponnesians began to run afoul of one another, and a great confusion of crashing boats and cursing captains erupted. The Athenians attacked, ramming every ship they came across and sinking one of the enemy flagships. As the Peloponnesians began to flee back to their base, the Athenians were able to capture twelve ships along with their entire crews, a crushing blow in addition to all the Peloponnesian ships that had been destroyed in the initial attack. The Athenians, elated in victory, set up a trophy and dedicated a ship to Poseidon, staying firmly in control on Naupactus. Without naval support, the land attack of the Peloponnesians' allies failed as well. All the Spartans and their allies could do was return to a safe port in the Peloponnese and brood upon their humiliation.

The Spartan authorities were furious at their fleet's loss, and concluded that cowardice rather than a lack of skill was behind the battle's outcome. Accordingly, they sent three advisors to oversee the fleet and ensure that future actions would appropriately demonstrate Spartan bravery. The fleet was also reinforced to a total number of seventy-seven ships – almost three times as many as Phormio had – and the transport ships were outfitted more like proper warships. The Spartans and their allies settled on a foolproof plan: they would sail into the waters of the gulf and make it look like they planned to assault Naupactus itself, which would force the Athenians to fight in narrow waters and be unable to take advantage of their superior seamanship. Essentially, the Peloponnesians wanted to do to the Athenians what the Greek defenders had done to the Persians at Salamis, only this time the Peloponnesians would greatly outnumber their opponents to boot. On the appointed day, the Peloponnesian fleet sailed into the gulf in four parallel lines, with a select group of twenty fast ships placed out front to beat the Athenian fleet to Naupactus and prevent the Athenians from taking shelter in the protected harbor. Once the Athenians had been lured far enough into the narrow waters closer to Naupactus, the three Peloponnesian lines planned to change direction and slam directly into the Athenian triremes, driving them against the shore. If the plan worked, the Athenians would be left no time or space to execute any fancy moves, and the Peloponnesian numbers would prove overwhelming. This second battle at Naupactus proved even more of a shock to the Spartans and their friends.

Phormio naturally had wanted to fight the Peloponnesian fleet again in the open waters just outside of the gulf, but when he saw the enemy making for Naupactus he had no choice but to sail into the gulf to protect that important site. The Peloponnesians waited until the Athenians were stretched out along the shore and racing to Naupactus, and then they pounced. All four lines, except the twenty fast ships out in advance, turned on the Athenians and pushed the nine rearmost Athenian ships against the shore, disabling them and taking several crews prisoner. The eleven leading Athenian ships escaped this first attack, and sped towards the harbor of Naupactus ahead of the twenty ships in the Peloponnesian vanguard. Ten of the Athenian ships reached the harbor and turned to defend themselves. An enterprising Peloponnesian vessel was in hot pursuit of the last Athenian ship, while the nineteen other Peloponnesian ships were sailing on at a leisurely pace, confident because of the success of their initial attack and expecting soon to be utterly victorious. Just off shore by the harbor was anchored a merchant vessel, which turned out to be a god-send for the last desperate Athenian ship. Turning around the anchored craft in a spectacular feat of seamanship, the Athenian ship wheeled to strike its pursuer amidships, disabling it and causing its captain to commit suicide out of embarrassment and despair. This sudden reversal utterly perturbed the rest of the Peloponnesian pursuers, who had maintained no order, and enthralled the other Athenian ships. The Athenians regrouped and rushed upon their pursuers. The nineteen remaining advance Peloponnesian ships gave in nearly without a fight, after which the eleven Athenian triremes came to the aid of their comrades, recapturing the ships and crews the Peloponnesians had taken, and driving the Peloponnesians back to their own shore. The second battle at Naupactus was a remarkable victory in the face of four-to-one odds. Athenian naval supremacy was reasserted in the strongest possible terms.

Naupactus offers a masterclass in naval tactics, revealing what could be accomplished by a society's dedication to developing and maintaining a great navy and keeping crews at the oars for long hours of drill and training. It is no surprise that the Athenian *thetes* developed political solidarity after spending the amount of time in the bowls of a trireme required to hone the coordination and skill they used to encircle and close in on the Peloponnesian *kuklos* in the first clash. Likewise, few other navies could have accomplished the dog-fighting maneuver around an anchored ship that turned the tide of the second engagement. Two crucial elements of the typical hoplite phalanx are that the hoplites provided their own equipment and fought in a relatively straightforward formation that could be utilized without constant drill. The Athenians were in a class of their own at sea, however, because only they had the resources and the willingness to invest as a polis in the great expense of building and equipping hundreds of triremes and providing for the livelihood of tens of thousands of rowers.

The navy in the Athenian visual landscape

In the last chapter, we considered hoplite imagery and the iconography of the citizen-soldier, concluding that in many important ways the figure of the hoplite dominates Greek representations of war and also of citizenship. This dominance, however, was not total. In Classical Athens, a city prominent because of its navy, naval imagery had an important place, though you have to go looking for it. Whereas hoplites appear frequently in vase-painting and sculpture, the typical media considered by students of Greek art history, ships and rowers show up in the Athenian landscape itself, represented by monumental buildings and massive harbors instead of painted or sculpted figures.

In the fifth century BCE, after the triumph of the Athenian navy at Salamis, some public monuments were dedicated to that victory at sea. Just as at Marathon, a permanent trophy for the Battle of Salamis was erected on the island's Cynosura peninsula, close to the scene of the action, and looking across to the

Piraeus. Themistocles himself, the architect of Salamis and of the Athenian navy in general, was honored with a monumental tomb at the entrance to the Piraeus port, the column of which can still be seen today. It is not surprising that Themistocles was so honored, given his general importance and prominence, but the siting of his memorial in the Piraeus indicates that he was memorialized primarily as a naval figure, in the part of Attica that was the consummation of his naval vision. Perhaps the most striking monumental celebration of Salamis has only recently been recognized. As John Papadopoulos and Samantha Martin-Mcauliffe argue in a convincing paper, the Propylaia – the magnificent gateway to the Acropolis on the same scale and magnificence as the Parthenon – was positioned in such a way as literally to frame the island of Salamis as one departs the Acropolis sanctuary. A powerful visual link was thus consciously made between the center of Athens and the island several kilometers away on the polis' western edge, reminding the Athenians again and again what happened in the Salamis straits. If Papadopoulos and Martin-Mcauliffe are right, the Periclean building program, long recognized to be a celebration of Athens' triumph over the Persians and ascent to greatness, included Salamis as much as Marathon or any other conflict, which is appropriate given that Salamis more than any other battle opened the door to the Athenian Empire. Finally, in the years immediately after Salamis, Aeschylus produced his play *The Persians*, which is a dramatization of Salamis from the perspective of Xerxes and the Persian court. Though, as I pointed out in the last chapter, Aeschylus perhaps overemphasizes a relatively minor infantry action that took place during the battle, nevertheless this play represents the only surviving tragedy to depict a real historical event, and that event is unquestionably a shining moment for Athens' navy.

It is the fourth century BCE, however, after the great empire that the navy had made possible had come to an ignominious end, that produced some of the most telling statements about the importance of the navy in the Athenian landscape. Demosthenes, the most famous Athenian orator who provided the inspiration for such later figures as Cicero, unequivocally praises Athens' naval architecture as representing the very best of the polis. Comparing the leaders of the time of the Persian Wars to his own day, Demosthenes says that Themistocles and Miltiades richly adorned the city instead of their own private houses. Among the examples of their architectural legacy, Demosthenes highlights the ship-sheds of the Piraeus and the Piraeus itself.

> The houses of Themistocles and Miltiades and other such famous men, if any of you happen to know of what sort they were, you would see that they are no grander than the houses of the common people. But the build and adornment of their public structures were of such a kind and such grandeur that they could be surpassed by none of those of later generations. I mean the Propylaia, the ship-sheds, the stoas, the Piraeus, and the other structures with which you see the city has been adorned.
>
> (Demosthenes *Against Aristocrates* 207)

Figure 3.4 The Propylaia, Athens, looking towards Salamis.

Source: photo by Braun, Clément and Cie. J. Paul Getty Museum (no. 87.XM.99.5).

He brings up the ship-sheds in another speech too, this time grouping them in with the Parthenon and Propylaia, suggesting that as monuments to the city's greatness the ship-sheds are in a league with the most famous of all Classical buildings:

> The buildings these men left behind as an adornment for the city – temples, harbors, and the buildings related to these – are so great that they are not surpassed by any that came later. I speak of the Propylaia, the ship-sheds, the stoas, and the others, which those men, adorning our city, bestowed upon us.
>
> (Demosthenes *On Organization* 28)

The ship-sheds were the massive buildings lining the Piraeus harbors in which the city's triremes were dry-docked and maintained. Today, archaeologists continue to study these structures, several examples of which can be seen just under the water at Zea harbor and extending into the foundations of modern buildings.[6] The ship-sheds have provided us with some of the best evidence of the dimensions of Classical warships. Not explicitly mentioned by Demosthenes, but equally important to the city's topography nonetheless, were Athens' walls, also championed by figures such as Themistocles. These walls – including the long walls between the city and its ports, and the walls of the Piraeus itself – made the Athenian Empire possible and allowed Athens to hold out for decades against Sparta, and were also a constant and monumental reminder for the Athenians that their power was based on the sea.

The Piraeus was home to another monumental naval building, the Arsenal of Philo, named after its architect and built after the emergence of Macedon as the dominant power in the Greek world and the consequent end of the age of the polis. We know more about this building than almost any other from antiquity because of the discovery of a detailed stone inscription outlining the dimensions and other data associated with the arsenal's construction. Recently, sizeable portions of the building itself have been discovered among the dense buildings of the modern Piraeus. The arsenal was built with the practical purpose of storing the rigging and other equipment needed to outfit the Athenian triremes, a clear sign that Athens continued to value its naval prowess even though Macedonian rule now curtailed most of Athens' and any other polis' foreign policy. Philo's building went well beyond its practical purpose, rising to a truly monumental scale that was a source of wonder in antiquity. As part of Philo's vision, the arsenal contained a walkway right through its center so Athenian citizens could stroll through to view and marvel at the massive equipment needed to keep the navy seaworthy.[7]

C. Jacob Butera, in taking into consideration these monumental structures and the topographical relationship between the city of Athens and its port at the Piraeus, as well as the not inconsiderable amount of naval imagery in other media, such as vase-painting, argues that the navy was far from invisible in Athens. While sailors and ships might not appear on the Parthenon frieze, the buildings housing the ships and frequented by the sailors were as important as the Parthenon to the Athenians' conception of their own greatness. Hoplites might have been more prominent in Attic art, and certainly were outside of Athens, where the navy was not nearly as important; but the navy need not always have conjured up images of an unruly and impoverished mob. Rather, without the naval mob, much of the rest of Athenian art and architecture of the Classical period might not have been made at all, a fact which all Athenians seemed to appreciate.

Notes

1 For up-to-date information on this exciting research, see: https://rpmnautical.org.
2 For discussions of these naval tactics, see Holladay (1988), Lazenby (1987), and Whitehead (1987).
3 For this debate, see Ober (2007) and Raaflaub (2007).
4 Strauss (1987).
5 For Aeschylus' work as one of Orientalism, see the important work of Edith Hall (1989).
6 For these excavations, see Lovén (2011).
7 For an account of this arsenal, see Pounder (1983).

Further reading

Butera, C. Jacob. 2010. *"The Land of the Fine Triremes:" Naval Identity and Polis Imaginary in 5th Century Athens*. PhD. Dissertation, Duke University, Durham, NC.

This doctoral dissertation offers the most comprehensive study of naval imagery in Classical Athens, which, as Butera argues, was far more important to the city's identity than is often recognized.

Hale, John R. 2009. *Lords of the Sea: The Epic Story of the Athenian Navy and the Birth of Democracy*. London.

A gripping treatment of the navy and its role in expanding Athenian democracy.

Hanson, Victor Davis. 2005. *A War Like No Other: How the Athenians and Spartans Fought the Peloponnesian War*. New York.

An accessible introduction to the various military considerations in the study of the Peloponnesian War, including the importance of navies and sea-power.

Horden, P. and N. Purcell. 2000. *The Corrupting Sea: A Study of Mediterranean History*. Malden, MA.

A fascinating and wide-ranging exploration of how the sea shaped the history of the Mediterranean region.

Lazenby, John F. 1993. *The Defence of Greece, 490–479 B.C.* Warminster.

The best single-volume study of the Persian Wars from a primarily military perspective. Essential reading for understanding the significance of the naval actions of Xerxes' invasion.

Martin-Mcauliffe and John K. Papadopoulos. 2012. "Framing Victory: Salamis, the Athenian Acropolis and the Agora." *Journal of the Society of Architectural Historians* 71: 332–361.

A brilliant study of the position of the Propylaia, the ceremonial entranceway to the Athenian Acropolis, demonstrating that the island of Salamis is perfectly framed as one departs the Acropolis. This article is an important reminder that the navy was a significant part of the Athenian consciousness and landscape.

Meiggs, Russell. 1972. *The Athenian Empire*. Oxford.

The definitive account of the Athenian Empire, created and maintained by the Athenian navy in the years after the Battle of Salamis.

Morrison, J. S., J. F. Coates, and N. B. Rankov. 2000. *The Athenian Trireme: The History and Reconstruction of an Ancient Greek Warship* (second edition). Cambridge.

An ancient historian and naval architect describe their project to build the *Olympias*, a fully functional trireme. This second edition includes observations derived from the ship's sea-trials.

Strauss, Barry. 1996. "The Athenian Trireme, School of Democracy." In J. Ober and C. Hedrick (eds.), *Demokratia: A Conversation on Democracies, Ancient and Modern*. Princeton. 313–326.

An argument for how working together to operate a trireme taught the lower-class Athenians how to work together, which translated into political power and increased democracy.

Strauss, Barry. 2004. *The Battle of Salamis: The Naval Encounter that Saved Greece – and Western Civilization*. New York.

A lively and comprehensive account of the battle, with informative discussions of Greek naval warfare in general.

4 Total war

Athens vs. Sparta

Introduction

In a book on the general history of Greek warfare, such as this one, there is precious little space to discuss a particular conflict in any great detail. The subject of Greek warfare is simply too vast, and the array of questions raised too complex, to allow for a blow-by-blow account of a specific campaign or war. An entire chapter on the Peloponnesian War, however, is justified by a host of reasons. First of all, while the Persian Wars, especially Xerxes' invasion of

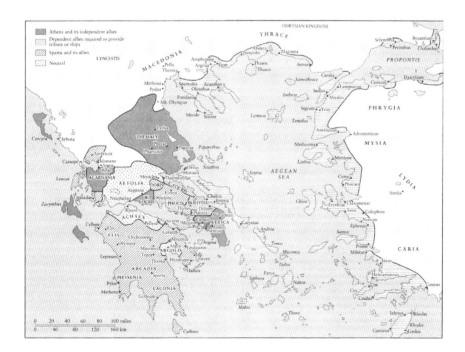

Map 4.1 Alliances at the outset of the Peloponnesian War.

Source: from *Readings in Greek History* (2nd edition) by D. B. Nagle and S. Burstein (2014). Map 5.3, p. 180. By permission of Oxford University Press, USA.

Greece, were the largest historical conflict yet seen in the Greek world and involved a far greater share of the Greek population than any previous conflict, the invasion itself lasted only a year. Though Athens was sacked and burned – twice – the Athenians were able to re-occupy their city and move on with their lives relatively quickly, as were the other Greeks of the mainland involved in the conflict. The Peloponnesian War, on the other hand, lasted the twenty-seven years between 431–404 BCE and involved so much more than military conflict, including debates and violent struggles over the best constitution, the place of soldiers, citizens, and non-citizens in a continuous and all-consuming war, and the subjugation of Greeks to other Greeks. Second, to be sure, the Persian Wars were critical to the development of Greek culture, including the idea of "Greekness" itself, but the Peloponnesian War represented a clash between the two poles of the Greek world, Athens and Sparta. The stakes were much greater than simply who would be more powerful than whom, but the war promised to test what was the best Greek way of war, way of organizing society, and way of life. Third, the Peloponnesian War, being a total war lasting decades, prompted an accelerated pace of military change. During and after the clash between Athens and Sparta, Greek warfare was profoundly different than it had been. And finally, more than virtually every other conflict in history, the Peloponnesian War is inextricably linked to its primary historian, the towering intellectual giant Thucydides, who presents students of the conflict with a range of unique advantages – and hazards.

We will begin this chapter with a discussion of Thucydides as a source and interpreter of the war, taking into consideration his profound impact on the Western literary and intellectual tradition and how that is sometimes a pitfall for scholars hoping to determine the truth of events of more than twenty-four centuries ago. We will then go over the key phases of the war, respectively labeled the Archidamian War, the Peace of Nicias, the Sicilian Expedition, and the Ionian/ Decelean War. The third section will treat strategic and tactical innovations, including siege warfare, the use of light-armed troops and mercenaries, the establishment of permanent bases in enemy territory, and the novel approach of attacking the enemy indirectly by striking imperial holdings and allies. The exigencies of continuous warfare led to the rise of larger-than-life generals who were treated as heroes (and sometimes villains) with semi-divine status, which we will explore through the careers of the Athenians Pericles and Alcibiades and the Spartans Brasidas and Lysander. Finally, at the end of the chapter, we will investigate the effect of long-term and total war on the Greek psyche, especially through the anti-war comedies of Aristophanes and tragedies of Euripides performed in Athens as the conflict continued to rage.

Thucydides, author of the war

Herodotus, the historian of the Persian Wars (and a host of subjects besides), is widely known as the Father of History, a title he held even in antiquity. Thucydides, historian of the Peloponnesian War, on the other hand, is regarded as the inventor of history as a true scientific and objective discipline. He is also considered the pioneer of political science, particularly the subfield of realism, and was the inspiration for no less a political philosopher than Thomas Hobbes and a host of others who followed. Herodotus was a native of Halicarnassus in Asia Minor, and composed his histories in the 430s BCE, fifty years after the Persian invasion of Greece. He performed his work orally for delighted audiences, especially in Athens, where he spent much time. Herodotus begins his work by stating that his purpose is to ensure that great deeds, both of Greeks and Persians, do not go unremembered, and to discover the real reason the two peoples fought each other. To perform this task, Herodotus treats an expansive range of subjects, including, in particular, novel customs that might help explain the differences between various peoples. Herodotus was thus as much a cultural anthropologist as a historian, and his many tales have entertained audiences for centuries.

Thucydides, an Athenian by birth and a generation younger than Herodotus, wrote about events of his own day, including many he was witness to and involved in. Thucydides was a general during the war, but was exiled by his fellow Athenians after he failed to protect the important Athenian ally Amphipolis from Spartan capture in 424 BCE. Though Thucydides lived to see the end of the war, he died before completing his history of it, which breaks off abruptly while treating the events of 411 BCE. It was left to Xenophon, another Athenian, to complete the history of the war up to the surrender of Athens in 404 BCE. Unlike Herodotus, Thucydides claims not to be interested in composing entertaining stories merely to charm listeners. Rather, he employed the finest methods at his disposal – personal experience, interviews with eye witnesses, and careful consideration of human nature – to determine the objective truth of events and record them as accurately, if perhaps dryly, as possible. Where Herodotus frequently presents several conflicting versions of a story, sometimes telling his audience which version he happens to prefer, Thucydides has done this leg-work for us, giving us only the definitive version of things. Until recently, therefore, Thucydides has been accepted as the more critical and rational of the two great historians, the author of a serious work of analysis, whereas Herodotus has been received as an avuncular figure too often taken in by a good yarn.

Things are, of course, not quite so straightforward. Thucydides' very claims of dispassion and scholarly rigor should, from the outset, invite caution from his readers. Thucydides felt that human nature, *to anthrōpinon* (literally "the human thing") in Greek, is a constant, and that human beings and human states have always and will always act in similar ways and from similar motivations no matter the time and place. Thus, if one carefully studied the Peloponnesian War, certainly the greatest event of Thucydides' own lifetime and one of the most important in the entirety of Greek history, including its events, personalities, debates, and outcomes, one would gain both a richer appreciation of the human condition and a deeper understanding of all other historical events and periods, including even those of our own day in the twenty-first century. Thucydides saw the Peloponnesian War as a paradigm, or representative model, of all major wars. More than that, every specific event that took place during the war, from

Figure 4.1 Marble bust of Thucydides.

Source: Musée du Louvre (no. MA 317). Photo credit: Erich Lessing/Art Resource, NY.

the plague at Athens to the civil war on the island of Corcyra, were paradigms of those sorts of events (that is, plagues and civil wars) in other times and places. Because of its paradigmatic nature, Thucydides famously calls his work a "possession for all time" (*ktēma es aiei* in Greek), in contrast to a short-lived performance piece of the sort written by his contemporaries (1.22).

The historian undoubtedly forged a genuine masterwork, one that has stood the test of time and continues to inform current affairs and those involved in them. But Thucydides' conception of his work as paradigmatic also led him to select the material he includes and present it in such a way as to establish and bolster the various paradigms he sees at work in human affairs. Thucydides does not always give us the full story. He was also, as the eminent historian Donald Kagan argues, above all a revisionist historian, keenly intent on correcting the errors and misconceptions of his fellow Greeks about the true nature of the war they had all witnessed. His work is therefore a polemic, a piece written specifically to refute rival points of view. No matter how detailed and careful Thucydides' investigations were, no such work can possibly be free of bias. As Kagan also argues, in many crucial cases the popular opinion Thucydides sought to refute was much closer to the truth of things than Thucydides' version. The very first sentence of the work provokes awe in the reader, but should also encourage careful skepticism: "Thucydides the Athenian *composed the war*…" The Greek literally means that he wrote not a history of the war or an analysis of the war, but the very war itself. While we can and should engage with Thucydides' timeless work of literature, students of the past should be very careful in determining to what extent the real Peloponnesian War was equivalent to Thucydides' composition.

Let's consider some of Thucydides' biases and look at some of his literary themes to determine how his work, aside from recalling the facts of the war, can inform us about Greek warfare more broadly conceived. An aristocrat by birth (in fact, connected along with the great Miltiades and Cimon to a royal family of Thracians), Thucydides was prominent enough in Athens to be elected general, and was assigned a post in the Thracian region because of his family ties.[1] Thucydides was thus adept, or connected, enough to be successful in the Athenian democracy. Nevertheless, he was exiled in 424 BCE by that same democracy, and as a consequence his work demonstrates throughout a mistrust of the more populist tendencies of the Athenian government and a marked preference for brakes on the common people such as the government of the 5,000 richest citizens that was established briefly in 411 BCE.[2] This political perspective is of no small consequence for a historian of a war that was widely seen as a conflict between the democratic Athens and the oligarchic Sparta. We can disagree with Thucydides' assessment of the Athenian democracy while recognizing that the war really was between a democracy and an oligarchy (or at least an oligarchy of a fashion), and these different political outlooks were operative in how the war was fought. Athens tended to force its allies to be democratic (yes, the Greeks did think that democracy could be forced on a state), while Sparta compelled its allies to be oligarchic. By the same token, democratic factions tended to support Athens, while oligarchs supported Sparta, and more than once the war between Athens and Sparta and their respective allies precipitated violent political strife between democratic and oligarchic parties.

Just as the war was in part a struggle between proponents of oligarchy and democracy, Thucydides saw the Spartans and Athenians as polar opposites in terms of their respective national characters as well. The historian presents the Athenians as possessing endless energy and innovation, pushing to extend their influence throughout the Mediterranean world and willing to try new ways to win, both tactically and strategically. As dynamic thinkers, the Athenians are also able to cope with reversals, pulling more than one victory out of a seemingly helpless situation. These characteristics are what frightened so many of the Athenians' fellow Greeks. Those who were not yet subjected to the empire were worried that they would be soon enough. The Spartans, on the other hand, are shown by Thucydides to be congenitally conservative, afraid even to venture out of the Peloponnese, let alone try their hand at new ways of war and new ways to increase their influence beyond their comfortable position of supremacy over their Peloponnesian neighbors. In the opening chapters of Thucydides' account of the Peloponnesian War, the Corinthians have to cajole the Spartans to act against Athens' aggression, in the process berating the Spartans for their painful slowness to action:

> Of all these things [the rise of Athenian imperial power], you are to blame. You first allowed them to strengthen their city after the Persian War, then you allowed them to build the Long Walls. It is you who, even up to now, rob the freedom of those who are enslaved by them, but also those who are still your allies … You, Lacedaemonians, alone of the Greeks, remain inactive and defend yourselves not by any action but by the impression of future action … The Athenians are always innovating and are swift in planning and in doing alike.
>
> (Thucydides 1.69–70)

Because Thucydides has established these paradigmatic characterizations, any Spartan or Athenian that acts outside the norms of his society is marked for special attention – sometimes for admiration, sometimes for censure. The Spartan general Brasidas, for example, whom we shall meet in the pages below, is portrayed as being virtually Athenian in his bold and creative leadership style, which leads him into conflict with the Spartan authorities even as he makes the greatest advances for the Spartan cause in the first phase of the war. Things were not so black and white, however. There were other energetic and innovative Spartans, just as there were plodding and conservative Athenians. Thucydides seems to color his portraits of some events of the war, especially the motivations and deliberations behind them, in order to maintain a consistent characterization of the two sides.[3]

Thucydides' most influential idea is that the war was inevitable. Early in his work, while outlining the proximate causes of the conflict, Thucydides says that the real cause of the war was "the growth of Athenian power and the fear this caused in Sparta" (1.23). As the First World War was precipitated by the unification of Germany and the destabilizing influence this had on the traditional balance of power, the prestige Athens gained after the Persian Wars, and the Aegean-wide empire Athens built based on this prestige and its all-powerful navy, threatened Sparta's traditional position of dominance in the Greek world, forcing Sparta to act before Athens became more powerful still. In the course of human affairs, Thucydides seems to reason, this conflict was bound to rise sooner or later. Today, the clash wrought by an emerging power threatening an established power is called by political scientists such as Graham T. Allison the "Thucydides Trap."[4] The rise of China, for example, might inexorably lead to conflict, perhaps destructive, between China and the United States. Perhaps the Peloponnesian War was inevitable – and several scholars think that it was. Thucydides is also able to use the war's seeming inevitability to downplay the war's proximate causes, many of which were precipitated by the policies of the Athenian statesman Pericles, a figure Thucydides held in the highest esteem, as Donald Kagan points out. Students of the war are now increasingly likely to point out the ways that the Greeks could have avoided war in 431 BCE, just as we all should hope that the great powers are able to avoid a state of war with one another.

It might prove impossible to disentangle the Peloponnesian War from the great author who wrote the definitive account of it. But that might not be a bad thing. Even where Thucydides gets it wrong, he still provides valuable food-for-thought, including penetrating insights into human behavior and the nature of warfare. Students of the ancient world should wrestle with the historian, taking into consideration what other primary evidence is available and also common sense to determine where we can safely differ in our own opinions regarding the war between the Athenians and Peloponnesians.

An overview of the Peloponnesian War

There are many excellent books on the Peloponnesian War (some of which are listed in the "Further Reading" section at the end of this chapter), and any comprehensive Greek history textbook will cover the war's central political, social, and cultural issues. Here I will offer only the briefest outline of the war and its major phases, in order to give some context to the rest of the discussion and situate the Peloponnesian War within the wider subject of ancient Greek warfare. It must be said at the outset that the war – a conflict between, on the one side, Athens and its empire, and Sparta and its allies in the Peloponnesian League on the other – is known today as the "Peloponnesian" War because our primary source and perspective is Athenian. The war could just as easily be called the "Athenian" War, or even the "Atheno-Peloponnesian" War. As always when dealing with antiquity, the incomplete and biased nature of our sources often skews our understanding of history.

Tensions had been high between Athens and Sparta for decades, including a period of hostilities in the middle of the fifth century BCE that scholars now call the "First Peloponnesian War," which involved mostly proxy battles instead of open warfare between Athens and Sparta themselves. In 446/5 BCE, Athens and Sparta signed a thirty-year peace treaty to bring an end to this conflict but which in the event lasted less than fifteen years. Though Thucydides says that the Peloponnesian War proper, which broke out in 431 BCE, was really caused by the growth of Athenian power and the fear this generated in Sparta, there were at least three more immediate causes of the violation of the thirty-year peace treaty, namely the so-called Affair of Epidamnus in 433 BCE and the siege of Potidaea and the Megarian Decree, both in 432 BCE.[5]

Epidamnus is not a household name today. Even in antiquity it was a relatively insignificant and out-of-the-way place, located in what is today Albania along the Adriatic Sea. But, just like the First World War was sparked by the assassination of Franz Ferdinand in Sarajevo, a struggle involving Epidamnus provided the spark of a much more serious conflict. In short, the citizens of Epidamnus were involved in a struggle between oligarchs and democrats in 433 BCE, and the democrats appealed to other states for help. Epidamnus was a colony of Corcyra (modern Corfu), so Corcyra was the first place from which help was requested, but the Corcyreans declined. Corinth, itself the colonial founder of Corcyra, and thus the "grand-founder" of Epidamnus, was asked for help next, but the Corcyreans objected, resenting the interference from Corinth. Things really got out of hand when the Corcyreans asked the Athenians for help against Corinth, an ally of Sparta, and Athens agreed. Corinth thus had good grounds for complaint against Athens, arguing to the Spartans that Athenian intervention violated the terms of the thirty-year treaty. Corinth had an even more legitimate grievance when the Athenians besieged the city of Potidaea in the northern Aegean in 432 BCE. Though Potidaea was a member of the Athenian Empire, it was originally a colony of Corinth. Thus, when the Athenians besieged the city because it tried to break away from the empire, the Corinthians protested this act of aggression against their colony – even though ancient Greek colonies rarely had any formal political ties to the original colonizing polis. Finally, in 432 BCE, the Athenians at the behest of the prominent leader Pericles levied a decree against Megara, a city just to the west of Athens and lying in the border zone between Athenian and Corinthian territory, barring the Megarians from using Athenian ports and markets, a crushing economic blow that caused real hardship in Megara. Since Megara was an ally of the Peloponnesians, the Athenians provided their rivals with yet another reason to argue that Athens had violated the treaty and thus needed to be brought to heel by force. When, again at the insistence of Pericles, Athens refused to concede to Corinth's complaints or yield to Sparta's demands that it provide the subjects of the Athenian Empire with sovereignty or at least rescind the Megarian Decree, Sparta and the Peloponnesian League voted for war.

The war aims of the two sides were rather different. The Spartans and the Peloponnesian League wanted to break Athenian power, ideally putting an end to Athens' Aegean-wide empire. At least in terms of propaganda, the Spartans were going to war to "liberate the Greeks," as they had been urged to do by the Corinthians and other allies. Athens' goal was on its face much more modest. All Athens, or at least its leading figure, Pericles, wanted was to be recognized by Sparta and the other Greeks as a great power and deserving of its imperial influence over other Greeks. To achieve this recognition, Athens needed merely to preserve the status quo, which could be accomplished by holding out against the Peloponnesians long enough to impress upon them that a war with Athens was too expensive and difficult to continue. In brief, Athens needed only to survive as an imperial power, while the Peloponnesians had to crush Athens. Having the best land army in the world, the Peloponnesians planned to invade Attica and lay waste to the land in an attempt to draw the Athenians out to battle. Pericles advised the Athenians to hunker down behind the walls of Athens, maintain the fleet and the empire in order to keep supplies and money pouring in, and make limited raids against the Peloponnese just to maintain pressure. Pericles reasoned that Sparta and its allies would soon run out of money and that all the various contingents in the Peloponnesian army would eventually return to their own homes and grudgingly accept that Athens was now a power to be reckoned with.

The Peloponnesian War (431–404 BCE) can be divided into four distinct phases: the Archidamian War (431–421 BCE), the Peace of Nicias (421–413 BCE), the Sicilian Expedition (415–413), and the Ionian/Decelean War (413–404). The war began in 431 BCE with Thebes attempting to invade and take over its local rival Plataea, an ally of Athens, and the Peloponnesian army under the command of the Spartan king Archidamus invading Athens. The war ended with the surrender of Athens in 404 BCE, made possible by the destruction of the Athenian fleet at the Battle of Aegospotami in the previous year. While Sparta's allies wanted Athens to be destroyed, Sparta was content to have the walls of Athens torn down, the Athenian fleet reduced to a mere twelve ships, and a pro-Spartan puppet oligarchy established in Athens.

The Archidamian War is named after Archidamus, who led the annual invasions of Attica for the first several years of the conflict. For the first couple of years, Athens abided by Pericles' strategy, but not without controversy. First of all, many Athenians found it intolerable to watch their lands and homes being destroyed without being able to go out from the walls to take on the Peloponnesians in battle. Pericles was fined and removed from office for a year because of the strain his strategy caused, but he was reelected for the following year anyway. And second, though the Peloponnesian army was unable to threaten Athens' fortifications, the influx of so many Athenians into the small area within the walls helped to exacerbate and spread a virulent plague that broke out in the war's second year, devastating the Athenian population. Pericles himself died of this plague, and his successors were far less likely to follow his original strategy. Thucydides says that Pericles was a uniquely capable and prestigious leader, and that those who succeeded him were short-sighted and self-interested demagogues. Most scholars today, however, think that Pericles' strategy was doomed to fail, and that many of his successors were in fact talented generals and leaders in their own right. The Archidamian War came to an end when both sides expanded beyond their respective strategies in the first years of the war. Athens, spurred on by the innovative general Demosthenes and the populist agitator Cleon, established a base in Peloponnesian territory at Pylos in 425 BCE, which led to a battle against that Spartans that resulted in nearly 300 soldiers

Figure 4.2 The northern tip of the island of Sphacteria, near Pylos, where nearly 300
         Spartan soldiers surrendered in 425 BCE.
Source: author's photograph.

surrendering and being taken prisoner by Athens, a shocking blow to Sparta.
Athens' advantage was short-lived, however, since in the following year Athenian hoplites lost a pitched battle in Boeotia, and the visionary Spartan general
Brasidas captured many of Athens' imperial possessions in the north Aegean,
most crucially the city of Amphipolis. The loss of Amphipolis imperiled Athens'
timber and gold supplies, and led to the exile of Thucydides, who had been the
Athenian general in the area. Both sides having suffered harsh defeats and
having accomplished important victories, the Spartans and the Athenians were at
last willing to come to terms.

   The Peace of Nicias, named after the Athenian general and statesman who
negotiated for Athens, was signed in 421 BCE, seemingly bringing an end to a
decade of war. Indeed, many Greeks at the time considered this to be the real
end of the war, and that the hostilities that broke out later were part of a second,
new war. Thucydides argues that the peace was simply a lull in a larger war, and
most scholars tend to agree. The peace terms, which were to be in effect for fifty
years, stipulated that both sides would maintain what they currently possessed,
except Athens would give up Pylos and the Spartans imprisoned in Athens and
under siege elsewhere, and Amphipolis would be returned to Athenian control.
According to Pericles' original war aims, Athens could consider the Peace of

Nicias a victory in the war. The Athenian Empire, after all, would remain largely intact, and Athens would be recognized as a power on a level with Sparta. The peace, however, did not work out. The people of Amphipolis, for one, had no intention of returning to Athenian control, removing one of the key reasons Athens had wanted to make peace in the first place. Furthermore, one of the greatest battles of the war took place at Mantinea in 418 BCE, during this supposed period of peace. Though Athens did not take part in this battle in full force – only 1,000 Athenian hoplites were present – that battle was a result of an alliance made between Athens and Argos to destabilize Sparta's control over the Peloponnese. This alliance was the brainchild of an ambitious Athenian named Alcibiades. The arch-nemesis of Nicias, Alcibiades saw continuing warfare as a path to his own personal advancement, and so he had no time for the peace brokered by his rival. Alcibiades' greatest influence was felt in his championing of a new and massive military venture for the Athenians, namely the invasion of Sicily in 415 BCE.

The Athenian expedition to Sicily in 415–413 BCE has gone down in history as one of the greatest military blunders of all time, though most historians think that the expedition need not have turned out as it did, but that there were many missed opportunities for success, especially on the part of Nicias. Thucydides records a debate in Athens in 415 BCE between Alcibiades, who advocated an expedition to Sicily to aid some Athenian allies on the island and possibly do some damage to Syracuse, a large and important city that was allied with Sparta, and Nicias, who cautioned that such an expedition during a supposed time of peace would lead to the Athenians taking on a new war on the same scale as the one they had just fought with Sparta, with little chance of success. In the end, Alcibiades won, but only sort of. To hedge their bets, the Athenians appointed both Alcibiades and Nicias as commanders, not a terribly great idea given how much these two hated each other, and added a third general, a seasoned veteran named Lamachus, to balance things out. The Athenians, in order to guarantee the success of the mission, voted to send the largest invasion force ever mustered at Athens, which in the end managed only to amplify the disaster.

The Sicilian Expedition started off poorly, and only got worse for the Athenians. Even before the fleet reached Sicily, Alcibiades was recalled to stand trial for his alleged role in a set of sacrilegious crimes, including profaning the Eleusinian Mysteries, one of the most influential cults in the ancient world, and vandalizing dozens of sculptures throughout the city on the eve of the expedition. Instead of returning to stand trial, Alcibiades fled to Sparta, where he promptly began to advise the Spartans on how best to fight the Athenians. Whether or not Alcibiades really did prompt the Spartans to undertake new measures, or whether the Spartans decided on such measures on their own, they did eventually establish a permanent base in Attica and send a general to aid the Syracusans. Both actions proved devastating to the Athenians. The Spartan general, a dynamic leader named Gylippus, helped to rally the Syracusans to finish off the Athenian expedition on both land and sea in 413 BCE, leading to an unprecedented loss of ships and soldiers for the Athenians, including the expedition's commanders.

And the Spartan base near Athens, at a place called Decelea, put enormous pressure year-round on the Athenians.

Despite losing hundreds of ships and thousands of men in 413 BCE, the Athenians held out for nearly another decade. The final phase of the war, called either the Decelean War because of the Spartan base in Attica, or the Ionian War because of the prevalence of naval battles near the western coast of Turkey, saw the emergence of the Persian Empire as a major player in Greek affairs once again. Because the Sicilian Expedition had been such a debacle, and because the war in general had led to great loss of blood and treasure in Athens, democracy was overthrown for a brief period in 411 BCE, replaced by an oligarchic government that brought about the recall of Alcibiades, who promised to arrange for Persian financial support to make up for the losses of the previous years. Alcibiades, who had been kicked out of Sparta, was actually playing a double-game. According to Thucydides, he advised the Persian satrap Tissaphernes to support whichever side was struggling, in order to keep the Greeks fighting and thus too weak to challenge Persia's interests. Waging war with money instead of men became the standard way the Persians dealt with the Greeks for the next several decades, with dire consequences to strength and stability of the Greek world. In the end, the personal relationship between another Greek, namely Lysander, an ambitious Spartan leader, and Cyrus, another Persian satrap and the younger son of the reigning Persian king, proved decisive. With Cyrus' money, Sparta finally built a fleet capable of challenging Athenian control of the sea. After several naval battles, Lysander managed to destroy much of the Athenian fleet at Aegospotami in 405 BCE, and then blockade Athens until the city surrendered in 404 BCE. Xenophon provides a stirring account of Athens' fall: "After this, Lysander sailed into the Piraeus, the exiles returned, and they tore down the walls of Athens with great eagerness and to the music of flute-girls. They thought that this day was the beginning of freedom for Greece" (Xenophon *Hellenica* 2.2.23). After the war, Sparta, or more particularly Lysander, tried its hand at controlling affairs in the Aegean, proving much more tyrannical than the Athenians had ever been. Far from being the liberators they had portrayed themselves as at the war's beginning, the Spartans managed only to make enemies of former allies. The fate of Athens was to have its fleet taken away, except for twelve ships, to have its walls torn down, and to have its democracy replaced by a narrow oligarchy loyal to Lysander. Sparta's moment in the sun was short-lived. Democracy was restored in Athens within a year, and the majority of the Greek world, encouraged and funded by Persia, soon turned against Sparta. The Greeks settled in to several more decades of nearly constant warfare. Nobody really won the Peloponnesian War.

Strategy and tactics beyond the phalanx

The staple of ancient Greek warfare, as we have discussed at length in Chapter 2, was the hoplite phalanx. Many find it surprising, therefore, to learn that the Peloponnesian War included only two full-scale pitched hoplite battles during nearly three decades of warfare: at Delium in 424 BCE, and at Mantinea in

418 BCE. Most of the fighting was by other means. Tactically, these means included especially sieges of walled cities, and light-armed skirmishing, often by mercenaries instead of citizen-soldiers. Strategically, the war aims of both sides were prosecuted by taking the war to the enemy's allies and imperial holdings instead of taking on the enemy directly in the field of battle, and by the establishment of permanent bases in enemy territory to ravage and harass long term.

City walls are of course an important strategic asset. In the last chapter, we considered how Athens' powerful navy and its impregnability by land due to its city walls and the long walls extending to the Piraeus port were central elements of Athens' grand strategy, essentially making Athens an island on land and a direct competitor of and threat to Sparta. Thus, the underlying strategic situation of the Peloponnesian War, namely a life-or-death struggle between Greece's greatest land-power and Greece's greatest sea-power, was largely a result of the strong walls of one of the two sides. In this chapter, however, we will focus on the tactical considerations at play in sieges of walled cities. The importance and frequency of sieges during the Peloponnesian War led to some developments in tactics and techniques, but perhaps most interesting for our purposes will be a comparison between the siegecraft of the fifth century BCE with that of the fourth, which we will address in the next chapter.

Tactically speaking, in the fifth century BCE the advantage in siege warfare always lay with the defenders. Before the fourth-century BCE development of

Figure 4.3 A section of the Athenian walls in the Kerameikos.

Source: author's photograph.

siege artillery, such as torsion catapults that could crumble and punch holes in stone walls, and huge siege towers that could allow many attackers to swarm over a wall's battlements and overwhelm defenders, well-constructed walls were virtually impossible for attackers to overcome with force. City walls at the time of the Peloponnesian War tended to be made of stone at the lower courses, with two faces of regular stone masonry filled with rubble in the center. The upper courses of the walls were often mud-brick, most of which has not survived to the present day, which gives the impression that the walls were shorter than they actually were. These walls could be supplemented with towers and gates, which gave the defenders more space to hurl projectiles on the attackers below. In the case of strong gates, towers on either side allowed the defenders to catch their enemy in a deadly crossfire. The walls of Classical Athens, particularly those visible at the archaeological site of the Kerameikos, are a good example of the fortifications defenders could rely on in the fifth century BCE. Not only have the stone courses survived – showing very irregular masonry owing to the fact that these walls were constructed in considerable haste over Sparta's objections – but some of the mud-brick at the higher levels has survived too, today covered by protective awnings. The entrance to the city of Athens at this point was through a double-gate well protected by towers.

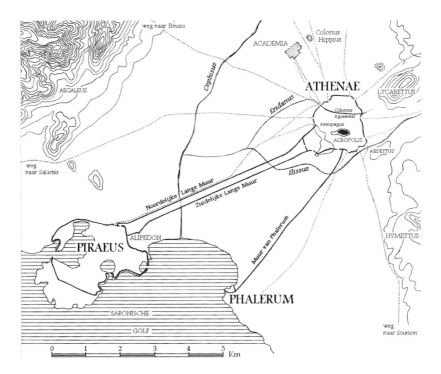

Map 4.2 The Long Walls of Athens.

Source: public domain, from Wikimedia Commons, by Napoleon Vier.

Aside from battering the doors of the gates or trying to scale the walls with ladders, there was little attackers could do against such obstacles. Instead, as immortalized by the story of the Trojan Horse, already hundreds of years old in 431 BCE, cities usually had to be taken by other means. Methods of forcing a city's surrender included starving the besieged population by establishing a blockade – we hear of desperate people boiling the leather straps of their beds in order to fill their stomachs with something – and arranging for the city to be betrayed by a sympathetic faction on the inside. During the Peloponnesian War, when so much of the conflict centered on whether democracy or oligarchy was the best form of government, there was often a political faction eager to hand the city over to the enemy as a way to overcome their rivals among the citizenry.

The difficulty of taking a city by assault, however, did not always prevent the attackers from giving it a spirited try. Plataea, the Athenian-allied city in Boeotia near where the Persians were once and for all driven from Greece in 479 BCE, even today offers visitors haunting ruins of walls overlooking a vast plain, though these walls are what remain of the fourth-century BCE, rebuilt city, rather than the city at the time of the Peloponnesian War. The war did not begin in 431 BCE with a Spartan invasion of Attica, but instead with a Theban attempt to take the city of Plataea to expand Thebes' control over Boeotia. The Thebans initially tried to take the city by treachery, by having pro-Theban sympathizers admit a group of Theban commandos that were to take over the city in a night raid. The Thebans were discovered, however, and killed or driven out by the Plataeans. The Theban attempt at subterfuge failed, and it fell to the Spartans to take the city of Plataea the old-fashioned way. While the Spartans laid siege to the city, beginning only in 429 BCE and after most of the population had escaped, they tried to overcome the walls with one of the more darkly comical plans in the annals of military history (Thucydides 2.75–2.78). The Spartans heaped up a great mound of earth against the walls, only to have the Plataeans dig under the walls from the inside and scoop away earth from the mound every day, leaving the Spartans scratching their heads as to why their mound failed to grow day by day. The Plataeans also built a second wall inside the city, in case the earth ramp should eventually succeed. Frustrated, the Spartans tried other means, including hurling torches into the city to set the Plataean buildings ablaze. The fires never managed to take hold. A more ingenious and effective incendiary method was used by the Boeotians in 424 BCE against the besieged Athenian garrison at Delium: pitch and other flammable materials were billowed and shot through a long pipe, annihilating the Athenians' temporary wooden defensive works (Thucydides 4.100). Plataea did eventually surrender, to be depopulated and destroyed, but only after a lengthy blockade through which many Plataeans escaped. The city fell in 427 BCE, despite being tiny compared to Sparta, defended only by a small garrison, and receiving no direct military support from Athens. The survivors of the Plataean garrison were all put to death, perhaps paying the price for just how frustrating a long siege can be. Several other populations during the war, including most infamously the Melians, suffered a similar fate once their cities fell.

A blockade took on much greater proportions, in terms of geography covered and troops involved, during Athens' attempts to take the city of Syracuse during the Sicilian Expedition of 415–413 BCE. Relying on their fleet to prevent supplies reaching Syracuse by sea, the Athenians resolved to cut off the massive city of Syracuse by land by constructing a series of stone blockade walls anchored by a stone fort to give the attackers a strong base in enemy territory. Unfortunately for the Athenians, constructing these fortifications was difficult for two reasons: the Syracusan cavalry could attack the men building the wall, and the Syracusans, especially when spurred on by the Spartan commander Gylippus, built counter-walls to cut off the Athenian works before they could be completed. Both sides continued to build walls and counter-walls and launch raids against one another until the Athenians faced up to the futility of their blockade attempts and tried to give up on the mission, only to be defeated by the invigorated Syracusans at sea and on land and utterly destroyed. The ultimate irony for the Athenians is that, before the arrival of Gylippus as an ally to relieve Syracuse, the Syracusans had very nearly decided to come to terms with the Athenians and possibly surrender their city. As the fate of others had demonstrated, it was sometimes prudent to come to terms early before the attackers built up enough rage to slaughter the population once a siege was successful. Thucydides records a debate in Athens in 427 BCE concerning what to do with the population of Mytilene once the city had surrendered to the Athenian besiegers (3.36–3.49). The firebrand Cleon argued that the men should be killed and the women and children enslaved, to receive just punishment for their treachery against the Athenian Empire. Cleon's opponent, an otherwise unknown figure named Diodotus, argued instead that leniency should be shown, lest future rebels hold out to the bitter end knowing that if they surrendered they would only be utterly destroyed. The failure of the Athenian siege at Syracuse, though, meant that no such debate took place during the Sicilian Expedition.

Arguably the most important siege of the war was the siege of Athens itself, though this was by no means a typical siege. Sparta did not attempt to surround or blockade Athens, and certainly had no plans to attack the city's walls, which were formidable and well-defended. Moreover, because it controlled the sea, Athens faced no real threat of starvation and could hold out indefinitely – in theory, at least. Pericles' entire strategy hinged on waiting out the Spartans from behind Athens' walls, the Athenians being a besieged people with the singular advantage of never running out of supplies. Also, the Spartans did not have the resources to invest the city permanently, so the sieges lasted only for a few weeks during the campaigning season, after which the Athenians could venture back out to their lands and properties. All of that being said, the Spartan king Archidamus did resort to a time-honored tactic of besiegers, namely laying waste to the defenders' lands in order to force a battlefield confrontation outside of the walls, something against which Pericles had to argue many times in front of an increasingly frustrated citizenry. Victor Davis Hanson has argued, based on experiments conducted on his own farm in California, that ravaging would not have been terribly effective in the long term. Olives are too hardy to be destroyed easily, and grapevines grow back quickly. Also, grains can only be destroyed when they are ripe, otherwise they cannot be burned. To be sure, for a city less well-supplied than Athens, the loss of even a single season's produce could be disastrous, which is what Brasidas counted on in 424 BCE when he threatened to destroy the ripening grapes of the people of Acanthus if they did not admit his army into their city and join the Spartan side. What mattered for Archidamus, and what made Pericles' job so difficult, was Greek pride and the terrible psychological strain that must have accompanied the Athenians witnessing their lands being invaded right before their eyes. Aristophanes' play *Acharnians*, produced in 425 BCE, has as its chorus the men of the deme Acharnae, which provided the greatest number of hoplites to the Athenian phalanx, irate that they must watch helplessly as their lands are ravaged. Yet, had the Athenians abandoned their walls, they almost certainly would have lost against the Peloponnesian hoplites, leading to much more painful casualties than some houses and crops, but Athenian pride very nearly drove the Athenian hoplites to march out to battle.

The most serious consequence of the Peloponnesians' annual siege of Athens was something Thucydides ascribes to chance and which the ancients could not possibly have predicted. Just one year into the war, a plague broke out in Athens that killed perhaps a third of the population, including Pericles himself. Scholars today still debate what specific disease the plague represents, with typhoid fever being a leading contender, but Thucydides offers a vivid description of its physical and moral effects (Thucydides 2.47–2.55).[6] The plague broke out and spread so destructively in large part because of the overcrowding in Athens that resulted when Attica's primarily rural population was crammed within the city walls for long stretches of time. The Athenians' control of the sea did not protect them from the effects of overcrowding and the unsanitary conditions that accompany too many people in too small a space. Sparta's siege of Athens, therefore, might have been more effective than even the Spartans realized.

As there had been many sieges before 431 BCE, so too had light-armed troops and mercenaries been part of Greek warfare since long before the outbreak of the Peloponnesian War. Archers, slingers, and other mobile troops fought against the Persians in 480–479 BCE, even if hoplites are given all of the credit. And mercenaries, or soldiers-for-hire loyal to their paymaster instead of any state or cause, had been hired by figures such as the Athenian tyrant Pisistratus as tools for gaining and keeping power. While the Greeks hired other Greeks and non-Greeks as mercenaries, Greeks themselves had frequently served as mercenaries for non-Greek powers in places such as Egypt and Asia Minor. So while light-armed skirmishers and mercenaries – the two often were one and the same – were not new developments of the Peloponnesian War, their use did expand over the course of the war and would continue to gain in popularity and prominence in Greek warfare over the following several decades, even though many Greek states persisted doggedly in their preference for the hoplite phalanx.

These light-armed troops included types of un-armored or lightly armored soldiers ranging from archers to slingers and stone-throwers. They also included peltasts, a type of medium-armed soldier originating in Thrace and named for a crescent-shaped wicker shield called the *peltē*. A peltast's primary offensive weapon was the javelin, or throwing-spear, of which he carried several. His primary tactic was to swarm in against the enemy to hurl javelins before with-drawing and regrouping for another attack. This tactic proved particularly effective against more encumbered and slow-moving hoplites.[7]

Two engagements illustrate well the expanded use of light-armed mercenaries, showcasing both their advantages and their pitfalls. At Pylos in 425 BCE, Lacedaemonian hoplites were defeated on the island of Sphacteria and nearly 300 taken prisoner after succumbing to the light-armed allies of Athens, allowing the expedition's leader, Cleon, to boast that no Athenian citizen-soldier needed to be used at all. While Cleon was the titular head of the force that attacked and forced the surrender of the Lacedaemonians, he worked in concert with Demosthenes, an innovative tactician who had been a general in previous years and would be again later in the war. Before Pylos, Demosthenes had suffered disaster in the wilds of northwestern Greece when his hoplites were surrounded by light-armed skirmishers in a thick wood. Demosthenes' enemies had sown confusion and terror as they struck down many of Demosthenes' men, the flower of the Athenian phalanx. Later at Pylos, Demosthenes, with Cleon, was the one to use light-armed troops to harry and destroy hoplites. Cleon brought to Pylos light-armed allies and mercenaries (some of whom might have been non-Greek) in great numbers, which he and Demosthenes deployed on the island in such a way as to surround the Lacedaemonian hoplites on all sides, raining down missiles and not giving the hoplites any chance to close for hand-to-hand combat. As more and more hoplites fell and lost heart, the light-armed troops gained greater confidence and pressed the attack with more aplomb. Eventually, tired, bleeding, and with no opportunity to fight in their accustomed manner, the surviving hoplites surrendered – to the shame of Sparta and surprise of the rest of Greece.

Pylos was an unqualified triumph for light-armed skirmishers, and proof that Demosthenes had learned his lesson in northwestern Greece. Demosthenes was sent to Sicily in 413 BCE to provide relief for the beleaguered Athenian expedition.[8] With him was to be a contingent of Thracian mercenaries, perhaps requested specially by Demosthenes since he had had so much success with such troops before. Unfortunately, these Thracians arrived in Athens too late to take part in the mission to Sicily, and therefore were sent back home. Their Athenian commander, however, a man named Dieitrephes, was given orders to cause as much damage as possible to the enemies of Athens as this mercenary force made its way north. One of the victims of the Thracians' depredations was the town of Mycalessus, lying a few kilometers from the sea in Boeotia. First thing in the morning, the Thracians, still in the employ of Athens and officially led by an Athenian, stormed into the town past its crumbling walls and began slaughtering all they came across. The people of Mycalessus fell in droves, utterly defenseless against the merciless professional soldiers. Not even the town's livestock was spared. To Thucydides' horror, the Thracians burst into a large boys' school and killed every last child they found inside. The mercenaries only returned to their boats when the cavalry from nearby Thebes arrived to rescue the town. Against the Theban horsemen, the Thracians acquitted themselves well, except, that is, for those mercenaries who were too intent on plundering the town to protect themselves against the Thebans. Driven off, the Thracians continued on their northern journey, but the Theban cavalry provided scant comfort to the people of Mycalessus. The town and its population had been virtually wiped out, the most pitiable fate suffered by anyone during the entire war, as Thucydides says (7.27–7.30). The massacre at Mycalessus demonstrated in the starkest way possible that, although mercenary soldiers might be tactically valuable, especially as a complement to more traditional Greek forces, soldiers loyal only to profit might pay no heed to the accepted norms of warfare.[9]

In the next chapter, we will explore in greater detail the rise of light-armed troops, and their use alongside hoplites and other arms. We will also consider the once widely held view that the fourth century BCE was a period of moral decline in the Greek world, in which the increasing prevalence of mercenaries over and above citizen-soldiers played a key part. As usual, I will point out that things were not so black and white, especially since light-armed troops and mercenaries were in use even during the heyday of Archaic and Classical Greece, as I have already said. But there is little doubt that mercenaries and other professional soldiers played larger roles in the fourth century BCE than they had in the past, and that Greek tacticians started making more frequent use of light-armed and combined-arms forces. Both of these trends were accelerated by the Peloponnesian War because such a long and all-encompassing conflict both made the citizen-soldier model less tenable – few private citizens could afford to be on such lengthy campaigns year after year – and, in their desperation to overcome their enemies, both sides were more open to tactical and strategic experimentation.

The war saw its share of strategic developments, especially striking given that traditional hoplite warfare is supposed to have eschewed strategy in favor of short and uncomplicated campaigns. After several annual invasions of Attica, with no sign that the Athenians would relent or come out to the field of battle, the Spartan general Brasidas suggested attacking Athens indirectly, but taking the war to the allies and subjects that made up the Athenian Empire. In essence, this strategy is similar to the fighting of proxy wars during the Cold War, when open military conflict happened in places like Vietnam instead of between NATO and the Soviet Union in Eastern Europe. Since Sparta and the Peloponnesians had no fleet with which to challenge Athens' control of the sea, only Athens' possessions that could be reached by land were a viable target for Brasidas. But several states along the coast of the northern Aegean, in the vicinity of Thrace, were tempting prizes, especially the city of Amphipolis on the Strymon River, which was a prime source of timber for the Athenian fleet and located close to lucrative mines. In addition, since many members of the empire wanted to be free of Athenian domination, there was a chance that some of these cities, including Amphipolis itself, might go over to Sparta without a fight if Sparta backed up its liberation rhetoric with actual military force. The impetus for Brasidas' mission to the north came from the eager commander himself, but also from the people of the Chalcidice peninsula who had secretly sent agents to Sparta to ask for Spartan help. Despite the promise of Brasidas' mission and his new strategic approach, it seems that the Spartan government was less than enthusiastic. Brasidas received no Spartan hoplites, but instead was given only a force of freed helots and various Peloponnesian allies. Nevertheless, in 424 BCE, a year after Sparta's humiliation at Pylos, Brasidas and his army set out for Thrace.

With a combination of shrewd diplomacy, Spartan-allied boots on the ground, and daring tactics, one by one Athens' possessions in the north went over to Brasidas, most crucially Amphipolis – a loss Athens would feel for the next century and which caused the Athenians to exile Thucydides, who had been stationed as a general in the area. When the Athenian relief force under Cleon failed to retake the city from Brasidas in 422 BCE, the Athenians were willing to make peace with the Spartans, leading to a treaty known to scholars as the Peace of Nicias. The Spartans had been ready to come to terms after their defeat at Pylos in 425 BCE, but the Athenians held out, exulting in their victory. Therefore, Brasidas' mission in Thrace accomplished what several years of full-scale invasion of Attica had failed to do, namely force the Athenians to come to terms, even if in the event those terms were not entirely in Sparta's favor.

Because of its nature as an aggressive imperial power, it was not out of the ordinary for Athens to prosecute the war by attacking Sparta's allies, especially since Athens' entire strategy was based on the knowledge that in a pitched battle Athens would likely lose to Sparta. However, the Sicilian Expedition could be seen as Athens attacking Sparta indirectly – the Syracusans were Dorian Greeks like the Spartans, and were officially allied to the Peloponnesian League. To the Athenians, Syracuse might have seemed a rich prize, like Amphipolis was for Sparta, and easier to attack than Sparta itself. A key point for the history of Greek warfare is that the Peloponnesian War was enough of a "world war" for the Greeks that far-flung expeditions in various parts of the Mediterranean were undertaken by rival poleis, poleis that were not terribly far from each other and that in ages past might have settled things in a more straightforward and speedy manner, such as an all-out battle in a plain.

Both sides made use of permanent bases in each other's territory, what we today might call forward operating bases. The Athenians, as might be expected, were the first to try this strategy. In 425 BCE, the Athenians were at Pylos in the first place because Demosthenes suggested that an Athenian fleet on its way to Sicily stop there to fortify the place. Pylos was located in Messenia, deep in the Peloponnese and next to Sparta's home territory of Laconia. The Messenians had been oppressed for centuries by the Spartans, principally as helots, and Demosthenes reckoned that an Athenian base and garrison at Pylos could serve to foment Messenian revolts against Sparta, which had happened in the past with unsettling results for the Spartans. Pylos lay on a promontory that was easily fortifiable, and the Athenian sailors built defensive works with whatever materials they had at hand. Sparta's attempt to disrupt the establishment of this base is what led to the Battle of Pylos and capture of nearly 300 Lacedaemonians. Long after the battle, Pylos continued to be occupied by the Athenians, existing as a constant annoyance for the Spartans.

In 424 BCE, the very next year, the Athenians tried to double-down on their success at Pylos by establishing a similar base in Boeotia, at a coastal site near Attica called Delium. Just as Pylos was to be maintained by only enough Athenian troops to encourage the Messenians to defect, so too was the plan at Delium to leave a small garrison to undergird the revolt of several Boeotian cities from Theban hegemony. Demosthenes himself was to conduct a mission in Boeotia to encourage anti-Theban factions to rise up, while another Athenian general fortified Delium. Unfortunately, the plan failed to come together. Demosthenes arrived at the wrong time, and the pro-Theban Boeotians had been tipped off and thus were able to quash any uprisings before they could happen. The Boeotian army, anchored by the Thebans, came out in full force against the Athenians at Delium, and the resulting battle, one of the only two hoplite battles in the war, was a crushing defeat for the Athenian hoplites. What was left of the Athenian garrison was besieged and eventually crushed, ending Athenian ambitions to gain influence in Boeotia.

Sparta eventually fortified a forward operating base of their own, but only once they were advised to do so by Alcibiades, according to Thucydides. In 413 BCE, as the Athenian expedition descended into utter quagmire in Sicily, the Spartans fortified Decelea, a strong point in northern Attica. The Spartan presence at Decelea, which lasted until Athens surrendered in 404 BCE, proved much more devastating than the annual invasions of the Archidamian War because the Athenians and their land were under constant pressure, with no hope for seasonal relief, and because the Spartan base prompted the desertion of many thousands of Athenian slaves. The long war had forced the Spartans, who traditionally hesitated even to travel outside of the Peloponnese, to step well outside of their comfort zone by occupying enemy territory permanently.

A new breed of leader

One of the factors that made the world of the Greek polis so unique in the ancient world is that no one person was able to monopolize power – either military, religious, or in terms of wealth – like the rulers of contemporary societies, such as the Persian Empire, were. While even the most democratic Greek societies still did not enfranchise anyone who was not a free-born male, virtually every Greek polis afforded more political power to more people than any other ancient state, and even many modern ones. In keeping with these principles of citizenship and egalitarianism, the Greeks tended to mistrust anyone who gained too much power, let alone claimed a special status as greater than his fellow mortals. Even Sparta frequently chastised its kings and regents if they overstepped, sometimes to the point of exile or death. The exigencies of total war forced a change to this mindset, and several leaders emerged who gained levels of wealth and military power that would have made Homer's Agamemnon jealous. By the war's end, one general, the Spartan Lysander, was even worshipped as a god and had religious celebrations named in his honor, a development that should have appalled the Greeks but in fact portended more of this sort of behavior in the future.

The first larger-than-life figure we will consider is Pericles, who, though he died a mere two years into the war, did more than any other person to precipitate the war in the first place and was responsible for Athens' strategy in the early years of the conflict. In his analysis, Thucydides says that Pericles reached such a level of influence and prestige that, although Athens remained a democracy in name, in actual fact the polis was subject to the rule of its leading citizen (2.65.9). Athens should have had safeguards against the rise of such a figure, especially since most of the highest offices in the polis were filled by a lottery instead of a vote, preventing anyone from achieving such offices because of wealth or connections. The institution of ostracism, whereby Athenians who aimed at too much influence could be exiled for ten years, was also designed to discourage sole rule, though ostracism was used only rarely by the time of the Peloponnesian War. Pericles was able to remain officially in the government year after year because he was elected time and time again to one of the few offices that were filled by a vote of citizens, namely the generalship.

Based primarily on Thucydides' analysis, Pericles has usually been seen as the last of a certain type of political figure, one who could guide the Athenians by the sheer force of his prestige. Pericles, according to Thucydides' eulogy of him, led the Athenians rather than being led by them, and was free to tell his fellow citizens things they did not want to hear without forfeiting his position of influence. After Pericles' untimely death at the hands of the plague his own policies had done so much to cause, Thucydides says that the politicians who followed were eager to win the favor of the mob by any means necessary (2.65.10). These demagogues, a word that literally means "leaders of the common people" in Greek, were a new type of politician in Athens, and, with Cleon as their arch representative, of a decidedly lesser sort according to most students of history. W. Robert Connor, an influential scholar of Thucydides, named his 1972 book *The New Politicians of Fifth-Century Athens*, making it clear that those who followed Pericles were unlike Thucydides' favorite Athenian. Recent scholarship, however, has both recast Pericles as the first of this new generation of politicians (rather than the last of the preceding generation) and considered him to be an imperialistic war-monger who pushed Athens into a preventable war, an opinion of the great statesman that was in fact widely held in antiquity and against which Thucydides crafted his own revisionist account.

Whatever one's assessment of Pericles, there is no doubt that he wielded an outsized influence over Athens and its war effort for many years, from the campaigns Athens undertook in the decade and more leading up to the war in the 440s and 430s BCE, until his death in 429 BCE. The time of the Persian Wars saw its share of prominent Athenian leaders too, such as Themistocles and Cimon, but the power of these leaders was limited both by the relatively short duration of the conflict with Persia and, often, by decrees of ostracism instigated by rival leaders. Pericles did run into his share of trouble with the Athenians – he was ridiculed in several comic plays, and he was formally censured and stripped of his generalship for a year after his war strategy failed to pay off immediately. Nevertheless, his influence on Athenian policy in the lead-up to the war and on Athens' war effort in the first two years of the conflict was profound. Most impressive, the physical city of Athens bears Pericles' stamp even today: the Parthenon and other great monuments on the Acropolis (and a fair amount besides) were erected as part of Pericles' building program, financed by the spoils and tribute taken as a result of Pericles' aggressive imperialism in the Aegean.

Raised as a ward of Pericles after the early death of his father, Alcibiades was rich, talented, and famously good-looking, and driven by ambition commensurate with his many assets. Other than Pericles, no Athenian had such a great impact on the war. Whereas Pericles' policies and strategy might justly be criticized, Pericles always fought for Athens. Alcibiades, by contrast, always fought only for Alcibiades, whether that was best achieved in the service of Athens or Sparta, or even Persia. The war gave Alcibiades plenty of chances to make a lasting name for himself, even after his own fellow Athenians had had enough of him. Despite his volatile nature, and the fact that many seriously suspected him of aiming at tyrannical power, Alcibiades was as talented a commander as the Athenians were likely to find, and the fickle Athenians turning against Alcibiades did more than anything else to cost Athens the war, or so Thucydides argues:

> The majority, fearful of the great lawlessness he exhibited with his own body in his way of living, and the lofty thinking he exhibited in anything he set his mind to do, they became his enemies on the grounds that he was aiming at tyrannical power. Even though his public conduct of the war was among the best, everyone was offended by his private conduct, and so they entrusted matters to others. This state of affairs went a long way towards ruining the city.
>
> (6.15.4)

Alcibiades saw the war as the perfect forum in which to rise to the prominence he felt he deserved, a view of war held by all too many ambitious figures throughout history. And it very nearly worked. When open hostilities came to an end with the Peace of Nicias, a treaty orchestrated by Alcibiades' political nemesis, Alcibiades worried his chance to shine would disappear. He therefore circumvented the peace by orchestrating the alliance with Argos that ultimately led to the Battle of Mantinea in 418 BCE, though in a cruel twist Alcibiades himself failed to be elected general for 418 BCE and therefore missed the battle he had masterminded. He got his next opportunity in 415 BCE by championing the Sicilian Expedition, which, according to Thucydides, Alcibiades saw as a springboard to no less than a Mediterranean-wide empire – though this notion is now largely discounted. The Athenians adjudicated between Alcibiades and his rivals by assigning command of the expedition to Alcibiades and Nicias both, with Lamachus added as a third general and counterbalance. Encumbered by rival generals, it is unlikely that Alcibiades' plans for Sicily would have come to fruition even if things had gone smoothly. They did not. The Athenians recalled Alcibiades to stand trial mere weeks into the expedition, since, on the night before the fleet was to set sail, vandals desecrated many religious sculptures throughout Athens, the so-called "herms" which were square columns topped by the head of Hermes and sporting an erect phallus in the middle of the stone block. Alcibiades and his friends were implicated in this sacrilege and, to boot, were also accused of profaning the Eleusinian Mysteries – a highly secretive and important religious institution in Athens – by mocking the rituals in a private home. Such scoundrels, many believed, must be aiming at undercutting traditional Athenian values, perhaps in a bid to overthrow the democracy.

Rather than come home and face the music, Alcibiades turned traitor and fled to Sparta to advise Athens' enemy on how best to prosecute the war against Athens. Thucydides puts in his mouth a self-justifying speech to the Spartans, remarkable for its sophistry. According to the historian, Alcibiades was the one who advised Sparta to fortify Decelea in Attica, which was ruinous for Athens, and to send aid to the Syracusans against the Athenian expedition, another measure that brought disaster upon Alcibiades' home city. Even after advising Athens' enemies, Alcibiades' propensity for scandal remained undiminished. After allegedly sleeping with a Spartan queen, he fled Sparta and ended up in the court of the Persian satrap Tissaphernes, to advise an enemy of the Athenians – and many other Greeks – even more inveterate than Sparta. Alcibiades suggested that the Persians use their vast financial resources to support whichever side in the Peloponnesian War seemed to be at a disadvantage at any given time, with the goal of keeping the Greeks at each other's throats and thus too weak to threaten Persian interests. It was good advice. While in the Persian Empire, Alcibiades engineered his own recall to Athens, setting himself up as the one person who could guarantee the Athenians financial support, provided that the democracy be overthrown and replaced by an oligarchy – which took place, albeit briefly, in 411 BCE. Alcibiades dominated the conversation at Athens at this point, with the pro- and anti-Alcibiades camps bitterly divided. He eventually did return to Athens and received a hero's welcome, but fled into exile again after one of his subordinates lost a major naval battle. The last years of his life were spent in his private castles in Thrace, where he had his own mercenary army, before he was arrested by the Persians and killed. Though his career was checkered, to say the least, Alcibiades gained influence in three different and mutually opposed societies, and personally championed several major developments in the course of the Peloponnesian War, a reach precious few individual Greeks ever managed to achieve.

If anything, the Spartans were even more wary of stand-out individuals than the Athenians were. The regent Pausanias, hero of the Battle of Plataea in 479 BCE, ran into trouble by listing his own name on the victory monument set up at Delphi (as Thucydides describes in a famous digression, 1.128–1.138).

The Spartans promptly erased his name from the inscription, and declared the victory to be that of all the Greeks that took part in the anti-Persian resistance. Pausanias got into even hotter water by acting imperiously abroad, when Sparta for a very brief period seemed as though it might take leadership over the Greeks on the other side of the Aegean. Worse than his arrogance, Pausanias began dressing and acting like a Persian grandee, which eventually led his countrymen to suspect him of Medizing, that is, joining the Persian cause. Pausanias, despite the great military service he had rendered Sparta, was starved to death by the Spartans after he was walled inside a religious shrine, to which he had fled for sanctuary. The Peloponnesian War produced two generals that the Spartans could control no better than Pausanias. The first, Brasidas, achieved remarkable things for Sparta, despite the short-shrift his fellow Spartans sometimes gave him. Next to Pericles, Brasidas was Thucydides' favorite general – certainly his favorite Spartan – and is portrayed virtually as a Homeric hero.[10]

Brasidas was involved in some of the most important events in the first period of the war. He was, for example, an advisor to the Peloponnesian fleet in its loss to the Athenian admiral Phormio at Naupactus in 429 BCE. At Pylos in 425 BCE, he cut a dashing figure as he urged his men to run their ships aground against the Athenians, before he passed out when he heroically received many wounds. Though Naupactus and Pylos were both failures for Sparta, he impressed the Spartans enough to be granted a command in Thrace in 424 BCE, radically altering Sparta's strategy by taking the war to Athens' northern possessions instead of just to Athens itself. Brasidas had almost total freedom in how he conducted his Thracian campaign, and he met with success after success through cunning diplomacy and the brilliant use of military force. On the field of battle, he evinced tactical as well as strategic ingenuity, being free to innovate largely because he commanded only helots (Sparta's state-owned serfs) and allies, rather than staunchly conservative Spartan hoplites. Once, while fighting a numerous and light-armed enemy, Brasidas arranged his men in a hollow infantry square, by which he easily overcame his foes' disorganized tactics and nullified their numerical superiority. After he took Amphipolis in 424 BCE from the Athenians, an action which led to Thucydides' exile and perhaps also Thucydides' admiration, Brasidas successfully defended the city against Cleon's army in 422 BCE by personally leading a surprise attack which divided and disoriented the Athenian force. Though he won the battle, Brasidas' bravery caused him to be mortally wounded in the melee, but he did not die until he learned of his success.

Brasidas' career stands out most because of what happened at its end. After he died driving the Athenians away and preserving the independence of Amphipolis, the Amphipolitans gave him a hero's burial right in the city's agora, within the city's walls, a rather unusual practice. They also gave him the formal religious honors due to a city-founder, even though Brasidas had founded no cities. These honors included annual athletic competitions, just like those celebrated in the name of semi-divine figures from mythology, such as Homer's warriors. In a fit of literal religious devotion, in honoring Brasidas as their founder the Amphipolitans tore down all the buildings in the city connected to the actual

Figure 4.4 Gold crown and ossuary from the so-called "Tomb of Brasidas," late fifth
century BCE.

Source: Archaeological Museum of Amphipolis. Courtesy of the Ephorate of Antiquities of Serres.
© Hellenic Ministry of Culture and Sports – Archaeological Receipts Fund.

founder, the Athenian Hagnon, who had settled the site in the 430sBCE (Thucydides 5.11). The life and death of Brasidas showed the Greek world that an ambitious general could gain fame and influence in the political and military spheres, but could also, in ways hitherto unthinkable, be revered as a demigod, at least posthumously. Brasidas deftly exploited the space a long and costly war allowed for military and diplomatic accomplishments, along with the material and psychological strain working upon Greeks such as those who lived in Amphipolis.

The career of Brasidas, cut short though it was, paved the way for an even more unconventional Spartan leader. Lysander, officially a "nauarch," or naval commander of Sparta, forged a close personal friendship with the Persian prince Cyrus and thereby gained enough Persian financial support to win the war at sea and force the surrender of Athens in 404 BCE. Putting an end to the decades-long war would have been plenty to ensure Lysander lasting fame, but he went much further than the typical military victor. Assuming de facto leadership over the entire Aegean world, Lysander behaved as if he were the king of all Greece, though he wasn't even a king of Sparta. In the process, he was honored by some Greeks as a god, all while, in actual practice, he sold out the Greeks of Asia and reneged on the mission of liberation for which Sparta had entered the war in the first place. Lysander was ahead of his time; in terms of the levels of power and wealth he enjoyed, and in the outrageous honors he received, he resembles a Hellenistic monarch in the time after Alexander the Great much more than a leader of Classical Greece.

After winning the war because of his personal ties – a point driven home when Sparta earlier lost a major naval battle during a year in which Lysander wasn't given command and Cyrus thus withdrew his support – Lysander did not free the Greeks. Instead, he installed "decarchies," that is, ruling boards of ten Spartans loyal to Lysander. In Athens itself, the Thirty Tyrants were allies, or puppets, of Lysander, giving him much control over Athens, just as he now had over many other Greeks. Some liberators the Spartans turned out to be. No matter: Lysander was still hailed as a god in several Greek states, and the people of Samos even renamed their festival of Hera in honor of Lysander, the *Lysandreia* (Plutarch *Lysander* 18). Lysander was all too happy to encourage such devotion, which he received while still alive, in contrast to the still extraordinary posthumous honors granted to Brasidas. His knack for self-promotion was prodigious: he used the vast sums of money he acquired to set up bronze statues of himself in Delphi, one of which was set up in a treasury building that the people of Acanthus, a northern Greek city, had earlier built in honor of Brasidas. The biographer Plutarch succinctly says that Lysander became richer and more powerful than any Greek had been before him.

Even though the war gave room to commanders like Brasidas and Lysander to rise to great heights, the Spartans did not forget their mistrust of powerful individuals. Lysander eventually overstretched and fell out of favor with the Spartan authorities. One of the kings, Pausanias, refused to support Lysander and the Thirty Tyrants against a democratic uprising in Athens, leading to democracy being restored after only a year of Lysander's puppet regime. Another Spartan king, Agesilaus, who came to the throne through the support and machinations of Lysander, soon outgrew his patron and nursed ambitions of his own. Lysander was eventually knocked off his pedestal and killed in battle in 395 BCE, sent into action without enough support. Agesilaus, learning from Lysander's example, both good and bad, took over as the virtual king of Greece, but instead of acting in a nakedly tyrannical fashion, Agesilaus upped the ante of Sparta's liberation rhetoric and launched an expedition against the Persian oppressors of the Greeks of Asia, portraying himself as a new Agamemnon.

Certainly other Greeks, in addition to Pericles, Alcibiades, Brasidas, and Lysander, rose to prominence through the opportunities afforded by the twenty-seven-year-long war. But those four figures exemplify the sort of power and prestige ambitious and skilled military leaders found in the Peloponnesian War. Perhaps Alcibiades was not as successful in obtaining a stable tenure of rule like his guardian Pericles had been, but like Pericles, Alcibiades saw aggressive military policies as an avenue to success. And though Lysander outstripped all the bounds that held back his predecessors, Brasidas' career provided a tantalizing example to all who followed of what could be achieved by playing one's cards right in the war effort.

War and the Greek mind

Long-term, ruinous warfare had a profound effect on the Greeks, which is, as always, reflected in culture. The Peloponnesian War broke out and raged during the height of Attic drama, both comedy and tragedy, and as a consequence many tragic and comic plays, including several that have survived intact, deal with the theme of war and reflect on real contemporary events and debates, explicitly in the case of comedy and implicitly in tragedy. It is tempting to see the coincidence of Greece's most destructive conflict and the flourishing of Athenian culture as a grand historical irony. However, we have already remarked that the Athenian "Golden Age" cannot be dissociated or considered in isolation from the conflict between Athens and Sparta. In general, too, great wars frequently produce great art. Not unlike other periods of terrible violence, the Hell of the Peloponnesian War inspired some of the most powerful and enduring dramatic reflections on the human condition in the Western literary tradition.

Like the very best modern political satire, which is blunt and incisive in its caricatures of real public figures, the fifth-century BCE genre of Old Comedy (distinct from the later fourth-century BCE, more slapstick-based New Comedy) pilloried living Athenian politicians and leaders, often while they themselves sat among the audience members. There are few better signs that Athens was a functioning democracy than the fact that even Pericles could be publically mocked, often in obscene ways. Though we know the names and have many fragments from several Old Comic playwrights, only the works of Aristophanes have survived in any complete form (a total of eleven out of around the forty plays he wrote). Nearly the whole of Aristophanes' literary career took place during the

Figure 4.5 The Theatre of Epidaurus, late fourth century BCE.
Source: author's photograph.

years of the Peloponnesian War, and what better fodder for a comedian than the often disastrous policies of Athens' military leadership? Though a member of the elite, who were typically not as pro-war as the common citizens, we must bear in mind that comedies – like tragedies – were performed in front of a public audience as part of a competition in which prizes were awarded by a citizen jury. Aristophanes and his peers, therefore, were keen to write crowd-pleasers, and so the themes of these plays must have resonated with the Athenian people to at least a certain degree. And what Aristophanes' plays tell us is that many Athenians had grown weary of – or at least could make fun of – the war and of the leaders who had led them to it.

In 425 BCE, Aristophanes performed a play called the *Acharnians*, named after the belligerent people of Archarnae, the Attic deme that contributed the greatest numbers of hoplites to the Athenian phalanx. Acharnae had been hit particularly hard by the annual Spartan invasions, precisely because the Spartan king Archidamus knew that the men of Acharnae, seeing their lands laid waste, would put great pressure on the Athenians to go out to meet the Spartans in battle. The protagonist of the play, at whom the chorus of Acharnians grows enraged, is a man named Dicaeopolis, who, exasperated at the ongoing war and the pointless debates on military policy held in the democratic assembly, decides to make his own personal peace treaty with the Spartans. As absurd as this premise is, not to mention practically impossible, Dicaeopolis' complaints surely struck a chord with the Athenian audience and embarrassed those who had participated in the sort of debates mocked in the play. Aside from giving a voice to those frustrated by the lack of success Pericles' policy had achieved by the time of the play's production, Aristophanes provides some glimpses, ostensibly through jokes, at the real misery engendered by the war. At one point, a desperate father from Megara, a city still chafing under Pericles' Megarian Decree, tries to sell his starving daughters to Dicaeopolis as sex-slaves just so he can have something to eat. The plight of the Megarians is perhaps exaggerated for comic effect, but few doubt that those in Megara and elsewhere were suffering, sometimes to a horrific extent. The exchange with the Megarian also gives Dicaeopolis an opportunity to claim that the war was a result of the kidnapping of prostitutes in the employ of Pericles' mistress Aspasia, a comedic rendering of the charge that Pericles had instigated the war to cover up various scandals in which he was implicated.

Much more famous today is Aristophanes' brilliant production of 411 BCE, the *Lysistrata*, in which the title character gathers women from all the major states involved in the war in order to stage a sex-strike until their husbands agree to make peace. The no-holds-barred profanity of Old Comedy, coupled with elaborate costumes showing in comic proportions the physical arousal of the hapless men in the play, made for a hilarious spectacle. The play is, unsurprisingly, one of the most commonly performed Attic tragedies today. Coming after the disastrous Sicilian Expedition and during the brief period of oligarchy at Athens, the *Lysistrata* is even more forceful than *Acharnians* about the pointlessness and futility of the war, and suggests, perhaps with some seriousness, that the women of Athens would be more capable of running things than the men have proved to be. In addition to a general anti-war message, this comedy hints at the very real demographic disaster faced by the Athenians and wider Greek world given the sheer number of young men abroad for long stretches of time and killed in battle, leaving many women without husbands and the state without children for the next generation. In addition to the *Acharnians* and *Lysistrata*, several of Aristophanes' other surviving plays deal with the war and the political chaos in its aftermath, and leading figures are frequently lampooned, especially the arch populist and war-monger Cleon.

Unlike Old Comedy, whose practitioners were free to invent novel plots and refer to contemporary events and personalities, with few exceptions (such as Aeschylus' *Persians*, discussed in earlier chapters) tragedy treated themes from Classical mythology, such as the Trojan War and the Oedipus story. Nevertheless, by carefully selecting and subtly modifying their mythological source material, tragedians encouraged careful reflection on current issues, all the while writing plays to delight the audience in order to win dramatic competitions, just like comic playwrights. All three of the canonical Attic tragedians (those whose complete plays have survived to the present), namely Aeschylus, Sophocles, and Euripides, pondered war extensively. We know for sure that Aeschylus and Sophocles were military veterans themselves, the former of the Persian Wars, the latter as a general in the years preceding the Peloponnesian War. Both Sophocles and Euripides produced several of their greatest masterpieces during the war, and scholars have mined these plays for commentary on particular issues raised by the war.

Euripides' *Trojan Women*, produced in 415 BCE, stands as one of the most stirring pictures of suffering and defeat ever created. The protagonists of the play are the women of Troy, especially Queen Hecuba, who await news of their fate after their city has fallen and their male relatives have been slaughtered by the Greeks. A major theme of the play is the great reversal of fortune that frequently befalls even the most powerful during times of war. Hecuba and the other royal women of Troy learn that they will be hauled away to be the slaves of the very men who killed their husbands, fathers, and sons; the younger women to be sex-slaves, the older to perform the most degraded and menial tasks in the household. The most pitiable – and terrifying – scene occurs when the young child Astyanax, son of the slain hero Hector, is pulled from his mother's breast to be hurled to his death from Troy's ruined battlements. His mother, Andromache, addresses her young son before he is snatched away:

> O child, do you cry? Do you understand the evils in store for you? Why do you draw close and clutch my garment with your hands, huddling under my wing like a newborn chick? Hector will not grasp his famed spear, rising again from the earth, and bring salvation for you. No kin of your father comes, no force of Phrygians. A dreadful leap to break your neck, falling piteously from on high, will steal your life away. O beloved embrace, dearest to a mother; o sweetest breath upon my skin. For nothing did my breast nourish you in your swaddling clothes. In vain did I toil and wear myself out with labor. Now, kiss you mother; you won't get another chance. Embrace the one who bore you; entwine your arms around my back and kiss my lips. O barbarous Greeks, ever devising new evils, why do you kill a child that bears no blame?
>
> (Euripides *Trojan Women* 749–765)

As Andromache is led away to be the slave of Neoptolemus, son of Achilles who had slain Hector, Hecuba, the child's grandmother, cradles the boy's broken body. The images of suffering and humiliation of the *Trojan Women* are universal themes that might apply to any given conflict. The play's message becomes even more striking, however, when one considers that it was produced in the year following Athens' infamous siege of Melos, a small island in the Aegean that bravely, if foolishly, held out against Athens. The Athenians eventually forced the surrender of Melos, and then killed all the Melian men of military age and sold the women and children into slavery. Thucydides wrote a stirring dialogue between the Athenians and Melians, emphasizing the naked power politics practiced by Athens and the sober warning about reversals of fortune delivered by the Melians. Coming many years before the appearance of Thucydides' *History*, the *Trojan Women* forced the Athenian audience to come face to face with the realities of their war-time policies. At the end of the war, the Athenians worried that they would themselves be killed and enslaved, just as they had done to the unfortunate people of Melos.

Euripides is a famous iconoclast, frequently recognized as taking on the deepest beliefs of the Greeks, including even the nature of the traditional Olympian gods. That Euripides would criticize the Peloponnesian War and the Athenians' conduct in it might seem only fitting. Sophocles, on the other hand, is widely regarded as a much more traditional figure, careful in his deference to Greek traditions. Even Sophocles, though, produced plays that showed war at its ugliest. His *Philoctetes*, performed in 409 BCE, tells the story of the eponymous protagonist's abandonment on the island of Lemnos by his fellow Greeks, who were making their way to Troy. Philoctetes was abandoned because he had suffered a wound that left him in constant agony and emitted an awful smell. The action of the play is driven by the Greeks' need to rescue Philoctetes and bring him to the war, since a prophecy foretold that Troy would not fall unless Philoctetes and his legendary bow (which once belonged to Heracles) took part in the action. Philoctetes' mental anguish – to accompany his physical torment – while confronting his betrayers is palpable. While some scholars have suggested that the play refers to the Athenian debates surrounding whether or not to welcome back Alcibiades (who was similarly removed from the war effort, even though his talents might have given the Athenians the best chance of winning), Sophocles also explores themes of trauma, suffering, and betrayal that threaten to affect every soldier in every war.[11] Sophocles' audience in 409 BCE would have been filled with soldiers who had fought in the war's battles, many of whom were still nursing wounds and all of whom had lost someone dear.

Greek tragedies, including especially those produced during the Peloponnesian War, are so powerful in their exploration of combat trauma that in recent years they have been performed for audiences of military veterans to assist them in confronting their own traumatic experiences. In his book *The Theater of War*, Bryan Doerries offers a memoir of his own encounters with Greek tragedy and how he and his theater company have helped the lives of thousands of veterans suffering from post-traumatic stress disorder (PTSD) by reading from and performing plays like *Philoctetes*. These productions are valuable therapeutic tools, according to Doerries, because the experiences of soldiers in combat can be remarkably similar even if separated by millennia.[12] It is a testament to the horrors of the Peloponnesian War that the Athenians who lived through it were driven to reflect on the suffering of war in such a way as to speak to the universal soldier across broad expanses of time and geography.

Notes

1 Most of what we know of Thucydides' life – and we know far less than we would wish – comes from the few references he makes to his own life in his *History* and a few scattered later sources, including a sixth-century CE biography compiled by Marcellinus.

2 A seminal study on this particular bias, though in German, is Diesner (1959).

3 I detail how these characterizations might lead Thucydides to distort some events in his *History*, particularly the motivations he attributes to his characters. See Sears (2011).
4 The most popular exploration of this theme is Allison (2017).
5 The great debate concerning whether the Peloponnesian War was the inevitable result of structural differences between Athens and Sparta, or a preventable conflict that flared up because of a series of relatively minor proximate causes, is best encapsulated by, respectively, de Ste. Croix (1972) and Kagan (1969).
6 For recent studies on the nature of the plague, see Papagrigorakis et al. (2006); but see also Shapiro et al. (2006).
7 The standard work on peltasts is Best (1969).
8 For more on Demosthenes and his military innovations, see Roisman (1993).
9 Kallet (1999) argues that by this passage Thucydides means to show that the Athenians have become diseased in their quest for victory.
10 For a discussion of Brasidas as a Homeric figure in Thucydides, see Hornblower (1991–2008, vol. 2, 38–61).
11 For a representative study linking the plots of drama to explicit events and people, Alcibiades in particular, see Vickers (2008).
12 Doerries (2015).

Further reading

Balot, Ryan, Sarah Forsdyke and Edith Foster (eds.). 2017. *The Oxford Handbook of Thucydides*. Oxford.

An up-to-date collection of chapters on various aspects of Thucydidean scholarship.

Connor, W. Robert. 1972. *The New Politicians of Fifth-Century Athens*. Princeton.

A seminal discussion of the changing nature of politics and political leaders before and during the Peloponnesian War.

Gomme, A. W., A. Andrewes, and K. J. Dover. 1945–1981. *A Historical Commentary on Thucydides* (5 vols.). Oxford.

The standard reference work for Thucydides as a historical source for the Peloponnesian War.

Hanson, Victor Davis. 2005. *A War Like No Other: How the Athenians and Spartans Fought the Peloponnesian War*. New York.

An engaging account of the various military considerations at play during the Peloponnesian War, and how the war fits into the context of ancient warfare more generally.

Hornblower, Simon. 1991–2008. *A Commentary on Thucydides* (3 vols.). Oxford.

An indispensable resource for anyone studying Thucydides or the Peloponnesian War.

Kagan, Donald. 2009. *Thucydides: The Reinvention of History*. London.

A readable distillation of Kagan's views of the Peloponnesian War's historian, demonstrating that Thucydides was very much a revisionist historian who presents a highly selective view of events, personalities, and motivations.

Kagan, Donald. 2012. *A New History of the Peloponnesian War*. Ithaca.

This e-book contains all four volumes of Kagan's magisterial history of the Peloponnesian War (*The Outbreak of the Peloponnesian War*, *The Archidamian War*, *The Peace of Nicias and the Sicilian Expedition*, and *The Fall of the Athenian Empire*, all originally written in the 1970s and 1980s). Kagan's work set the standard for Peloponnesian War scholarship.

Lazenby, J. F. 2004. *The Peloponnesian War: A Military Study*. London.

Lazenby is an excellent military historian, and he offers here a concise look at the purely military considerations at play in the Peloponnesian War.

Lendon, J. E. 2010. *Song of Wrath: The Peloponnesian War Begins*. New York.

A novel thesis arguing that the first few years of the Peloponnesian War can best be explained as resulting from reciprocal actions taken by the Athenians and Peloponnesians, respectively, in order to save face. Lendon reminds us that much more than tactical and strategic considerations are at play in war.

Morley, Neville. 2014. *Thucydides and the Idea of History*. London.

An accessible treatment of the influence Thucydides has had on the study of history, from a leading expert on the reception of Thucydides.

Ste. Croix, G. E. M. de. 1972. *The Origins of the Peloponnesian War*. Ithaca.

The counterpoint to Kagan's first volume, de Ste. Croix argues that the Peloponnesian War was the result of long-term structural conflicts within the Greek world.

Westlake, H. D. 1968. *Individuals in Thucydides*. London.

An important exploration of prominent individuals in Thucydides, including what roles they play in the Peloponnesian War and how they are portrayed literarily.

Winter, Frederick E. 1971. *Greek Fortifications*. Toronto.

The standard reference work for Greek fortifications and siegecraft.

5 The fourth century BCE
Mercenaries and scoundrels

Introduction

There was a time when teachers of Greek history presented the Greek world as entering a period of inexorable decline in the fourth century BCE, especially after the death of Socrates in 399 BCE – the result of a controversial trial that was in part brought about by lingering tensions in Athens after the city's loss in the Peloponnesian War. This narrative of decline is no longer generally accepted. How, for example, could the time of Plato and Aristotle, not to mention the longest stable period of Athenian democracy, coincide with the collapse of the Classical Greek character? Even fourth-century BCE trends in warfare that have often been trotted out as the prime suspects in bringing about Greek decline, such as a growing reliance on mercenaries, are but extensions of practices that were much more prevalent in earlier periods than once thought. That said, the fourth century BCE started with the independent Greek polis in full swing and ended with the Mediterranean world carved up among all-powerful warrior-kings, all successors of the ultimate warrior-king, Alexander the Great. The fourth century BCE, therefore, in which Greek warfare continued to develop and change until culminating in the Macedonian war machine, deserves careful consideration on its own. The Macedonian kings Philip II and his son Alexander, who shaped the world in the second half of the century, will be considered separately in the next chapter.

We will begin with the topic scholars had long seized on as the definitive one for fourth-century BCE warfare: mercenaries. We saw in the last chapter that mercenaries had been a factor in Greek warfare for a long time, including during the Peloponnesian War, before the fourth century BCE began. Nevertheless, mercenaries, both Greek and non-Greek, were more common and influential in the fourth century BCE than in earlier periods, whether or not that entailed a decline in the character of the Greek citizen-soldier. Mercenaries cost money, and not every state could afford to employ mercenaries for any length of time. As the fourth century BCE was a time of great innovation in fields such as philosophy and art, it also provided fertile ground for the development of the art of war. Professional generals and writers of technical military manuals flourished during this time, a largely new phenomenon that reflects a different view of war than as the province of citizen amateurs. The fourth century BCE saw a greater role taken by military strongmen who monopolized the resources of poleis, such as Dionysius of Syracuse, and both gained and maintained power by using these resources to fund essentially private armies. Leaders of federal states, such as Jason of Pherae, who ruled nearly all of Thessaly, could also summon great stores of wealth to pay for soldiers, amassing armies greater and more skilled than could be easily dealt with by poleis and citizen-soldiers. In such a climate of innovation and change, what role did the traditional hoplite phalanx have? To the very end of the polis, the phalanx remained a staple of Greek warfare, though leaders such as the Theban Epameinondas experimented with cunning new phalanx tactics and supplemented hoplites with other types of arms. We will end this chapter by discussing two battles representative of fourth-century BCE warfare, Lechaeum and Mantinea.

The heyday for mercenaries?

The Athenian rhetorician Isocrates wrote *On the Peace*, a speech or political pamphlet (it is not clear whether it was ever delivered in the Assembly) written around 355 BCE, to offer Athens advice after its allies revolted in the so-called "Social War" of 357–355 BCE. He identifies one of Athens' chief problems as an over-reliance on mercenaries instead of citizen-soldiers:

> We seek to rule over all others, but are unwilling to go to war ourselves. We undertake war against virtually all peoples, but we do not train ourselves for this. Instead we hire stateless, disloyal men who have gathered together from all manner of evildoers, who will follow against us anyone who offers them more pay … And we are so much worse than our ancestors … since when they voted to wage war against anyone, although the Acropolis was full of silver and gold, they thought it necessary to run the risk with their own bodies to support their own political decisions, whereas we, though in a state of great poverty and being so numerous, we hire mercenary armies, just like the King of Persia does!
>
> (Isocrates *On the Peace* 44, 47)

Isocrates exploits many of the Athenians' most cherished beliefs about themselves in order to highlight just how decadent the Athenians had supposedly become. The same people who had resisted the Persians, even to the point of abandoning their own city for the greater good of Greece, and the same people who had built an empire and took on the whole of the Greek world for decades, cannot be bothered to field an army of their own citizens. Not only are mercenaries unsavory and treacherous characters, according to Isocrates, but they are also the sorts of soldiers employed by the very paradigm of the despotic ruler, the Persian king himself. While Isocrates was surely exaggerating for rhetorical effect, and while recent scholarship has challenged traditional ideas about mercenary dominance in fourth-century BCE warfare, there is no doubt that soldiers-for-hire were an important factor in the decades after the Peloponnesian War.

Figure 5.1 A red-figure vase depicting Thracian peltasts.

Source: drawing by Adrienne Lezzi-Hafter after an Attic kyathos by the Eretria Painter. Sozopol Archaeological Museum (no. 261).

To get a sense of the ways that mercenaries impacted Greek warfare in the fourth century BCE, let's look at three examples from the early years of that era. Since, as we have already noted, mercenaries were expensive, it might be unsurprising that the first two examples involve Persian money (nobody had more money than the Persians). In one case, a Persian satrap hired Greek mercenaries to fight on his behalf against the Great King of Persia in an attempted coup; in the other, the Persians paid for mercenaries, likely from non-Greek sources, for one side in a war of Greeks against other Greeks. Starting from the final phase of the Peloponnesian War, the Persians and their money became a constant and unsettling presence in Greek affairs. The third case, namely the turbulent situation in fourth-century BCE Sicily, primarily concerns the use of mercenaries by Greeks against other Greeks, often in order to secure or overthrow the extra-constitutional rule of various strongmen.

The most famous mercenary campaign in the ancient world is arguably the March of the Ten Thousand, in which 10,000 Greek soldiers (actually more like 12,000, including some non-Greek troops), mostly hoplites, were hired by the Persian prince and satrap Cyrus to overthrow his elder brother, Artaxerxes, Great King of Persia, and put Cyrus on the throne (though the mercenaries did not at first know the true reason they were hired). Non-Greek peoples such as the Persians and the Egyptians had been hiring Greek mercenaries for centuries, but Cyrus' mercenary force was the largest yet. Starting out in 401 BCE, only a few short years after the Peloponnesian War ended, this force, along with a much larger army of Persian troops, marched all the way to what is now Iraq, where they fought a great battle at Cunaxa. Though the Greek mercenaries were victorious in their part of the field, Cyrus himself was killed while charging against the king, leaving the Greeks deep inside the Persian Empire with no purpose and no leader. Miraculously, these Greeks over many months made their way back to the sea and to the Greek world, even after their original Greek commanders had been murdered by the Persians. One of the replacement leaders of the Ten Thousand was an Athenian named Xenophon, who wrote about this experience in the *Anabasis*, the world's first military memoir.

When we think of mercenaries in the Greek world, we usually think of light-armed and frequently non-Greek soldiers like peltasts, hired precisely because they complement the standard Greek hoplite phalanx in terms of armament and tactics. Cyrus and other Persians were interested in hiring Greeks, however, precisely because the Greeks were experts at hoplite warfare, a style of fighting much different from the way of war among the peoples of the Persian Empire. That is, the Persians had plenty of mobile and light-armed troops like archers and cavalry, but were not particularly skilled in the deployment of heavy infantry – as they learned to their great cost at Marathon, Thermopylae, and Plataea. The Ten Thousand, though they did include some contingents of peltasts and other non-hoplite arms, were predominantly Greek hoplites, providing a force of shock troops that promised to do great damage to the conventional Persian armies of Artaxerxes, which indeed did happen at Cunaxa but to no strategic avail.

The three years of continuous campaigning of the Ten Thousand led to many tactical insights, frequently described in great deal by Xenophon, which we will explore below. But here we should note the political and social disruption that the March of the Ten Thousand reflects. Many hundreds of hoplites left their home states, including great powers such as Sparta and smaller places such as the cities of Arcadia, to fight in the service of a foreign power – and not just any foreign power, but the Persians, once Greece's mortal enemy. The Spartan authorities might have unofficially sanctioned the expedition, since a Spartan general, Clearchus, was one of the commanders of the mercenary force, and Cyrus had been the personal friend of the Spartan leader Lysander, who had won Sparta the war with Persian money. Other Greek states, on the other hand, would not have supported so many of their hoplites venturing abroad, and these soldiers acted on their own as private persons – clearly at odds with the supposed Classical ideal of the citizen-soldier leaving his plow to fight his polis' enemy in a brief campaign. Xenophon might have been exiled from Athens for his participation in the expedition, though there were other possible causes of his exile, such as excessive closeness with the Spartans. In general, the Greek world in the aftermath of the Peloponnesian War was full of enough internal political strife and, in many cases, crushing poverty that thousands of Greeks thought the best course of action was to obtain employment from a traitorous Persian prince in far-away lands. Decades of warfare left many Greek poleis without money or good livelihoods for its citizen-soldiers, while in Athens, for example, the political situation was so tense that many aristocrats, such as Xenophon, thought it was safer to leave the city altogether. Even when the expedition was over, and they had made their way back to the sea, many of the Ten Thousand elected to remain abroad in the service of a Thracian king, while others continued campaigning in Persian lands under the leadership of the Spartan king Agesilaus.

The second example of mercenaries comes from a single contingent of peltasts paid for by the Persians and commanded by an Athenian general named Iphicrates during the Corinthian War (395–387 BCE). The Persians provided the Athenians with this force in order to make trouble for Sparta, whose king Agesilaus was conducting successful campaigns against Persia. The entire Corinthian War was largely a result of Persian machinations to get the Greeks to fight each other and stop threatening Persia. Indeed, once the war broke out, Agesilaus was forced to abandon Persian territory and deal with the situation in mainland Greece, where Athens, Thebes, Corinth, and Argos had all banded together against Sparta. The peltasts paid for by Persia might have been Thracians, or Greeks recruited from cities close to Thrace, or perhaps a mixture of both. Whatever their ethnic origin, they were soldiers-for-hire that served on continuous campaigns and under a single commander for several years, an extraordinary situation that allowed for a remarkable degree of unit cohesion and tactical innovation. Iphicrates, who was one of the most prominent and controversial generals of the fourth century BCE, took full advantage of his time as commander of these peltasts.

In many ways, Iphicrates' force fits in with the Greeks' use of mercenaries in the fifth century BCE, principally in how it complemented the heavy-armed phalanx. Just as hoplites made up for the deficiencies in Cyrus' army, peltasts and other light-armed and mobile troops allowed for tactical possibilities unavailable to the hoplite phalanx on its own. During the Peloponnesian War, as we discussed in the last chapter, Demosthenes and Cleon were able to use light-armed mercenaries to great effect against Spartan hoplites at Pylos. Mercenaries did not only bring new tactics to bear. Being professional soldiers serving for long-stretches of time, they were often able to execute more complicated maneuvers than the average citizen-soldier, though many literary sources do disparage non-Greek mercenaries for the apparent lack of discipline, which may be nothing more than an overdone stereotype. For his part, Iphicrates was able to exploit his long-term command over a group of professional soldiers to develop a highly disciplined and effective fighting force. He also earned himself great fame, and became known more for his exploits abroad for various paymasters than as a loyal soldier of Athens, which probably only fueled the flames of anti-mercenary sentiment.

Iphicrates was long held up by scholars as the poster-child of rogue mercenary generals in the fourth century BCE who fought only for their own interests rather than those of any polis. Iphicrates and others were often labeled *condottieri*, the term applied to the soldiers-of-fortune that led the mercenary armies of Renaissance Italy. To be sure, Iphicrates really did lead many mercenary operations in far-flung places across the Aegean and Mediterranean, often for paymasters seemingly at odds with his home state of Athens. For instance, he served as more or less the personal general of a Thracian king named Cotys, even marrying Cotys' daughter. The orator Demosthenes says that Iphicrates once fought a naval action on behalf of Cotys against the forces of Athens itself, certainly bad behavior for an Athenian citizen. Just like the reliance on mercenaries in general, the behavior of Athenian mercenary commanders seems to be incontrovertible evidence that the Greek character, specifically in Athens, had taken a turn for the worse after the Peloponnesian War. Scholars today, however, such as W. K. Pritchett, tend to discount the *condottieri* comparison. Instead, the evidence, even from such anti-mercenary authors as Demosthenes, suggests that the fault for the rogue operations of commanders lay with the Athenian people, who regularly sent these commanders out without sufficient resources to pay the mercenary soldiers. Enterprising leaders such as Iphicrates, therefore, were forced to pick up paying work wherever and from whomever they could, to avoid having to contend with a bunch of disgruntled soldiers. Fighting for foreign rulers was one way Iphicrates and others could pay the troops to carry out their original mission for Athens. Raiding and pillaging was another less-than-savory way. Still, if Iphicrates really did fight against Athens, that would be clearly unacceptable in any situation, though commanders of all times and places have been known to misbehave, such as the Spartan regent Pausanias and the Athenian general Themistocles, who both cozied up to the Persians in the early fifth century BCE. Rogue and ambitious commanders were by no means a fourth-century BCE phenomenon, even if increased use of mercenaries was.

Though far less known than the affairs of mainland Greece, largely due to the lack of contemporary sources, the history of the Greeks in Sicily in the fourth century BCE makes for a fascinating study. Caught between rival claimants to tyrannical power, populist agitators for democracy, and the powerful Carthaginians who dominated the western part of the island and had designs on the rest, the Sicilian Greeks, especially the people of Syracuse, endured more warfare and political strife than even the Greeks of the mainland – and in the fourth century BCE, that's saying something. Mercenaries, primarily of Greek origin and frequently from Greek states such as Sparta and Corinth, were key players in these upheavals.

During and after the Peloponnesian War, Syracuse had its fair share of internal strife, made worse by the serious threat posed by Carthaginian invasions of Sicily. Because of the military emergency and civil strife among several factions in the city, at the end of the fifth century BCE a man named Dionysius was able to make himself tyrant of Syracuse, and expanded his power to be effectively the king of much of Greek Sicily. We will consider Dionysius in greater detail below, since he enjoyed certain military advantages because of his position as extra-constitutional sole ruler, but for this part of the chapter it is important to note that he gained and maintained power in large part because he was given a group of Greek mercenaries, officially to serve as his bodyguards, but in reality to secure for him tyrannical authority. Dionysius kept mercenaries in his employ throughout his reign, procuring what was essentially a private army. He also demonstrated to other aspiring tyrants and military strongmen the importance of paying mercenaries well, since he won the loyalty of several mercenary groups simply by offering them more pay than others were able or willing to do. Figures like Dionysius inspired the Greek historian Polybius, writing during the period of Rome's expansion into Greece, to comment that sole rulers are always dependent upon mercenaries to maintain control (11.13). More than that, Polybius adds that mercenaries in the employment of sole rulers fight better than those employed by democracies since, once victorious, democracies no longer need mercenaries, whereas sole rulers will need to keep paying mercenaries even if they are victorious.

Despite some ups and downs early in his reign, Dionysius enjoyed a relatively stable reign for decades, always with a contingent of paid Greek soldiers at his beck and call. After his death, however, the situation in Syracuse and indeed all of Sicily deteriorated markedly. Dionysius was succeeded by his son, who became Dionysius II, portrayed by a hostile source tradition as the very paradigm of the fickle and wicked tyrant. Despite receiving political and moral instruction from no less than Plato, Dionysius II in no way measured up to the ideal figure of a philosopher-king. The misrule of the younger Dionysius opened up the possibility that someone else might be able to claim power or serve as a liberator in Syracuse, and also in the other cities dominated by Syracuse during the reign of the elder Dionysius. Two figures stand out during the decades of Dionysius II's off-and-on again rule in Syracuse: Dion, a native Syracusan and advisor of both Dionysius I and II who became tyrant himself, and Timoleon, a Corinthian soldier summoned to intervene in Sicily who reestablished a constitutional government. Both Dion and Timoleon relied on and fought against mercenary armies.

The Greek biographer Plutarch, writing during the first centuries of the Roman Empire, has provided us with gripping accounts of the lives of Dion and Timoleon, which provide a disturbing picture of the tumultuous history of Sicily in the first half of the fourth century BCE. Though Plutarch and other sources for this period are vehemently anti-tyranny and are thus heavily biased, there is no mistaking the turmoil roiling through Sicily as Dion and Timoleon successively struggled against Dionysius II and other rulers and would-be rulers throughout the island. On both sides, mercenaries invariably played leading roles, frequently switching sides depending on the shifting balance of power and who offered the most money. Dion, after wresting power in Syracuse from Dionysius with the help of mercenaries, was eventually assassinated by a mercenary conspiracy in 354 BCE. Timoleon, who spurned the tyranny himself, came to a more peaceful end, but only because he assiduously cultivated the loyalty of the mercenaries and other soldiers through inspired leadership and granting plenty of opportunities for plunder. At the beginning of his biography of Timoleon, Plutarch says that, after the struggle between Dionysius II and Dion, many Greek cities in Sicily were in the control of bands of mercenary soldiers who were eager for any and all changes of government provided that they receive their pay. Mercenaries should not be blamed for all of the problems faced by the Sicilians – certainly the ambitions and misrule of figures like Dionysius II are a root cause – but it is difficult to see how such continuous warfare between tyrants and their rivals would have been possible without a ready supply of Greek soldiers-for-hire. Citizen-soldiers do not seem to have been an option: when Timoleon rid Syracuse of its tyrants in 343 BCE, he found the city bereft of citizens and animals grazing in the middle of what was once a bustling urban center. The same was true of other cities throughout the island, pointing to the wreckage left by decades of mercenary-driven civil warfare.

Professional generals and the art of war

When the Ten Thousand arrived at the Greek polis of Byzantium at the end of their harrowing journey, they were met by a rather strange character. A certain Theban named Coiratadas had been journeying around the Greek world offering his services as a professional general. He offered to lead the Ten Thousand on a campaign in Thrace, but his freelance command was short-lived since he failed to provide adequate rations for the soldiers and showed himself to be less than competent (Xenophon *Anabasis* 7.33–7.41). While Coiratadas is hardly the best example of a seasoned warrior who could deliver expert military advice to the highest bidder, he does signal an important shift away from citizen warfare – namely, the idea that average citizens fought as soldiers and even generals for their own homes and polis – to professional generalship reflecting full-time dedication to the art of war. The fourth century BCE saw the rise of such professional military output as tactical manuals, most famously that written by Aeneas Tacticus about sieges. Xenophon himself, after he served among the Ten Thousand, in addition to his historical writing produced several military treatises on subjects like the equestrian arts, for the apparent purpose of educating would-be commanders. Warfare had so increased in scope, duration, and complexity that it could no longer remain the preserve of citizen militias and amateur politician-generals.

In the fifth century BCE and earlier, military leaders and political leaders tended to be one and the same. The Peloponnesian War began to change that, but even in that lengthy conflict political figures regularly took the reins of military expeditions. For every general Demosthenes, who does not seem to have been a major voice in the Athenian Assembly, we have figures like Cleon and Nicias, who were well-known politicians. By the end of the war, however, and into the fourth century BCE, professional soldiers become more and more common and often had little to do with the political decisions regarding military campaigns. We have already discussed the Athenian general Iphicrates, who has been called a *condottiere*, or professional mercenary general. He is but one of several career soldiers who behaved in ways similar to Coiratadas, only with more success in actually securing commands. Though these so-called *condottieri* were regularly employed by their polis as generals, they also fought as professional commanders for other powers. Iphicrates, for example, fought in the service of a Thracian king, virtually as a court general. The Spartan Clearchus had led the Ten Thousand to fight for the Persian prince Cyrus. Even the Spartan king Agesilaus, who saw plenty of military action in his official role, late in his life fought as a mercenary leader in Egypt. For most of the Archaic and Classical periods, Greek warfare was conducted by amateurs, but in the fourth century BCE it was increasingly seen as a profession. Even in those rare cases in which Greeks were full-time soldiers, such as was the case for the full Spartiates, military service was typically in the service of one's own state. Neither of these two axioms – soldiers as amateurs and fighting as citizens – held as much sway after the Peloponnesian War.

Instead of fighting in a single battle or venturing out on campaigns that lasted a few weeks at most, these new professional generals spent years in military activity, fighting on land and sea and living with hardened soldiers, both citizens and mercenaries. Long years in the field allowed these leaders to hone the art of war and develop unprecedented levels of expertise in tactics, leadership, and logistics. This expertise gave rise to the military manual, a new literary genre written by experienced military men for the benefit of professional soldiers.

In fifth-century BCE Athens, a group of professional teachers called sophists began to set up shop, claiming to be able to teach the sons of wealthy Athenians the skills necessary to succeed as persuasive politicians in the democracy. (These sophists were the main antagonists of the famous philosopher Socrates, who worried that they cared more for winning arguments than discovering the truth.) With the professionalization of warfare, a new literature emerged aimed at making successful commanders, analogous to the work of sophists geared to making successful democrats. These military manuals became very popular in later centuries, and we possess several from the Roman Imperial Period. But the first comes from the fourth century BCE and is attributed to Aeneas Tacticus, the "Tactician." Perhaps identical to the Aeneas of Stymphalos, who was a general of the Arcadian League in the 360s BCE, Aeneas Tacticus wrote several military manuals, but only his work on siege warfare survives. Written before the advent of sophisticated siege towers and torsion artillery, Aeneas' text emphasizes the experience of the defenders, offering advice on how to survive for long periods trapped behind the city walls and how to prevent traitors from opening the gates to the enemy, by far the most likely way for a besieger to take a city.

In the decades after Aeneas produced his work, siege warfare became much more sophisticated. As we will discuss in the next chapter, Philip and Alexander made use of tremendously powerful torsion artillery, gigantic siege towers, and specialized siege troops who were skilled at undermining fortifications and other measures designed to weaken defenses. Defenders too developed clever ways to hold off attackers, including employing special screens and nets to parry the missiles launched by artillery. We know the name of Philip's siege engineer, one Polyidus of Thessaly, who applied his expertise to hone Philip's siege train. In the fourth century BCE, siege warfare became the domain of professionals, leading to an arms race between besiegers, with ever more sophisticated tools of attack, and defenders, who built larger walls and stouter towers.

Xenophon the Athenian, best known for his works on history, including his first-hand account of the March of the Ten Thousand, also wrote a series of smaller works, including the technical treatises *On Horsemanship* and *The Cavalry Commander.* Xenophon as a young man, before joining Cyrus' expedition, had been a member of the Athenian cavalry, perhaps fighting on behalf of the Thirty Tyrants who ruled Athens for a year following the Peloponnesian

Figure 5.2 The walls of Aigosthena, near Athens, late fourth or early third century BCE.
Source: author's photograph.

War. His experiences with the Ten Thousand, including as a general for the return march, ensured that he was well-acquainted with combat. He thus writes about horses and cavalry warfare from the perspective of one with substantial experience. As a student of Socrates and of a philosophical bent in his own right, in addition to writing about the care and raising of horses, and some of the finer points of organizing and leading cavalry formations, Xenophon uses these treatises to convey deeper truths about humanity and the world. For that matter, his seemingly straightforward memoir of his time with the Ten Thousand contains many musings on the nature of military leadership, as well as vivid passages about innovative tactics. Xenophon's works contain much information that would have been useful to aspiring cavalrymen and military commanders.

Federal states and strongmen

Regardless of which side of the hoplite debate one happens to fall – "orthodox" or "revisionist" – it is pretty clear that the phalanx and the relatively egalitarian Greek polis were mutually supportive. A cohesive citizen militia arrayed in dense formation reinforced the egalitarian and participatory values of the polis, just as the demands on the citizen of citizenship and everyday life precluded complex formations beyond the phalanx and lengthy military campaigns. If Greek warfare was to develop significantly, professional troops and long-term service in the field were needed to provide the means and opportunity for tactical experimentation and innovation. Likewise, as the tumultuous and virtually anarchic history of the fourth century BCE demonstrates, for any one power to gain an insuperable military advantage and put an end to the constant conflict between rival poleis, greater and more reliable military resources than those typically commanded by an independent polis would be necessary. Various trends in the fourth century BCE led to the emergence of just the sort of military forces that could pave the way for a single dominant power in the Greek world. One of these trends was the rise of federal states, or *ethnē*, that grouped together large populations and vast expanses of territory based on ethnic ties instead of citizenship in a polis. Jason, ruler of the city of Pherae, managed to be made lord, or *tagos*, of all Thessaly, a huge region in northern Greece. Jason came to wield a level of political power and the commensurate massive and largely professional army that made him the leading man in Greece. The other trend we will consider is tyranny in Sicily, especially as exemplified by Dionysius I of Syracuse. Ruling his own city and effectively much of Sicily besides, Dionysius was able to support a sizeable army, centered on a professional mercenary force, with which he maintained and expanded his power, and championed several tactical innovations.

During the 370s BCE, while Athens, Sparta, and Thebes – among others – vied with one another for a position of dominance in Greece, a crafty and ambitious leader emerged among the Thessalians. Thessaly, an expansive region boasting the broadest plains in Greece, was known for its skilled cavalry, but not for its military or political might. There were poleis in Thessaly, even some important ones, but no Thessalian city on its own ever held the sort of sway enjoyed by the greater poleis in central and southern Greece, Ionia, and southern Italy and Sicily. One of the curiosities of Greek history is that there was no nation-state of Greece during the Classical period, despite the fact that the Greeks recognized certain common traits among themselves, a "Greekness," that was identified and defined especially after the Persian Wars. But as similar as they were, the Greeks were still divided into several ethnic sub-groups, either real or imagined. The Athenians, for example, appealed to their supposed Ionian ethnicity as they gathered allies and subjects, while Sparta reached out to its fellow Dorian Greeks as natural allies. Though they were Greeks, Jason of Pherae recognized that the Thessalians would be far stronger if they organized formally into a federal nation-state based on common ethnic ties, to make a nation of Thessaly instead of living in relatively weak independent city-states as was the norm throughout the Greek world. Other regions in or next to Greece were at times organized along ethnic lines, most notably the non-Greek peoples of Epirus and the semi-Greek peoples of Macedonia. King Philip II rose to such great heights of power largely because he consolidated the Macedonians under a single ruler and behind a single purpose to an unprecedented degree. In important ways, Jason of Pherae anticipated Philip of Macedonia.

In a clever literary device, Xenophon presents the rise of Jason of Pherae through the speech of another Thessalian leader, Polydamus of Pharsalus, delivered to the Spartans (*Hellenica* 6.1). Polydamus outlines the predicament that he is in, namely the overwhelming pressure to join with Jason voluntarily since the ruler of Pherae has already gained power over most of Thessaly. Pharsalus did in fact come to terms with Jason, and Jason was made the lord, or *tagos*, of all Thessaly by the general consent of all Thessalians. In his speech, Polydamus, who claims to relate also the words that Jason himself spoke to him, outlines the advantages enjoyed by Jason and the potential power latent within the region of Thessaly. Jason boasts of controlling a mercenary army of some 6,000, which he keeps trained to peak condition and motivates to fight with various rewards and honors, including splendid funeral rites should the soldiers die in battle. If all Thessaly were to join together, Jason says he would control in addition a force of 6,000 cavalry, more than 10,000 hoplites, and a host of peltasts – a combined-arms force to rival any in the world. Polydamus' speech makes it clear that few powers on earth could contend with a ruler like Jason once he achieves control of Thessaly, which in fact he did shortly after Polydamus delivered his speech in 375 BCE.

Xenophon later recounts how, in the aftermath of the Battle of Leuctra in 371 BCE, Jason was looked to as the leading man in Greece, and behaved as a diplomatic arbiter between even the most powerful Greek poleis (*Hellenica* 6.4). When Jason arrived in Boeotia, the Thebans wanted him to join them to finish off the Spartans. Jason, on the other hand, advised the Thebans to seek a truce with the Spartans, which in the event is what happened. Xenophon suspects that Jason's real aim was to keep both sides weak and dependent on him militarily and diplomatically, a position Philip of Macedonia later carefully cultivated to great effect. But, like Philip, Jason was assassinated shortly after Leuctra. Most Greek states were all too happy to celebrate Jason's assassins since it was widely feared that left unchecked Jason would become the sole ruler of all Greece, a "tyrant" of Greece in Xenophon's formulation. In his assessment of Jason, Xenophon says he was the greatest man of his day:

> When Jason returned to Thessaly, he was a great man, both because he had been legally appointed the ruler (*tagos*) of the Thessalians and because he maintained many mercenaries in his service, both infantry and cavalry, and these troops were trained to such a degree that they were the best soldiers around. He was still greater because of his many allies, both those he already had and those who wanted to join him. He was the greatest man of his time and not to be despised by anyone.
>
> (Xenophon *Hellenica* 6.4.28)

Where Philip was succeeded by his son, Alexander, every bit his father's equal and then some, Jason was not so lucky. Jason's authority fell to his two brothers, one of whom soon killed the other. Jason's son, Alexander, killed the remaining brother and took over power himself. Alexander of Pherae failed to carry on his father's military and diplomatic legacy. Instead, according to the overwhelming literary tradition, Alexander behaved as one of history's most reprehensible tyrants, only to drive the Thessalians to seek a way out of Jason's carefully crafted federal state. Eventually, Alexander's own wife engineered his assassination, bringing an end to a unified and dominant Thessaly (Plutarch *Pelopidas* 35). The Greek poleis seemed to have dodged a bullet with the rulers of Pherae. Jason very nearly became de facto king of all Greece, and had his successors been competent, it is difficult to see how the poleis could have resisted the military power of a unified Thessaly any more than they were able a couple of decades later to withstand a unified Macedonia under Philip.

A tyrant for the better part of four decades, Dionysius I of Syracuse suffers from an invariably hostile tradition in the ancient sources, including historiographical, biographical, and even philosophical writers like Aristotle. Today, his reputation has somewhat revived at the hands of modern scholarship. After all, it is difficult to imagine that he would have been able to reign for so long and so successfully if he was a bad as the sources suggest. Also, there is every indication that the Syracusans and many other Sicilians besides were far better off under Dionysius than other rulers. In his book-length treatment of Dionysius, Brian Caven argues that Dionysius should be seen more as a legitimate king than a tyrant. Coming as he did before Philip of Macedonia, however, kingship for Dionysius was likely inseparable from tyranny in the minds of his contemporaries. For our present purposes, another major argument of Caven is even more important, namely that Dionysius did not desire power for its own sake, but rather in order to be in a better position from which to strive for specifically military glory. Dionysius had two great advantages in achieving this goal. First was his kingly or tyrannical power, not only in the large city of Syracuse, but eventually over much of Greek Sicily too. Second was the frequent large-scale military actions brought about by conflict between the Greeks and the Carthaginians. The Carthaginians were a Phoenician people that original hailed from what is now Lebanon but came to be based in North Africa. A powerful naval people who would eventually become the main antagonists of the Romans during the Middle Republic, the Carthaginians posed an existential threat to the western Greeks similar to that represented by the Persians in the East. One of the greatest Sicilian Greek victories over the Carthaginians took place in 480 BCE, the very year Xerxes invaded mainland Greece. Lots of wars and lots of military authority allowed Dionysius to hone his art of warfare and develop many new (or new to the Greeks) tactics and tools.

Dionysius, hailing from an unexceptional and middling background, rose to power during a time of military emergency. First, he denounced those charged with prosecuting the war against the Carthaginians as incompetent and corrupt, managing to have himself made a military commander with supreme authority. Then, taking a page out of the playbook of Archaic tyrants like Pisistratus of Athens, he managed to have a bodyguard of 600 mercenaries assigned to protect himself. In the event, the number of his military bodyguard rose to 1,000, removing any semblance of democratic rule of law undergirding Dionysius' position. In addition to securing control over Syracuse, by presenting himself as the only viable hope against the Carthaginian threat, Dionysius became the virtual king of Greek eastern Sicily, always keeping an army of mercenaries at the ready and generally maintaining their loyalty by offering them more pay than anyone else was able to (he did run into trouble from time to time, particularly when he was short of funds or his rivals paid off the mercenaries to turn against him). Dionysius won the right to recruit mercenaries from many parts of the Greek world, including territories controlled by Sparta. With a great influx of soldiers and military experts from around the eastern Mediterranean, Dionysius championed many drives to supply his forces with weapons and equipment, amassing a huge stockpile of the tools of war, including a massive expansion of the Syracusan navy to rival that of the famously naval Carthaginians. It seems that Syracusan citizens were still used as soldiers from time to time, but Dionysius certainly preferred mercenaries as the backbone and greater part of his armies. Diodorus records an episode in which Dionysius tricked the citizens of Syracuse into going out into the fields so he could confiscate all their weapons while they were away (14.10). Later, though, Diodorus does mention that Dionysius enrolled into his army Syracusans in fighting shape (14.44).

War with Carthage and the attendant influx of mercenaries and military professionals from around the Greek world allowed Dionysius to invent powerful new siege equipment that revolutionized siege warfare among the Greeks. The Carthaginians – just like other peoples from the ancient Near East, such as the Assyrians – were well-versed in various siege techniques, including the use of massive siege engines and towers. As we saw in the last chapter, the Greeks were generally quite bad at sieges, both because investing a walled city tended to take more time and money than the typical polis was able to invest, and because the Greeks made use of few specialized siege tools able to overcome well-built and properly manned defenses. From the very beginning, Dionysius' struggles against the Carthaginians involved many sieges on both sides, and Dionysius learned from his opponents and was eager to add his own touches to this kind of warfare. The historian Diodorus, a native of Sicily writing in the first century BCE but using now-lost sources from the fourth century BCE, credits Dionysius or his military engineers with the invention of the catapult. Though less effective than the torsion catapults of the later fourth century BCE, which used twisted strands of hair or animal sinew to deliver projectiles with enormous force, the non-torsion, crossbow-style catapults of Dionysius' army were capable of launching stones, bolts, and other projectiles both against defenders on a city wall or against attackers trying to breach the wall. Though the rest of the Greek world would only adopt such artillery later in the century, catapults greatly changed Greek warfare. Not only was another tool in the hands of attackers, city walls became much higher, with mud-brick giving way to sturdier stone masonry even in higher courses, and reinforced with large towers equipped with broad platforms to hold defensive artillery. This fourth-century BCE arms-race has left an indelible mark on the Mediterranean landscape, with large stone circuit walls built with regular courses of ashlar masonry dominating many archaeological sites, including the impressive city of Messene in the Peloponnese.

Diodorus' detailed description of the siege of Motya, a Carthaginian city in western Sicily, in 398 BCE provides a brilliant case study of Dionysius' comprehensive approach to siege warfare (14.49–14.53). Motya was a walled city situated on an island within a harbor, a seemingly unassailable site. Dionysius, however, attacked the city walls directly by constructing a great earthen causeway to the city from the mainland, anticipating the famous land-bridge made by Alexander the Great during the Siege of Tyre in 332 BCE. Against the walls of the city, Dionysius employed catapults, which were able to wound and kill the defenders on the battlements and were even used to attack the crews of the Carthaginian ships sent to relieve the city; great siege engines six-stories tall, as high as the walls and tallest buildings of the city; and battering rams to smash apart sections of the wall. Even with such technically sophisticated tools in play, the battle for the city was a grisly affair for Dionysius' army, since the defenders hurled fire-arrows and burning pitch on the attackers and their siege engines. Once the walls were breached, many on both sides were killed in protracted street-by-street fighting and slaughter. Eventually, the forces of Dionysius prevailed by sheer numbers. Knowing well how to command mercenaries, Dionysius allowed his victorious army to plunder the city – a perfectly acceptable course of action, especially against a non-Greek enemy like Motya – and he richly rewarded those who had distinguished themselves in the struggle, especially the soldier who had first scaled the city's wall. A ruler without Dionysius' peerless authority and resources in terms of personnel and materiel would not have been able to conduct a siege in this way nor command the loyalty of the soldiers by allotting rewards and recognition, as well as spoils from the vanquished, as if he were king.

Does the phalanx still matter? Epameinondas and the rise of Thebes

Despite the tactical advances outlined above, the hoplite phalanx remained central to the armies of the Greek polis, right up to the triumph of Macedon in 338 BCE. The fourth century BCE in fact saw several of the greatest, and most "canonical," hoplite battles of Greek history, especially during the Corinthian War in the century's first decade. At the Nemea River in 394 BCE, in particular, the Spartans reminded the world that there were few substitutes for a disciplined Spartan phalanx (which we examined in some detail in Chapter 2). A little more than two decades later, though, the Spartan phalanx was broken for good, at the Battle of Leuctra in 371 BCE. The architect of Sparta's defeat was a brilliant general from Thebes named Epameinondas, who, while making use of the full spectrum of soldiers available, wielded the hoplite phalanx in a new and devastatingly effective way. The Thebans had always been excellent hoplites, and in the hands of Epameinondas, they emerged as the greatest military force in Greece, if only for a brief period.

No matter how tough the Thebans were, it was always difficult for citizen-soldiers to contend with the professional Spartan hoplites, who trained continually for war. A few years before Epameinondas emerged as an influential leader, Thebes struck a compromise between a professional standing army and an amateur militia. Three hundred warriors came to be trained at state expense, to serve as the elite core of the Theban army, a measure that other states, such as Argos, had also tried at various times but not with the success of the Thebans. These 300 hoplites comprised what the Thebans called the "Sacred Band." Not only was the Sacred Band better trained and more tactically effective than the farmer-soldiers that made up the majority of the phalanx, they were also especially motivated. According to literary sources such as Xenophon, the Sacred Band was made up of 150 pairs of lovers, the idea being that the hoplites would fight all the more valiantly in front of their beloved (Plutarch *Pelopidas* 18–19). In Epameinondas' time, the Sacred Band was commanded by a man named Pelopidas, a talented and bold leader in his own right. The two worked brilliantly together.

As we have seen, the Greeks usually arranged phalanxes with the best troops on the right wing, supposedly the most dangerous position given than the soldiers on the very end of the line had no shield covering their right sides. The combination of the best troops on the right and the tendency for phalanxes to drift rightward as they advanced as each man tried to find shelter in the shield of the man to his right meant that in many hoplite battles the right wing of both sides was victorious. Clashes such as the first Battle of Mantinea in 418 BCE and the Battle of Coronea in 394 BCE were only over once the two right wings faced off against each other in a second phase of battle after the two left wings had been routed. Epameinondas decided to counter his enemies by placing his best troops, anchored by the Sacred Band, on the extreme left wing of the Theban phalanx, therefore matching his elite directly against the other side's strongest contingents. To ensure that his left wing would be victorious against the enemy's right, Epameinondas stacked the Theban left an astonishing fifty ranks deep, turning the phalanx into a hammer with which he would "crush the head of the serpent." In the case of Thebes' most dangerous enemy, Sparta, the Spartan king tended to be positioned on the right wing. Therefore, if Epameinondas' phalanx was able to take out the Spartan right, the Spartan king would likely be killed along with the Spartan army's best soldiers, bringing about a decisive end to the battle in Thebes' favor. To this end, Epameinondas marched his phalanx towards the enemy in an oblique fashion, that is, diagonally across the plain with the left out front and the center and right hanging back and refusing battle. In theory, the hammer of the Theban left should overwhelm the enemy right in short order, achieving victory even before the rest of the Theban army needed to engage at all. Xenophon says that Epameinondas led his army against his foes "prow-first, like a trireme," aiming to ram through the enemy formation (Xenophon *Hellenica* 7.5.23). At the Battle of Leuctra in 371 BCE, one of history's most decisive engagements, Epameinondas' tactics, as supported by Pelopidas and the Sacred Band, defeated the Spartan phalanx and killed a Spartan king, bringing an end once and for all to Sparta's battlefield superiority. Nine years later, the Theban phalanx again defeated the Spartans tactically on the field of

Mantinea in 362 BCE, which we will consider in detail below, but in the battle Epameinondas was killed, and Thebes' pretensions of hegemony in Greece died along with him.

With his novel formation and tactics, Epameinondas upended conventional hoplite wisdom not only in arranging the best troops on the left, but also in his refusal to be preoccupied with avoiding being outflanked. In Chapter 2, we learned that a traditional phalanx's greatest vulnerability was in being outflanked by a more numerous or more mobile enemy. Hoplites are well-suited to head-on attack and defense within a dense formation, but are distinctly vulnerable on the sides and rear. By stacking the left fifty deep, Epameinondas, out of necessity, shortened the overall length of his line, making sure that any enemy army that had comparable numbers would be able to present a broader frontage that over-lapped the Theban wings. Epameinondas' phalanx was thus not made for a long and drawn-out fight, during which the enemy would almost certainly envelop the Theban formation. Instead, Epameinondas relied on the shock of his initial charge to break the enemy quickly, before any outflanking maneuvers could be attempted. Traditionally, the highest mark of a hoplite's courage was to stand firm and hold his place on the field, a form of passive courage often contrasted with the active courage represented by the bold attacks launched by individual warriors in Homeric epics. Epameinondas' men could not simply hold their place in line; they had to plow through the enemy as quickly as possible in a bold headlong charge.

That this novel approach to the phalanx was effective – and we know that it was, even and especially against the Spartans – forces us to reconsider how hop-lites fought on the battlefield. In Chapter 2, we spent a great deal of time discuss-ing the so-called Hoplite debate, in which once side, the "orthodox" side, argues that hoplites in the front ranks locked shields and literally pushed against their enemies, while those stationed in the rear ranks pushed against their comrades in front of them, to move the entire formation forwards until the enemy's side broke and was routed. The other side, the "revisionists," insists that the mass-shove, or *ōthismos* in Greek, was figurative rather than literal, that hoplites fought in much looser and more fluid formations than conventionally thought, and that the rear ranks must therefore have served a reserve or moral function rather than add literal weight to the charge and clash. How, then, did Epamei-nondas' fifty-deep left wing work? Prior to Epameinondas, the densest phalanx we hear of in the sources was also Theban, particularly the twenty-five-deep for-mation at Delium in 424 BCE, and perhaps also at the Nemea River in 394 BCE. Thucydides gives the impression of a real shoving match at Delium, and the twenty-five made short work of the conventionally marshaled Athenians (4.89–4.101). In Epameinondas' battles, since he needed to win quickly without allowing time for reserves to replenish the ranks of the fallen, it is even more difficult to understand the Theban victory by reference to reserves or moral support than it is in the case of Delium. I doubt whether we will ever have a good idea of what the soldier in rank forty-eight was doing during the battle, but the literary descriptions and the battles' outcomes give the clear impression of weight and shock, that the fifty ranks of Thebans were able to overwhelm and push through the enemy right very effectively.[1]

Much more could be said about Epameinondas. For example, he had strategic vision to match his tactical ingenuity. After Leuctra in 371 BCE, he invaded the Peloponnese and established great cities hostile to Sparta right on Sparta's doorstep, making sure that the battlefield defeat Sparta had suffered in 371 BCE was compounded by the removal of any chance Sparta might have had to rebuild its former position of dominance. After Leuctra, Thebes emerged as the clear great power in the Greek world. As we will consider below in the case of the second Battle of Mantinea, Epameinondas was well aware of the importance of a combined-arms approach to warfare to supplement his phalanx, even as effective as his phalanx was. Space permits us here only to emphasize Epameinondas' signature innovations in the use of the hoplite phalanx and his reliance on a skilled professional elite that would remain influential in Greek warfare for several more decades. The Sacred Band was only brought to an end in 338 BCE, when all of its soldiers were killed fighting Philip of Macedonia at the Battle of Chaeronea. Importantly, Philip himself had spent much of his youth as a hostage in Thebes, training along with the Sacred Band and picking up the Theban genius for innovation and experimentation, which Philip would exploit deftly in the creation of his own new type of phalanx.

Figure 5.3 The walls of Messene, 369 BCE.

Source: author's photograph.

Case studies: Lechaeum and Second Mantinea

There are many military engagements to choose from to be case studies for trends in fourth-century BCE warfare, especially since the Greeks were nearly continuously at war with each other in this period. I have chosen here to high-light one battle, at Lechaeum in 390 BCE, in which mercenary peltasts defeated a contingent of several hundred Spartan hoplites, reinforcing the lesson that should have been learned when light-armed mercenaries defeated the Spartans at Pylos in 425 BCE. The Battle of Lechaeum demonstrates what could be accomplished by light-armed mercenaries given enough training and an enemy unable or unwilling to deploy light-armed soldiers of its own. The other battle we will con-sider was fought at Mantinea in 362 BCE, a great clash which, in the estimation of Xenophon, led only to further chaos and confusion throughout the Greek world. The second Battle of Mantinea (to distinguish from the earlier battle fought on the same plain in 418 BCE during the Peloponnesian War), a pitched battle fought between the Theban forces of Epameinondas and the Spartans and their allies, is worth studying because of the combined-arms tactics employed by Epameinon-das. Though he is primarily famous for his innovations with the hoplite phalanx, Epameinondas also recognized the importance of light-armed troops and cavalry to supplement his heavy-armed infantry. Though, because of Epameinondas' death in the battle, the strategic situation after Mantinea was negative for Thebes, in the battle itself all parts of Epameinondas' army initially worked together bril-liantly, foreshadowing the combined-arms approach of the Macedonians later in the century.

Lechaeum is one of Corinth's two ports, located just a few kilometers from the city on the Gulf of Corinth. During the Corinthian War, Corinth was an ally of Athens and the base of an Athenian force that included citizen hoplites, under the command of the Athenian general Callias in 390 BCE, and Iphicrates' contin-gent of mercenary peltasts (Xenophon *Hellenica* 4.5). Lechaeum was in Spartan hands. The battle was a result of an unforced error on the part of the unnamed Spartan commander leading the army based at Lechaeum. A group of soldiers in the Spartan force were returning home to celebrate a religious festival, and they were escorted part of the way along the coast of the gulf by a division, or *mora*, of 600 Spartan hoplites and a squad of cavalry. Demonstrating supreme cocki-ness, on the way back along the coast the Spartan hoplites marched on their own, with their unshielded right sides towards the Athenian force stationed in Corinth. Since the Spartans had recently met with much success, they figured that the Athenians would not dare to venture out of Corinth's walls to attack, even though the Athenian force far outnumbered the Spartan *mora*. Iphicrates and Callias, on the other hand, knew a golden opportunity when they saw one.

Callias led out the Athenian hoplites and arranged them in battle order in front of the city, to serve as support for the peltasts if needed. Iphicrates led his peltasts boldly against the 600 Spartan hoplites. The peltasts were instructed to use hit-and-run tactics, approaching the hoplites only close enough to throw javelins, and then retreating before the more encumbered Spartans had a chance to catch and kill any of the mercenaries. From the start, the battle was a one-sided affair. The peltasts, protected only by light wicker shields and armed with distance weapons, swarmed against the hoplites at great speed and killed many before running away to regroup for another attack. The Spartan commander attempted a tactic that had sometimes worked before, namely sending out the youngest age classes of the hoplites to run after the peltasts. At Lechaeum, this measure only compounded the Spartans' disaster. The young Spartans, out in pursuit and thus separated from the relative safety of the phalanx formation, managed only to be killed all the more easily by the increasingly confident peltasts. On open ground, without useful mobile support, hoplites simply could not contend with well-trained and disciplined light-armed soldiers. Once Iphicrates' men saw that the Spartan hoplites bled and died just like anyone else, the myth of Sparta's invincibility was shattered, which had always been one of Sparta's most important battlefield advantages.

Eventually, the Spartan cavalry, which had traveled further away along the coast and were therefore not with the hoplites when the battle broke out, came to the aid of their beleaguered comrades. Sparta was not known for its love of horses, and its cavalry was accordingly less-than-stellar. Instead of harnessing the speed and mobility of the horses to drive off the peltasts, the Spartan cavalry maintained a continuous front with the hoplites, allowing the peltasts to withdraw after their waves of attack as easily as they had done before. The cavalry served some use, as a few Spartan hoplites were able to make it back to safety by intermingling with the horses during the retreat. Most of the Spartans that survived the battle, however, did so by running desperately to the sea, where friendly boats had anchored in an attempt to bring the force some relief. In the battle, some 250 of the 600 Spartans were killed by the peltasts – the Athenian hoplites did not need to engage in the fight at all. The rest of the Spartans survived only by retreating in a most un-Spartan fashion, recalling the surrender of the Spartans at Pylos against a similarly confounding enemy.

The Battle of Lechaeum restated what was first demonstrated at Pylos thirty-five years earlier, namely that well-deployed, light-armed troops could be devastating against unsupported hoplites, even the world's best hoplites. Hoplites can certainly contend with light-armed soldiers such as peltasts, but only if the hoplites are marshaled on ideally narrow terrain or, better yet, supported by light-armed troops of their own. At Lechaeum, the Spartans did have a cavalry force, which, if used correctly, could have ridden down the peltasts and at least killed enough to take the wind out of the mercenaries' sails. The Spartan cavalry, however, did not deploy as it should have, and proved nearly useless in the battle. Iphicrates demonstrated to the world what peltasts could do. Even so, Iphicrates was not so arrogant as to believe his light-armed mercenaries could stand on their own. The Athenian hoplites under Callias were ready to enter the battle if need be, if, for example, the Spartan cavalry had actually been deployed effectively and chased the peltasts back towards the walls of Corinth. Iphicrates, celebrated for his comparison of an effective army to the human body, as noted above, was ready to use combined-arms tactics at Lechaeum. We should also note that Iphicrates' mercenaries were deployed in conjunction with Athenian citizen-soldiers, demonstrating that, in theory at least, an increased use of merce-naries need not entail or reflect citizens' dereliction of duty.[2]

Epameinondas is most famous for his victory at Leuctra in 371 BCE, where he defeated the Spartan phalanx and made clear to the world that Sparta was in the midst of inexorable decline. At Leuctra, the star of the show was the Theban hoplite phalanx, but Epameinondas did use a combined-arms force in that battle. Before the fateful collision of phalanxes, the battle began with a cavalry skir-mish between the Theban and Spartan horse, in which the former won handily. The second great pitched battle orchestrated by Epameinondas was fought at Mantinea nine years later, in 362 BCE, and involved Thebes and its allies, princi-pally Argos and Tegea, on one side, and a large anti-Theban coalition, including Sparta, Athens, and Mantinea, on the other – a total of about 50,000 troops between the 2 armies (Xenophon *Hellenica* 7.5). This later battle demonstrates far more clearly than Leuctra the Theban general's combined-arms approach to warfare, and how various types of soldiers could be used effectively in conjunc-tion with a cleverly arranged heavy-armed phalanx.

The plain of Mantinea, nestled among the mountains of the Arcadian plateau in the Peloponnese, looks as though it was designed for ancient battles. The plain is shaped like a figure-eight, with a wide and flat upper bout around the polis of Mantinea in the north and a similarly shaped lower bout extending to the south near the polis of Tegea. The waist of the figure-eight is about 2 kilometers wide between the mountains, just enough space for a good-sized ancient army to be marshaled and be protected on the flanks. In 418 BCE, the first Battle of Mantinea was fought between two hoplite phalanxes in the middle of the upper bout, a straightforward infantry battle with no non-hoplite arms and in which both right wings outflanked and defeated the enemy left wing – and had plenty of space to do so. The battle of 362 BCE was fought by many types of soldiers and in the waist of the figure-eight, with careful attention paid to protecting the flanks, especially on the part of the anti-Theban coalition army on the defensive.

Thebes' enemies lined up for battle in the waist of the plain, facing south towards the lower bout. Most of the coalition army were hoplites, and they filled the available space between the mountains. The Athenians, stationed on the left wing, had with them a sizeable number of cavalry, which had fought a success-ful action against the Thebans the day before – despite losing many good Athe-nians, including one of Xenophon's own sons. The Athenians placed these horsemen on the extreme left of the battle line, to cover the army's left flank up against the rising hills. The Athenians, therefore, used their cavalry in the tradi-tional way, namely to guard the hoplite phalanx's unprotected sides. Epameinon-das, on the other hand, was bolder and more innovative with his own cavalry. He marshaled his horsemen and light-armed infantry to work closely together, a combination that proved very effective in later armies, such as those of the Mac-edonians. Cavalry could attack and pursue at great speed, while light-armed troops could harass and waylay the enemy infantry, including the enemy's own light-armed troops, to provide cover for the horses. Epameinondas also arrayed his cavalry in wedge formations, a tactic pioneered by horse-loving peoples like the Thessalians and Thracians and which would be a key ingredient in Alexander the Great's heavy cavalry. Much more than a continuous front, the points of many wedges were effective at opening gaps in enemy formations. The Athenian cavalry, by contrast, were arrayed in standard ranks just like hoplites. At Mantinea, Epameinondas did not only match the enemy cavalry with an innovative combined-arms force of cavalry and light-armed troops, he also employed more effective formations and tactics.

Seeing his enemy lined up for battle, Epameinondas, who was several kilometers to the south at Tegea, began to march his army diagonally across the lower bout of the plain, from southeast to northwest. He made it seem that his army was planning to camp for the night once they had crossed the plain. The soldiers in the anti-Theban coalition began to relax and even prepare for the night themselves. As his army made its way diagonally towards the enemy, Epameinondas secretly brought more and more ranks into his left wing, making the famously dense infantry formation he had used at Leuctra. Before the army had finished crossing the plain and was still stretched out in an oblique fashion, with the Theban left far closer to the enemy than the Theban right, the Theban phalanx charged. Just as at Leuctra, the fifty-deep phalanx on the Theban left, anchored by the Sacred Band, drove the enemy right wing from the field. On the Theban right was stationed the combined force of cavalry and light-armed troops, which prevented the Athenian cavalry from coming to the aid of their comrades. The Athenian cavalry feared that if they moved out of formation to bring help to their army's right wing, they would be swarmed by the Theban force. Epameinondas' combined-arms force defeated the Athenian cavalry in these early stages of the battle, meaning that the anti-Theban coalition was losing on both wings.

As so often happens in war, despite the tactical superiority of Epameinondas and the Theban army, fortune intervened and turned the tide of the battle. During the struggle on the Theban left, in which the dense phalanx was making short work of its foes, Epameinondas was mortally wounded and carried out of the melee by his soldiers. With their leader dead, the Theban phalanx failed to press home their victory, not even advancing beyond the spot where they first turned the enemy back. Chaos and confusion spread across the entire Theban line. Despite pushing the Athenian cavalry from the fight, the Theban cavalry did not pursue and destroy their defeated enemy. The Theban light-armed troops were victorious on the right too, but when the Theban cavalry more or less stopped fighting, the Athenians rallied and killed a great number of these light-armed troops. Thus, while the Thebans had won a clear tactical victory in the first phase of the battle, as Epameinondas lay dying, the Thebans failed to exploit the victory and suffered a strategic setback. The battle was reckoned a draw, and with their leader dead, the Thebans lost their bid to be Greece's greatest power. Xenophon ends his major work on history with this battle, saying that in the aftermath Greece became more anarchic and chaotic than ever before:

Figure 5.4 Funerary monument for Dexileos, an Athenian cavalryman killed during the Corinthian War, 394 BCE.

Source: courtesy of the Ephorate of Antiquities of Athens – Kerameikos Museum (no. P 1130). Photo credit: Foto Marburg/Art Resource, NY.

After these events had taken place, the opposite of what everyone expected took place. Since nearly the whole of Greece had come together and had been arrayed in battle-lines against each other, there was no one who did not expect that the victors would rule, and the defeated would become subjects. But the god brought it about that both sides set up a trophy, as if they had won, and neither side prevented the other from doing so. Both sides gave back the dead under a truce as if they were the victors, while both also received their dead as if they had been defeated. With both sides saying that they had won, neither side appeared to be any greater in terms of acquiring a city or territory than they had been before the battle was fought. In Greece there was more confusion and disorder after the battle than before.

(Xenophon *Hellenica* 7.5.26–7.5.27)

It fell to the Macedonians to take up the mantle of Epameinondas and exploit combined-arms tactics to the fullest – eventually against the Persian Empire, but at first against the Greeks themselves.

Notes

1 Devine (1983) makes the interesting suggestion that Epameinondas did not stack the Theban soldiers in fifty actual ranks, but rather instructed his army to form a hollow wedge formation to punch through the enemy lines. Buckler (1985) convincingly reasserts the orthodox view that the Thebans were stacked in fifty literal ranks and advanced to the left in front of the rest of the army, like a ship's ram.
2 The most comprehensive scholarly treatment of this battle (though in German) is Konecny (2001).

Further reading

Anderson, J. K. 1970. *Military Theory and Practice in the Age of Xenophon.* Berkeley.

   Still an indispensable resource for understanding fourth-century BCE Greek warfare.

Buck, Robert J. 1994. *Boiotia and the Boiotian League, 432–371 B.C.* Edmonton.

   A comprehensive treatment of Thebes and the Boiotian league, including Epameinondas and the Battle of Leuctra.

Buckler, John. 2003. *Aegean Greece in the Fourth Century BC.* Leiden.

   A leading historian provides a thorough account of the period covered by this chapter, including major military developments and campaigns.

Cartledge, Paul. 1987. *Agesilaos and the Crisis of Sparta.* Baltimore.

   An invaluable account of the decline of Spartan prestige and military power in the fourth century BCE, centered on the life and times of its most influential ruler.

Caven, Brian. 1990. *Dionysius I, War-Lord of Sicily.* New Haven.

   A useful book-length treatment of Dionysius I of Syracuse and his historical context.

Flower, Michael A. 2012. *Xenophon's Anabasis or the Expedition of Cyrus.* Oxford.

   A wide-ranging yet accessible look at perhaps the most important literary source for early fourth-century BCE warfare.

Flower, Michael A. (ed.). 2017. *The Cambridge Companion to Xenophon*. Cambridge.

A recent collection of chapters on many aspects of Xenophon's writing and his life and times. A important resource for understanding this fourth-century BCE source.

Griffith, G. T. 1968. *The Mercenaries of the Hellenistic World*. Groningen.

Though focusing on the centuries following the period covered by this chapter, this is still an important work for understanding the phenomenon of mercenaries in general.

Hamilton, Charles D. 1979. *Sparta's Bitter Victories: Politics and Diplomacy in the Corinthian War*. Ithaca.

An important study of the Corinthian War of the first part of the fourth century BCE, putting fourth-century military developments in context.

Lee, John W. I. 2007. *A Greek Army on the March: Soldiers and Survival in Xenophon's "Anabasis."* Cambridge.

A detailed study of the dynamics of the Greek mercenary army portrayed in Xenophon's *Anabasis*, covering a range of issues pertinent to military history.

Lewis, Sian (ed.). 2006. *Ancient Tyranny*. Edinburgh.

A collection of essays on ancient tyranny, including chapters on the fourth-century BCE rulers of Pherae, the tyrants of Sicily, and the connection between tyranny and military power in the fourth century BCE.

Marsden, E. W. 1969. *Greek and Roman Artillery: The Historical Development*. Oxford.

A comprehensive account of ancient artillery, which developed a great deal in the fourth century BCE.

Marsden, E. W. 1971. *Greek and Roman Artillery: Technical Treatises*. Oxford.

An exploration of the ancient technical manuals describing artillery and its use.

Mitchell, Lynette. 2013. *The Heroic Rulers of Archaic and Classical Greece*. London.

A readable exploration of sole rule in ancient Greece, arguing that sole rulers and tyrants never really went away, at least as a viable option to consider. This thesis has relevance for the sole rulers of the fourth century BCE discussed in this chapter.

Parke, H. W. 1970. *Greek Mercenary Soldiers, from the Earliest Times to the Battle of Ipsus*. Oxford.

The standard work on Greek mercenaries.

Pritchett, W. K. 1974. *The Greek State at War, Part II*. Berkeley.

This volume contains an invaluable discussion of the so-called *condottieri* of the fourth century BCE. Pritchett concludes that the general impression of these generals being entirely independent from their states is overblown.

Sears, Matthew A. 2013. *Athens, Thrace, and the Shaping of Athenian Leadership*. Cambridge.

This book includes a discussion of the innovations of fourth-century BCE Greek warfare, and the extent to which they were due to the influence of the Thracians, especially peltasts, and those Greeks (such as Xenophon and Iphicrates) who spent time in Thrace and led Thracian troops.

Stylianou, P. J. 1998. *A Historical Commentary on Diodorus Siculus, Book 15*. Oxford.

A vital commentary on one of the fourth century BCE's most important – if flawed – literary sources.

Trundle, Matthew. 2005. *Greek Mercenaries: From the Late Archaic Period to Alexander.* London.

A comprehensive and up-to-date discussion of mercenaries in the Archaic and Classical Greek world.

Whitehead, David. 2002. *How to Survive under Siege, by Aineias the Tactician. A Historical Commentary with Translation and Introduction.* London.

Essential for those wishing to gain a greater understanding of Aeneas Tacticus and his work, one of the earliest tactical manuals that we possess.

Winter, Frederick E. 1971. *Greek Fortifications.* Toronto.

The standard reference work for Greek fortifications and siegecraft.

6 Philip and Alexander of Macedon

Crushing the polis, conquering the world

Introduction

Alexander the Great, the most famous household name from ancient Greece, was perhaps not even Greek. Certainly the citizens of the major poleis on the Greek mainland, such as Thebes, Athens, Corinth, and Sparta, were not eager to consider the warlike horsemen of the northern region of Macedonia to be their cultural equals, a snub that bothered Alexander, who slept with a copy of the *Iliad* under his pillow no less, throughout his life. Cultural snobbery aside, Alexander came to rule virtually all of the Greeks living in what is now Greece and Turkey before conquering the Persian Empire and spreading Greek ideas and soldiers throughout the Near and Middle East. It was the Greco-Macedonian kingdoms that succeeded Alexander, in places like Egypt and Syria, that Rome encountered as it built a Mediterranean-wide empire. And it was the hybrid Greek and native cultures – called "Hellenistic" by nineteenth-century scholars, a term meaning "Greek-ish" – encountered in these places that so captivated the Romans and ensured that Greeks would have a lasting legacy in the West.

Alexander, officially Alexander III, King of Macedonia, forged the largest empire the world had yet seen largely through sheer force of will and personality, but also by using one of history's most effective war machines. He inherited the ancient world's deadliest army from his father, Philip II, who was a military visionary on a par with his more famous son. Philip of Macedonia turned a weak backwater into a fully functioning and wealthy nation-state, welded aristocratic horsemen and rural peasants into a cohesive combined-arms professional army, and managed to crush the proud hoplite armies of Greece, bringing an end to the era of the independent polis in the process. Philip's political and military reforms, along with unparalleled diplomatic acumen, provided the groundwork for Alexander's conquests.

This chapter will begin by considering the sources for Philip and Alexander, which are surprisingly problematic. The surviving contemporary sources for Philip are largely negative, written as they were by Greeks who saw Philip as a dangerous and barbarous enemy. Alexander employed his own court historians, hardly the stuff of unbiased reflection, and the works we still have today were written centuries later in a time when Alexander's greatness was taken as a given

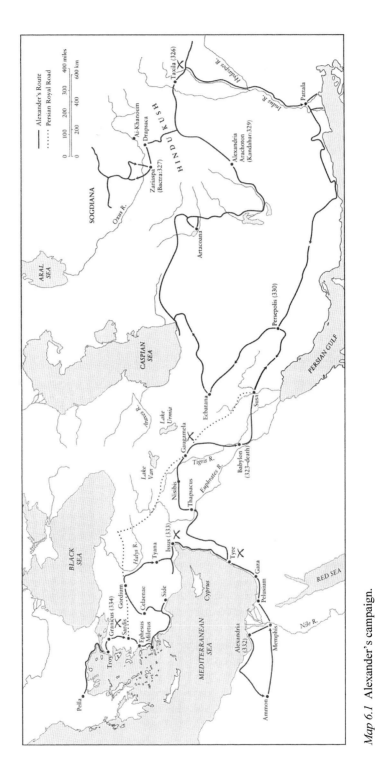

Map 6.1 Alexander's campaign.

Source: From *Readings in Greek History* (2nd edition) by D. B. Nagle and S. Burstein (2014). Map 7.3, pg. 270. By permission of Oxford University Press, USA.

and he had taken on the trappings of legend. We will try to piece together Philip's military reforms, including the development of a new type of phalanx and the pioneering use of heavy cavalry as the main striking force of the army. Instead of focusing on tactical developments alone, we must also understand how Philip leveraged the advantages of controlling a large territorial state to create a professional standing army that made short work of the Greeks at Chaeronea in 338 BCE. Likewise, as we chart Alexander's conquests in Asia, we need to explore how an understanding of politics, society, and culture allowed Alexander to gain acceptance not just as a Macedonian conqueror, but even as the new legitimate king of Persia and the peoples of the Persian Empire. Two important watershed events of Alexander's campaign, the Siege of Tyre and the Battle of Gaugamela, will serve as case studies of Alexander's art of war. Finally, since it is supremely difficult to separate the myth of Alexander from the historical person, we will conclude with Alexander's historical and cultural legacy. Was Alexander's unprecedented military success in the service of a genuine cosmopolitan vision of the world? Was he concerned above all to demonstrate Homeric excellence and obtain lasting fame, or was he merely a maniacal killer? Finally, how has the concept of "genius," perhaps first realized in Alexander, clouded the way historians talk about military leaders?

Sources for Philip and Alexander

The fifth century and the first half of the fourth century BCE are, relatively speaking, blessed with rich primary sources, including especially the big three Greek historians Herodotus, Thucydides, and Xenophon. While scholars are certainly wary of accepting the word of these authors at face value, and are glad to have alternative sources (such as the so-called Oxyrhynchus Historian) where such exist, there is no denying the value of these contemporary accounts, no matter how biased or incomplete. By contrast, no ancient historian's work has survived from the age of Philip and Alexander. We are at the mercy of much later historiographical sources written during the Roman Empire that compile, sometimes problematically, now-lost histories. Such contemporary literary evidence that does survive was not written to provide full historical narratives and is almost universally hostile to the Macedonians, especially Philip. Given these source problems, historians have had their work cut out for them when trying to discern exactly how the Macedonian army developed, how some of Philip's and Alexander's most important battles unfolded, and what the larger aims and legacy of the Macedonian kings were. The most difficult challenge is to sort out the difference between the Alexander legend that sprang up and endured in the decades and centuries after his death, and the ways the Macedonian military machine developed and the ends to which it was deployed before a Macedonian empire stretching from Egypt to India was a foregone conclusion.

Theopompus of Chios, a historian and contemporary of Philip, actually lived for a while at Philip's court, giving him an insider's view of Macedonia and its ruler. Unfortunately, the work of Theopompus does not survive in the manuscript tradition. We have only a few fragments of his history preserved in other authors, which nevertheless do tell us important things about units in Philip's army and other military matters. The best surviving contemporary source for the rise of Philip is the famous Athenian orator Demosthenes, far from a dispassionate observer. Demosthenes was an inveterate enemy of Philip and the Macedonians, and delivered a series of speeches in Athens over the course of many years warning of the dangers of Philip's growing power and urging the Athenians to stop the Macedonians before it was too late. Demosthenes' surviving speeches denigrate Philip as an uncouth and wanton barbarian, while at the same time recognizing the Macedonian's ingenuity and skill. Demosthenes also chastises the Athenians for having become soft and unworthy of their forebears by not standing up to Philip. Some Athenians, including Demosthenes' personal enemy Aeschines, were actually in favor of coming to terms with Philip. The greatest speaker of his day, and of many others, Demosthenes' speeches against Philip are full of wit and vitriol. He does not aim necessarily to present the whole picture but to persuade the Athenians to adopt a certain course of action. The Battle of Chaeronea in 338 BCE, for example, was the brainchild of Demosthenes, who spoke and engaged in diplomacy tirelessly to craft a Greek alliance against Philip. Despite the one-sided evidence Demosthenes provides, he does give us a crucial view of the debates raging in Athens as Philip emerged as a new and dangerous power. And while Demosthenes does not discuss the tactical nuances of Macedonian warfare, he provides some insight into Philip's diplomatic skill and strategic vision, as well as the advantages held by a king engaged in a struggle against a slow-moving and contentious democracy.

The other literary sources for Philip and Alexander were long ago grouped into two traditions, showing that modern scholars as much as ancient authors can be unhelpfully biased: the so-called "good" sources, and the oft-maligned "vulgate" sources. The "good" sources are based primarily on the now-lost works of Alexander's official court historian, Callisthenes, whose history was taken up and expanded by figures such as Ptolemy, one of Alexander's generals and founder of the Ptolemaic dynasty in Egypt. It is only in the work of much later authors, principally Arrian of Nicomedia, who wrote in the second century CE, that the "good" sources are preserved. Arrian has long been the preferred source for Alexander, because his work is derived from a less sensationalist tradition, short on gossipy personal details and long on a narrative of major events and supposedly rigorous analysis. Arrian was also a powerful political figure in the Roman Empire, and had been a military leader (indeed, he wrote surviving works on the art of war), which suggest that he would have had more insight than most regarding the subject matter of his history. Though not uncritical of Alexander, Arrian is perhaps too flattering in his portrait of the Macedonian king, and some of his details are contradicted by other sources.

The "vulgate" tradition, a term meaning "common" or even "of the rabble," is based mostly on the work of Cleitarchus, a historian working in Alexandria in the decades immediately following Alexander's death. Cleitarchus might have used official histories like that of Callisthenes as his sources, but he also likely spoke with soldiers who had taken part in Alexander's campaigns. Cleitarchus focused on personal anecdotes much more than the historians of the "good" tradition had, and his portrait of Alexander is far less flattering than Arrian's. Though Cleitarchus' original text does not survive, he was the main source for Diodorus of Sicily, a Greek universal historian writing in the first century BCE, and Quintus Curtius Rufus, a Roman author writing in Latin in the first century CE. I should note that Diodorus is also one of our main sources for Philip, but Diodorus' source material for that period is more obscure than for Alexander's reign. Because of its focus on Alexander's character and personal traits, the histories in the "vulgate" tradition preserve many stories not found in Arrian, and provide valuable evidence despite previous generations of scholars vastly preferring Arrian.

In addition to Arrian, Diodorus, and Curtius, an invaluable account of Alexander survives in the work of Plutarch of Chaeronea, the ancient world's preeminent biographer who wrote in the first and second centuries CE. Plutarch was concerned above all not to narrate history but to portray Alexander as a man. Drawing from every available source, including those in both the "good" and the "vulgate" tradition, Plutarch's life of Alexander is a tremendous read and offers valuable insights and details not contained in the other sources. Plutarch also provides information about the life and times of Philip, both in his biography of Alexander and in his treatment of other fourth-century BCE figures, especially Demosthenes. As a native of Chaeronea, the site of Philip's decisive victory over the Greek poleis, Plutarch is naturally fascinated by the rise of Macedonia and that battle in particular.

As always, we must read Greco-Roman literary sources in conjunction with other forms of evidence, including written sources from within the Persian Empire and the material evidence provided from such contexts as tombs, temples, and coinage. From Eastern contexts, cuneiform tablets, especially those from an "astronomical diary" found at Babylon, provide contemporary written accounts of the time of Alexander, including the information not found in our other sources that Persian soldiers deserted at the Battle of Gaugamela in 331 BCE. In recent decades, a great deal of archaeological work has increased our understanding of various regions of the Persian Empire at the time of Alexander's conquests, and, as we will see in the next chapter, the material record suggests a complex and two-way interaction between Greco-Macedonian conquerors and native populations in the wake of Alexander's expedition. While the standard literary sources do not provide a clear picture of the mechanics of the Macedonian phalanx, the mass grave, or *polyandrion*, of the Macedonians at Chaeronea contains the gigantic spear points from the soldiers' *sarissas*, providing a chilling glimpse of those terrible weapons. Finally, portraits of Alexander and Philip in marble and on coins, as well as public monuments from their reign, allow us to see from another angle the ways in which the Macedonian kings presented themselves and conceived of their empire.

Philip's military reforms

A common parlor game among ancient historians is to debate whether Philip was actually greater than his son, Alexander.[1] Though such a dispute, while amusing, may in the end be pointless, it does point to an important truth. As A. B. Bosworth, a leading scholar of Alexander, says near the beginning of his book *Conquest and Empire*, "the Macedon that Alexander inherited was the creation of his father." To understand how important Philip was for laying the foundation on which Alexander's empire was based, we should turn to the words of Alexander himself, at least as he is portrayed by Arrian. Trying to quell a mutiny of his soldiers at Opis, near Babylon, in 324 BCE, Alexander says:

> Philip took hold of you while you were nomadic and poor, most of you in animal hides and pasturing meager flocks in the mountains, defending them poorly against the Illyrians, Triballians and neighboring Thracians. He gave you proper clothing to wear instead of animal hides, led you from the mountains and into the plains, and left you the equals in war to the neighboring barbarians so you could be safe because of your native excellence rather than relying merely on strong terrain. He made you inhabitants of proper poleis and ordered you with sensible laws and customs. Of those barbarians who formerly pressured you and plundered your goods, he made you the masters instead of their slaves and subjects.
>
> He added most of Thrace to Macedonia, took the best places along the sea, and allowed for commerce throughout the land. He enabled you to work your mines without fear. He made you the rulers of the Thessalians, of whom formerly you were deathly afraid. By cutting the Phocians down to size, he made a broad and easy path into Greece instead of a narrow and difficult one. The Athenians and Thebans, always positioned against Macedonia, he humbled to such a degree – I was by now working along with him – that instead of you paying tribute to the Athenians and being subject to the Thebans, they for their part had to find their safety in you. Going into the Peloponnese, he put things in order there, and was made the supreme leader of all Greece for the expedition against Persia. However, he gave the glory to all the Macedonians instead of keeping it for himself.
>
> (Arrian *Anabasis* 7.9)

As is perhaps unusual for speeches assigned to ancient commanders, Alexander's words are largely true. When Philip came to power in 359 BCE, he inherited a kingdom in shambles, suffering from endemic dynastic quarrels, regional fragmentation, and continuous interference from outsiders, including the Athenians. When Philip died in 336 BCE, he was king of a massive and united Macedonia, more or less the direct ruler of Thrace and Thessaly, and dominated a league of mainland Greek states, save Sparta, that he forged and kept in line because no single Greek state or even coalition of states could any longer stand up to him. Philip's decisive victory came when he defeated in battle a hoplite coalition led

Figure 6.1 The Lion of Chaeronea, marking the grave of the Theban Sacred Band, 338 BCE (or possibly later).

Source: author's photograph.

by Athens and Thebes at Chaeronea in 338 BCE, a marvelous demonstration of Philip's mastery of the pitched battle. But while Philip created almost from scratch the ancient world's best army, it is remarkable how seldom he had to use its full strength as he amassed his great power.

We can group Philip's broad tactical reforms into three main areas: a new phalanx, called the "Macedonian phalanx" to distinguish it from its Greek precursors; heavy cavalry equipped with lances instead of ranged weapons, and used as the main striking force of the army; and a fully realized combined-arms force which, through drill and training, was able to operate with remarkable coordination. Let us look at all three in turn.

The origin and early form of the Macedonian phalanx is obscure, and scholars often reconstruct Philip's heavy infantry based on the more reliable information we have about Alexander's army. Diodorus does make a general statement about Philip's creation of the Macedonian phalanx and re-organization of the army after a disastrous defeat that killed many Macedonians, including Philip's brother and predecessor as king, Perdiccas:

> The Macedonians, due to the disaster in battle and because of the scale of the dangers they faced, fell into a great state of perplexity. Nevertheless, in the midst of such fears and dangers, Philip was not struck out of his wits by the magnitude of the looming perils. Instead, he gathered the Macedonians together in assemblies and encouraged them with eloquent speeches to be courageous. He boosted morale, organized his military units for the better, and outfitted the men with the appropriate weapons of war. He made the men engage constantly in armed manoeuvers and competitions. He thought up the dense formation and the equipment of the phalanx, copying the overlapping shields of the heroes at Troy. Philip was the first to marshal the Macedonian phalanx.
>
> (Diodorus 16.3)

Diodorus puts these reforms in 359 BCE, the year Philip came to the throne, though it is more likely that such sweeping changes took place over a much longer span during Philip's reign.

Prior to Philip, whatever organized army there was in Macedonia consisted of aristocratic horsemen. Macedonia had nothing equivalent to the hoplite class in Greece from which to draw a citizen infantry militia. The majority of Macedonia's population was rural and poor, neither organized enough to form a disciplined infantry nor wealthy enough to furnish hoplite equipment. Many of those that did fight in the army had been killed along with Philip's brother and predecessor, Perdiccas, at the hands of the Illyrians when Philip ascended to the throne in 359 BCE. Philip can fairly be said to have created a professional Macedonian infantry where virtually nothing had existed before, and instead of forming a Greek phalanx, he devised an entirely new heavy infantry formation. Philip was indeed well aware of the Greek phalanx, having lived in his youth as a hostage in Thebes, just as the Thebans were at the height of their military prowess under

Epameinondas and Pelopidas. The Theban Sacred Band showed Philip what a well-trained phalanx could do. Yet, Philip opted for something different to provide the backbone for his new army.

The soldiers in Philip's phalanx were, paradoxically, both more lightly armored and less maneuverable than Greek hoplites. The Macedonians were not equipped with heavy breastplates or obstructive Corinthian helmets – though by the mid-fourth century BCE, neither were hoplites – and they abandoned the large 1-meter shield in favor of a light model with perhaps two-thirds of the diameter. Philip equipped his men with this smaller shield, held in place around the neck and shoulders with a strap, in order to free up both hands for a much longer spear called the *sarissa*. While a hoplite spear was around 2–3 meters long, the *sarissa* was perhaps 4–5 meters long, and grew even longer in the generations following Philip and Alexander. Material evidence from places such as the Macedonian grave at Chaeronea or the royal tombs at Vergina provide chilling evidence of the *sarissa*'s size, including iron spear points a half-meter long and joints for holding the long *sarissa* shaft together in battle, since it could be disassembled into two pieces to allow for easier transport. Wielding this terrifying new spear with two hands, a soldier in the Macedonian phalanx could keep his enemy well at bay, but was even less likely to succeed in one-on-one combat than a hoplite.

Without the large hoplite shield, the Macedonian phalangite was potentially more vulnerable to spear and missile attacks. Philip compensated for the lack of armor by arranging his soldiers even closer together, mimicking passages from the *Iliad*, according to Diodorus, in which the Greeks at Troy were packed together like stones on a wall, so close that their horsehair plumes touched. The smaller shields meant that the Macedonians could stand shoulder-to-shoulder, and the longer spears meant that more spear points extended beyond the front rank, up to five, in fact. While a hoplite phalanx was usually eight or twelve ranks deep, except for occasionally deeper formations such as those regularly employed by the Thebans, the Macedonians phalanx was eventually sixteen ranks deep. The resulting formation resembled nothing so much as a porcupine or prickly forest of spears. The spears themselves, held upright at various angles by the men in ranks behind the fifth, would have served as a screen against missiles, making up for the lack of defensive armor. The Macedonian phalanx confronted each hoplite unlucky enough to be marshaled against it with at least five massive iron points, the longest of which kept the hoplite several meters away from his relatively unshielded Macedonian opponent.

Many scholars have attributed the basic equipment of the Macedonian phalanx to the fourth-century BCE Athenian general and mercenary commander Iphicrates. In an aside about Iphicrates' military talent, Diodorus says that the Athenian invented an entirely new type of infantry soldier, one called a "peltast" due to his use of a small shield called the *peltē* (15.44). In addition to furnishing his soldiers with a shield lighter and easier to handle than the standard hoplite shield, Iphicrates also lengthened the hoplite spear by half, doubled the length of the sword, and made a new kind of easy-tie boot, later called the "Iphicratid" boot. This passage from Diodorus is problematic. For one thing, "peltast" had long referred to a type of light or medium-armed soldier most known for using javelins and typically associated with Thrace. In previous chapters, we have considered the importance of peltasts in the Peloponnesian War and other conflicts, including Iphicrates' own triumph against Spartan hoplites at Lechaeum in 390 BCE. Maybe Iphicrates' new infantryman did carry a shield called a *peltē*, but the idea that Iphicrates invented peltasts or that the majority of peltasts fought like Iphicrates' new soldier is clearly false. The other major problem is that, aside from this single decontextualized passage in Diodorus, we hear nothing of these new soldiers in action, unless, of course, the Macedonian phalanx is an example of the "Iphicratid" soldier. Ultimately, the Diodorus passage raises more questions than it answers. All we can say for sure is that Philip's infantry did use smaller shields than Greek hoplites and did wield longer, two-handed spears than their Greek counterparts.[2] I am tempted to credit Philip alone with the innovation represented by the Macedonian phalanx.

Demosthenes, perhaps surprisingly given the supposed importance of Philip's heavy infantry reforms, emphasizes other elements of the Macedonian army as decisive for Philip's military ascendancy, namely his use of light-armed troops and cavalry, along with his facility with siege warfare (*Third Philippic* 47–50). Philip formalized a combined-arms approach to battle and warfare, which, though combined-arms forces had made appearances here and there earlier in Greek history, represented the culmination of the Greek art of war. Just as Philip might have taken his inspiration for his phalanx from the Thebans, the Athenian mercenary general Iphicrates might have provided the groundwork for the Macedonian combined-arms approach. Polyaenus, a compiler of military stratagems who wrote during the Roman Empire, says that Iphicrates compared an army to the human body:

> The phalanx he called the chest, the light-armed troops the hands, the cavalry the feet, and the general the head. If any of the lower parts were missing, he said that the army was lacking; but if it missed a general, it had nothing.
>
> (Polyaenus *Stratagems* 3.9.22)

Unlike the Greek hoplite phalanx, Philip's Macedonian phalanx was never meant to be the main striking force of the army. This role belonged, as it always had in Macedonia, to the aristocratic cavalry. Macedonia, blessed with many large plains just like Thessaly, had long been cavalry country, and even before Philp came to power, the elite backbone of the Macedonian cavalry had been the "King's Companions." This title was not merely honorific, since the Companions were literally the closest advisors and associates of the Macedonian king, who typically fought along with them on horseback himself. While Philip did not invent the Companion Cavalry, he expanded their ranks by affording more and more Macedonians large grants of land as his kingdom expanded, allowing for a much larger number of aristocratic nobles to serve on horseback. He also innovated by adopting the wedge formation, apparently first used among the neighboring Thracians, which proved much more effective in combat, especially against infantry, since the narrow point of the wedge could break through an infantry line effectively, while the wider parts of the wedge would punch an even larger hole in the enemy formation.

It is not always clear how the Macedonian cavalry were equipped before Philip. Most ancient cavalry, including the forces deployed by the Greeks and the Persians, were lightly armed, prized for their mobility more than their weight and potential for shock. More often than not, horses in the ancient world were used as mobile missile platforms, allowing their riders to loose arrows or javelins against the enemy before falling back at speed to regroup for another attack. This kind of harassing tactic could be very effective, especially against heavy infantry too encumbered to fight back against fast cavalry. Cavalry were particularly deadly against a retreating enemy, since horsemen could harass and kill the fleeing soldiers at ease, wreaking great havoc. The Campion Cavalry under Philip and Alexander, however, were heavily armed, using a thrusting lance called the *xyston* (or perhaps sometimes a *sarissa*, since a unit of cavalry called the *sarissa*-bearers is attested) and rode in dense formations meant to punch through the enemy by weight and shock.[3]

By the time Alexander invaded Asia in 334 BCE, the king always commanded the Companion Cavalry in person, leading the charge from the right wing of the army, looking for a gap in the enemy line created by the movement and attack of the Macedonian phalanx. Philip might have regularly led from horseback on the right too, though at Chaeronea, the only pitched battle for which we have any information concerning the role of Philip's cavalry – and even this information is sketchy and consists of a patchwork of sparse sources – the Macedonian cavalry was likely stationed on the left and under the command of the prince Alexander, while Philip led from the right at the head of the phalanx. Chaeronea was a special case, since Philip had to deal with the Theban Sacred Band on the Greek right, the elite unit of 300 professional hoplites that represented the only part of the Greek army that could pose any threat to Philip's superior force. Philip thus utilized his cavalry against them, and so moved the Companions to the left wing of the Macedonian army.[4]

As Philip's empire expanded, he added another crack cavalry force to his army: the Thessalians, traditionally the best horsemen among the Greeks. Under Philip, the Thessalian cavalry seems to have been equipped and arranged more or less identically to the Companions, that is, with a thrusting lance and in wedge formations. Where the Companions were in the place of honor on the right wing with the king, and usually made the decisive offensive strike, the Thessalians were marshaled on the left wing. Other cavalry units also fought in the Macedonian army, including light cavalry that fired arrows and hurled javelins, and advance scouting units called *prodromoi*, or those that "run in front" of the army.

While heavy infantry and heavy cavalry formed the core of Philip's new army, Philip also made use of light-armed troops, especially slingers, archers, and peltasts. These units, consisting largely of allied soldiers from the lands such as Thrace being added to Philip's kingdom, were useful as skirmishers in front

Figure 6.2 Artist's conception of a member of the Macedonian Companion Cavalry.

Source: from J. Warry, *Warfare in the Classical World* (Norman: University of Oklahoma Press 1995), 82. Reprinted with the permission of Salamander Books and the University of Oklahoma Press.

of the main army, deployed to soften up the enemy before the full clash of arms, and as protection for the army's flanks. Another important unit is represented by the *hypaspists*, or "shield-bearers," who were elite infantry, perhaps equipped similarly to hoplites, that covered the vulnerable gap between the right wing of the phalanx and the Companion Cavalry. This unit had a storied history in the Macedonian army, and after the death of Alexander, *hypaspist* veterans were renamed the "silver shields" to reflect their ornate armament and their prestige. Philip truly took the central idea behind Iphicrates' army-as-body metaphor to heart, and because he could afford to keep his men in arms for long periods of time and drilled them constantly, he was able to wield all these moving parts effectively and with great coordination.

As Demosthenes implies above, Philip used his non-phalanx soldiers, including his light-armed troops and cavalry, to great effect as he expanded his power and territory. He did not merely use such units in full battle array and for pitched battles, but was flexible enough to use different units for different tactical purposes. One of those purposes was the capture of fortified cities, something with which the Greeks often struggled and came up short. The last specialized unit Demosthenes mentions is the siege train, which included not only the awesome equipment Philip had constructed to batter down and scale the walls of cities, but also, by necessity, a corps of military engineers expert in the use, construction, and maintenance of siege equipment. One reason why the Classical Greeks never really excelled at siege warfare was the sheer expensive and logistical challenge sieges entailed. As in the case with his professional army, Philip could afford to go beyond Greek warfare.

One event that intensified the conflict between Philip and Athens was Philip's siege of Olynthus in 348 BCE, an ally of Athens in the northern Aegean (Diodorus 16.53). Philip's attack on this city occasioned Demosthenes' first series of speeches, called the "Olynthiacs," against the Macedonian king. Though this siege was a formative part of Philip's empire-building, we are only given a sparse description in the sources and cannot say for certain exactly what methods Philip used, but we are told that he assaulted the city walls several times and lost many men. Even with his resources – we know he had artillery such as ballistae and catapults since many missiles have been found at the site – Philip resorted to treachery to take Olynthus. After two of the city's top officials betrayed Olynthus, Philip enslaved the inhabitants and utterly plundered and razed the city to serve as a warning to others. Today, Olynthus has the unfortunate distinction of being a remarkably well-preserved Classical city precisely because it was destroyed in one violent episode instead of being allowed to develop and evolve as a city for decades or centuries more.[5]

Several years later, in 341/0 BCE, Philip laid siege to two more northern cities, Perinthus and Byzantium (Diodorus 16.74–16.77). Diodorus' description of this campaign suggests that Philip by now had acquired a great deal more siege capability, and other sources – such as the Roman architectural writer Vitruvius – say that by this time Philip had hired a man named Polyidus of Thessaly to serve as his chief siege engineer (Vitruvius 10.19.13). With Polyidus' help, Philip made use of siege towers nearly 40 meters high, much higher than the city walls and towers. These towers had many stories, all loaded with attackers and artillery. Most scholars also think that by this time Philip began to use torsion siege artillery, a much deadlier form of weaponry that the tension artillery pioneered by Dionysius of Syracuse. Torsion engines made use of twisted hair or animal sinew to add much more force to their missiles, enough force in fact to damage walls and battlements in addition to killing men. These new torsion catapults and ballistae set a new standard for the destructive power of besieging armies and soon became standard throughout the Mediterranean. As with tension weapons, torsion engines were used both by attackers and by defenders during sieges. From the time of Philip, city walls and towers had to be built in such a way as to withstand torsion-fired missiles and also provide enough space for siege artillery platforms for the defenders. It is with good reason that the time of Philip and Alexander and the subsequent Hellenistic period furnish some of the most impressive stone walls of the ancient world.

At Perinthus and Byzantium, Philip's siege was unsuccessful. His new methods, including the use of siege towers, battering rams, sappers, ladders, and artillery, were still not enough. It was not for lack of trying. Diodorus says that Philip divided his forces into several shifts, so he could keep up the pressure day and night. He was energetic and alert, ordering ladders to be put against the walls where defenders had been cleared by artillery missiles. He was also able to breach the walls in several places at Perinthus, including crumbling a large section of the defenses. The people of Perinthus, however, had hastily built new walls inside the outer ones, and their closely packed houses also served to ward off the attackers. But in the end, the only thing that saved Perinthus was an influx of men and supplies from neighboring areas, including mercenaries paid for by the Persians. Byzantium sent a large force to Perinthus, and was rewarded for helping its ally by having Philip divide his forces to besiege Byzantium too. After months of siege and several spirited but unsuccessful attacks, Philip called off the operation against Perinthus and Byzantium. He did gain those cities in short order, but only after he defeated a Greek coalition led by Athens and Thebes at Chaeronea in 338 BCE.

Philip had many advantages over even the mightiest of Greek poleis. As Demosthenes says in his most famous speech, *On the Crown*:

> Examine the advantages enjoyed by Philip, against whom we were fighting. First, he ruled his troops as a supreme commander, which is the greatest of all advantages in war. Second, his men always had their weapons in their hands. Additionally, he had plenty of money, and did whatever he chose without informing the people ahead of time through decrees or deliberating in public. He did not fear being prosecuted by informers, falling under indictment for introducing unlawful motions, or submitting for a formal audit of his activities in office. Quite simply, he himself was master, commander, and lord of all.
>
> (Demosthenes *On The Crown* 235)

Demosthenes outlines three factors of great benefit to Philip. First, as king he was free to make war when and how he chose, without having to deal with rivals for power or to persuade a body of citizens to ratify his plans. The reason Demosthenes had to make so many speeches against Philip at Athens was because the Athenians could not agree on what they should do about Philip, and some Athenians actively supported the Macedonian. The occasion for *On the Crown* was a legal action brought against a friend of Demosthenes who, years after the Battle of Chaeronea, had proposed that Demosthenes be awarded a gold crown in recognition of his services to the city. Demosthenes' rivals, especially Aeschines, brought Demosthenes' ally to court, alleging that Demosthenes' record in no way justified such an honor, prompting Demosthenes to make his impassioned defense of his own policies and actions. The longstanding quarrel between Demosthenes and Aeschines illustrates well the challenges and personal risks inherent in advocating any policy in a democracy, especially in the spheres of foreign affairs and war. Philip could be both more efficient and more confident as a political and military leader.

Second, Philip kept his soldiers in arms continually, allowing for a degree of professionalism and skill impossible in citizen militias. The Athenians and Thebans were fine hoplites, perhaps the finest in Greece aside from the Spartans in their heyday. Nevertheless, Philip's phalanx was far more disciplined and effective at Chaeronea than the best soldiers the Greeks could muster. Philip was able to maintain a standing army because of the third advantage enumerated by Demosthenes, namely access to a lot of money. The Greeks were well aware of the advantages possessed by professional troops, but it was next to impossible for poleis to provide regular pay for a large number of soldiers for long periods. In the fourth century BCE, Athenian generals regularly got into trouble while on campaign because they had to resort to plundering, in effect piracy, in order to pay the troops with whom they had been sent out with insufficient funds. Once Philip came to possess lucrative gold mines in places like Mt. Pangaeum, his cash reserves outstripped the resources of any of his rivals and allowed him to keep great numbers in arms.

Aside from these considerable advantages, Philip enjoyed another privilege denied to the Greek poleis, namely being free of the polis itself. If, as discussed in Chapter 2, the hoplite phalanx and the polis were inextricably linked – that is, the tactics and makeup of the phalanx both reflected and influenced the increasingly egalitarian archaic Greek state – Greeks would face many barriers to military innovation, both cultural and practical. Citizen-soldiers, by their very nature as regular farmers for the vast majority of the time, could not acquire the skill and experience required for intricate combined-arms warfare. Standing firm in the battle line was probably the best the member of an amateur militia could hope for. There are good reasons the Spartans repeatedly bested their fellow Greeks in battle on so many occasions, chief among them the fact that full Spartiates trained for warfare continually. Even the professional Spartan warriors, however, were constrained by cultural factors from innovating beyond the standard phalanx. When the Spartans did make use of cavalry, they infamously put their weakest soldiers on horseback, rendering their cavalry ineffective. The Spartans disdained archers and other light-armed troops, if they used them in battle at all. Other Greek poleis too continued to conceive of the hoplite as the ideal Greek soldier, well beyond the time when light-armed and other ways of fighting had proven their worth even against hoplites in battles like Pylos in 425 BCE and Lechaeum in 390 BCE.

Philip faced no such constraints. The Macedonian peasantry had never fought as hoplites and had never lived in poleis at all, let alone served as proud citizen-soldiers. One positive element of being excluded from the Greek cultural sphere was that the Macedonian infantry had no hang-ups about fighting as light-armed soldiers or in a new type of phalanx, and Philip had enough money to train soldiers full-time to develop the cohesion necessary for combined-arms tactics. Greeks who were famous for their military innovations, such as the Athenian Iphicrates, who won the Battle of Lechaeum by unleashing mercenary peltasts against Spartan hoplites, tended to be those outside of the standard hoplite system, either because they led mercenaries or because they spent extended periods on campaign, or both. The same factors that allowed Iphicrates a free hand to innovate were only magnified in Philip's case, allowing the Macedonian king to develop an army well beyond the capabilities of the old-fashioned forces marshaled by the Greeks.

Perhaps the most remarkable fact about Philip's new army, including the many advantages he exploited in building and deploying it, was how rarely he made use of it. For all he was reviled by the Greeks as an uncouth drunkard, Philip was an astute diplomat and shrewd politician. He preferred to make territorial gains, remove threats on his borders, and acquire allies and subjects without bloodshed. As a king, Philip had diplomatic tools that most fourth-century BCE Greeks lacked, including polygamy. Philip married several times, frequently to cement alliances with potential challengers to his northern dominance. Olympias, the mother of Alexander, for example, was the daughter of a king in Epirus, a region in northwestern Greece abutting Macedonia. Philip married Macedonian women too, usually to neutralize potential rivals in other aristocratic Macedonian families. While having several wives did lead to some dynastic tension in Philip's household, especially when he married the Macedonian Cleopatra, whose family hoped her child would supplant Alexander as the heir to the throne, overall much of Philip's empire and its stability can be attributed to clever marriage alliances.

While marriage alliances helped to cement his position among the non-Greek and semi-Greek peoples of the north, Philip flexed his diplomatic muscle to ensure that his power increased among the central and southern Greek states too. In fact, Philip managed to be invited to intervene in Greek affairs, rather than force his way in with his army, and he was able to pose as the defender of the god Apollo, no less. Since the Greeks, notoriously, were often at war with each other, Philip maneuvered himself into the position both of indispensable ally and of the one enemy that could not be ignored. When central Greece was embroiled in conflict over control of Apollo's sanctuary at Delphi, in a series of struggles called the "Sacred Wars," most of the leading Greek states took the side either of Phocis, the power that had seized the sanctuary, or of the Amphictyonic League, the group of states allied for the sanctuary's safekeeping. Athens was an ally of the Phocians, while Thebes was on the side of the league and eventually asked for Philip's help in bringing the Third Sacred War to an end. Philip did end the war in 346 BCE by positioning his army to threaten the vital pass of Thermopylae, which caught the Athenians off guard and forced the surrender of the Phocians without any bloodshed. Philip afterwards became the de facto head of the Amphictyonic League, which gave him all the justification needed to invade central and southern Greece in 338 BCE, in yet another Sacred War, an act that culminated in the Decisive battle of Chaeronea. Already in 346 BCE, however, the writing was already on the wall in terms of who was the new great power in Greece. For his role in bringing the Third Sacred War to an end, Philip, a Macedonian whom most Greeks did not even consider Greek, presided over Delphi's Pythian Games, a festival on a par with the Olympic Games.

Philip also cultivated personal political allies in various poleis that might oppose him. In Athens, Demosthenes' archrival Aeschines often advocated on Philip's behalf, and was instrumental in crafting the Peace of Philocrates between Athens and Philip. Aeschines' enemies in Athens, especially Demosthenes, argued that this arrangement harmed Athenian interests and did little more than legitimize and make room for Philip's anti-Athenian imperialism. Naturally, Aeschines and other supporters of Philip were accused, openly and frequently, of being on Philip's payroll and therefore acting as traitors. But hindsight should not obscure the fact that a very influential faction in Athens not only was not opposed to Philip, but actually sought his alliance. The famous orator Isocrates penned a letter to Philip in which he urged the Macedonian king to take up the mantle of panhellenism, uniting all the Greeks against Persia as a common enemy, something the Athenians, Spartans, and Thebans had failed to achieve.

Whether or not Aeschines and his associates accepted bribes, Philip did indeed resort to bribery many times during his reign, something he was able to do especially after he added lucrative gold mines to his territories. The siege of Olynthus, for instance, only ended once Philip arranged for the city to be betrayed by two Olynthians he had bribed, who, incidentally, apparently came to a bad end despite the enormous sums of money they received. Philip reportedly said that his most effective weapon was a donkey laden with gold (Cicero *Ad Atticum* 1.16.12). As Philip's unsuccessful sieges of Perinthus and Byzantium demonstrate, despite having the most sophisticated siege army in the Classical world, strong walls and a motivated defense are often too difficult to overcome with conventional weapons of war.

In the end, though, Philip's conventional forces, namely his combined-arms army centered on the Macedonian phalanx and the heavy cavalry, provided him with his most consequential victory. In 338 BCE, on the plains of Chaeronea in western Boeotia, Philip's army rendered obsolete the hoplite phalanx and the polis system that had both nurtured and relied on it (Diodorus 16.84–16.87; Pausanias 9.40.10; Plutarch *Alexander* 9; Polyaenus 4.2.7). The Athenians and

Figure 6.3 The Philippeion at Olympia, 338 BCE.
Source: author's photograph.

Thebans, along with several other Greek allies, had joined together at the urging of Demosthenes to form a grand hoplite coalition that lined up to stop Philip once and for all, on the very doorstep of the most important Greek poleis. Though the sources for this battle are frustratingly vague and scattered, the most convincing reconstructions have Philip employing a feigned retreat – a maneuver all but impossible for amateur armies – to lure the Greek left, where the Athenians were stationed, into a false sense of victory before the Macedonian phalanx obliterated the hoplite line. At the other end of the field, the Macedonian heavy cavalry smashed through the Greek right and killed every single soldier in the storied Theban Sacred Band. Philip's eighteen-year-old son, Alexander, had led this cavalry charge.

Alexander and his war machine

Arrian (*Anabasis* 1.11) and Diodorus (17.3–17.5) agree that after pacifying Greece (principally by burning the rebellious Thebes to the ground to set an example) Alexander crossed into Asia in 334 BCE at the head of around 30,000 infantry and 5,000 cavalry. Alexander left Antipater in Macedonia with a force of 12,000 infantry and 1,500 cavalry, and there may have been an additional 10,000 troops waiting for him in Asia, who had been sent as an advance force, but it is uncertain whether they were still deployed when Alexander began the campaign proper. Alexander's army was large, and had an especially high ratio of top-quality cavalry, but it was far smaller than the forces the Persian king, Darius III, could muster, and Alexander was aiming at taking his army very far from home, deep into hostile territory. Tactical skill, matchless equipment, good generalship, and sheer audacity would have to overcome the challenges facing the Macedonian king.

At the start of his campaign, Alexander's war machine was essentially Philip's. From his father, Alexander inherited not only the desire to lead a Panhellenic crusade against the Persians, but also the world's finest combined-arms army. But where Philip was reluctant to use his excellent army, preferring instead to use diplomacy to gain allies, and bribery to corrupt enemies, Alexander lived for combat, fighting a total of four large set-piece battles between the Granicus River at the western edge of Asia Minor and the Hydaspes River in India. Aside from these famous clashes, Alexander's army fought in countless smaller engagements as the Macedonians sought to pacify an enormous territory encompassing dozens of nations and peoples. Like his father, Alexander was conscious of political and public relations considerations, but above all he desired to be seen in the mold of Achilles, a Homeric hero with legendary bloodlust. According to Plutarch, Alexander slept with a copy of the *Iliad* under his pillow (Plutarch *Alexander* 8.2). As a good Homeric warrior, those called the *promachoi*, or "front-fighters," Alexander always led from the front, setting the standard for the Hellenistic generals that followed him – and he received many wounds for his trouble.

The best example of Alexander's leadership from the front, aside from his direct assaults against the position of Darius at the pitched battles of both Issus and Gaugamela, came near the end of the campaign, after the army had already turned back from the Hyphasis River in India, when Alexander assaulted a town of the Mallians, an Indian people (Arrian *Anabasis* 7.9–7.10). Assaulting their fortress, Alexander found his sappers and wall-climbers were moving too slowly for his liking, so he grabbed a ladder himself, placed it against the wall, held up his shield, and scaled the wall under a hail of missiles. When he reached the top of the wall, he killed the enemies he found there, and then jumped into the fortress itself, put his back against the wall and prepared to fight all comers. After killing several men, the Indians were afraid to approach Alexander in hand-to-hand combat, and instead loosed missiles at him, one of which punctured his chest. Seeing their king taking the lead, Alexander's soldiers, especially his bodyguard, doubled their efforts, so much so that they broke several ladders in their haste to scale the walls. Eventually, Alexander, bleeding from a serious chest wound, was rescued by his guards who followed him into the fortress. Going berserk, the Macedonians forced their way into the walls by smashing through the gate, and the fortress fell with a great slaughter.

It is difficult to imagine Philip leading an assault like this. There is certainly no record of him doing so, even though he was wounded more than once. Alexander's bravery and leading-by-example were both effective and irresponsible. Effective in that the Mallians' fortress was taken, and several battles were won, by Alexander boldly taking the lead. Irresponsible because Alexander was very nearly killed more than once, which would have left his army far from home, with no clear successor and no firm plan to keep the new empire together, a result that would have caused the entire enterprise to end in failure, and would have led to unimaginable suffering and chaos.

Alexander's leadership style led not only to a different perception of the Macedonian king, but also to different military outcomes than those likely had Philip led the invasion of Persia himself. For example, on more than one occasion, namely after the Battle of Issus in 333 BCE and shortly before the Battle of Gaugamela in 331 BCE, Darius offered Alexander great swaths of the Persian Empire, and even his daughter in marriage. Philip likely would have taken the deal, if only to buy time to consolidate his gains before further pushes to the east. Alexander, on the other hand, continued to seek out battle with the Great King, to settle things by force of arms. Aside from boldly rushing into pitched battles, Alexander pressed his sieges harder than Philip did, or at least with more success. Philip had an extensive siege train, and laid siege several times, but never managed to take a city by storm. When he was successful, it was usually due to the city being betrayed from the inside. Alexander, on the other hand, at sites like Miletus, Halicarnassus, and especially Tyre (which will be discussed below), pressed the attack boldly and, despite setbacks and losses, was able to take cities by force while using essentially the same siege train as his father.

Another major difference between the armies of Philip and Alexander was that the latter campaigned for many years many hundreds of miles from home. A decade of campaigning meant that Alexander had to replenish his losses, and was often not able to count on reinforcements from Macedonia itself. In addition to the need to maintain a certain number of soldiers, Alexander also had to grapple with the realities of ruling a territorial empire far too vast to police by brute force alone. Alexander needed to position himself as the legitimate successor of Darius III, as the new Great King of Persia. One way Alexander tackled both challenges at once was to incorporate Persians and other locals into his army, transforming his force from a Greco-Macedonian one into something much more multi-ethnic.

Near the end of his campaign, at the Persian capital of Susa as he journeyed back west, Alexander entertained many local leaders, and enrolled in his army, according to Arrian, some 30,000 local boys who were to be equipped and trained as members of the Macedonian phalanx (*Anabasis* 7.6). Arrian says that this caused consternation among the Macedonian veterans, who had seen their mission as one of Macedonian conquest of the Persians, not amalgamation. Alexander even had the gall to call these local troops the *epigonoi*, or "successors." As a measure that surely increased tensions among the Macedonian elite even further, Alexander also enrolled some Asian horsemen into the ranks of the Companion Cavalry, the most prestigious of his forces. Matters came to a head at Opis in 324 BCE (Arrian *Anabasis* 7.8–7.11). When Alexander announced that he would send home the older and more infirm Macedonian veterans and replace them with local troops, the Macedonian soldiers mutinied. As A. B. Bosworth argues, Alexander pursued such policies not merely to ensure that his army was at full strength, but also to reflect his status as King of Asia, and to create a base of soldiers loyal to him alone (*Conquest and Empire* 273).

Alexander's new role as Great King, instead of first among aristocratic equals, as had been the Macedonian tradition, necessitated a new approach to his army. Once he assumed the mantle of Darius, Alexander faced a pushback from his most stalwart soldiers. Cleitus the Black, one of Alexander's closest friends, who had actually saved Alexander's life at the Battle of the Granicus, on a night of excessive drinking called out Alexander's growing arrogance and adoption of Persian manners. Enraged at Cleitus' insolence, which likely would not have been out of place back in Macedonia, Alexander grabbed a spear and killed his friend (Arrian *Anabasis* 4.8–4.9; Plutarch *Alexander* 50–51). As he pushed deeper into Asia, Alexander found it increasingly difficult to control his army, especially its Greco-Macedonian core. At the Hyphasis River in 326 BCE, Alexander's army mutinied, prefiguring the mutiny at Opis two years later, and refused to go further into India, forcing Alexander to halt his eastward expansion (Arrian *Anabasis* 5.28–5.29). If he was to continue in his role as conqueror and king of new lands, Alexander would need to forge an army that would follow him without the pesky independent spirit and local attachments of his Macedonians.

After Alexander's death, despite his efforts at creating a true multi-national force, his successors continued to rely mostly on Greco-Macedonian soldiers to form the core of their armies – even if those armies were based in far-off places like Egypt or Syria.[6] The hesitation to recruit mostly from local troops meant that Hellenistic kings often had difficulty finding enough soldiers to fill their massive armies, and that a single defeat in pitched battle could so deprive one side of personnel that the entire war would come to an end. Recruitment proved to be one of the major weaknesses that hobbled the Hellenistic kingdoms in their struggles with Rome, which could draw from a nearly limitless base of soldiers.

As Alexander marched further and further from home, and came to possess more and more territory, his military needs accordingly changed. Particularly as he made his way through central Asia, as he headed in the direction of India, Alexander found having one large battle-ready army would not do the trick. Finding the various isolated peoples of central Asia, in places like Bactria and Sogdiana, no easier to pacify than modern states have found in central Asian countries like Afghanistan, Alexander divided his forces, sometimes into several smaller units, to subdue various rebellious and not-yet-conquered areas. Frequently, he assigned several of his top generals to lead small strike forces, centered on contingents of heavy cavalry, to bring rapid relief to threatened places and swift counterstrokes against rebels. Though it would take many years and lives, arduous backtracking, and a few brutal and example-setting atrocities, Alexander pacified central Asia, at least enough for his liking, and moved on to India. He was able to do so because of the agility and adaptability of his army and his command style. Alexander's war machine was not a blunt instrument, but a precise multi-tool.

As a final note on his invasion force, let us consider Alexander's controversial attitude towards naval warfare. Alexander was notoriously a land-lubber. He did have a navy, and used some 160 triremes, mostly supplied by his Greek "allies," to help ferry his forces across the Hellespont at the start of his campaign against Persia, and had this force with him when he laid siege to Miletus on the coast of Asia Minor. The Macedonian fleet proved its worth at Miletus, and managed to keep the Persian fleet at bay while also refusing to engage in a pitched naval battle (Arrian *Anabasis* 1.19). However, with some 400 ships, the Persians had a far larger and better navy, the backbone of which were the expert Phoenician mariners who lived along the Levantine coast in what is now Lebanon. Despite his success at Miletus, Alexander decided to disband his fleet, ostensibly because it was no match for the Persian fleet and he did not have the money to maintain it. Also, since the Macedonians were in control of the coast of Asia Minor, and were making their way further along the eastern Mediterranean, Alexander planned to "defeat the Persian fleet on land," that is, by robbing the enemy navy of its bases (Arrian *Anabasis* 1.20).

In the event, this is exactly what happened: Alexander robbed the Persians of their bases on the coast, driving the Persian navy out of the contest. But Alexander did not achieve this easily, and at one of the most important bases, the Phoenician city of Tyre, Alexander's besieging forces were very nearly defeated by the opposing navy and were only saved in the nick of time when other Phoenician and Cypriot navies threw in their lot with the Macedonians, as we will discuss further below. An even more dire consequence of ceding the Aegean Sea to the Persians was that Alexander's enemies could cross the sea to foment revolt in Greece. The Greeks were, after all, not entirely willing allies of Alexander, and in his campaign's early stages, losing his supply lines back home could have been disastrous. In fact, this was the exact plan advocated by Memnon of Rhodes, a Greek mercenary who was working for Darius in Asia Minor. Memnon was an eminently capable general, and knew that Alexander was left vulnerable without his fleet. Darius put Memnon in charge of the entire war effort along the coast of Asia Minor, and Memnon immediately set to work employing the navy to take back several islands, including Chios, which was betrayed to him, and Lesbos, where he laid siege. In a stunning stroke of fortune, however, Memnon died before putting his plan into action, and Darius did not have any other generals eager to stir things up in Greece. Memnon was Darius' best asset in the war, and Alexander's most formidable enemy. Arrian says that Memnon's death was the greatest setback the Persians faced at this stage of the campaign (*Anabasis* 2.1). Alexander's war would now be fought entirely on land.

Case studies: the Siege of Tyre and the Battle of Gaugamela

Following his victory over the armies of Darius at the Battle of Issus in 333 BCE, Alexander did not move immediately against the heart of the Persian Empire. Rather, he consolidated his position along the Levantine coast of the eastern Mediterranean before adding Egypt to his empire. In the Levant, Alexander stopped at the great Phoenician city of Tyre, today located in southern Lebanon. In Alexander's day, Tyre had moved from its original site on the mainland to occupy an island lying about a kilometer off the coast. Surrounded by water and fortified with defensive walls dozens of meters high, Tyre seemed to be impervious to assault. Nevertheless, Alexander decided to lay siege to the city primarily, as the sources say, because the Tyrians had denied Alexander's request to sacrifice in their city to the Phoenician god Melqart – whom Alexander linked to his own patron Heracles. Such an affront to Alexander's prestige could not be allowed to stand, especially since Alexander had to firm up his Mediterranean gains before aiming for the grand prize further east.

Siege warfare had advanced a great deal under Philip, especially with the innovations of Polyidus of Thessaly. Philip's siege train had included towers, sappers, and torsion artillery. For all these innovations, and the resources to back them up, Philip was still unable to take by storm the major cities he besieged. Olynthus fell because of bribe-induced treachery from the inside, Philip's favorite method for ending a conflict, and Perinthus and Byzantium held out long enough for Philip to be called away elsewhere, despite feverish assaults and innovative tactics and equipment on the Macedonian side. Tyre presented Alexander with a far greater challenge than any of those cities had for his father, yet lay siege he did – in the end successfully, after investing the city for the first half of 332 BCE (Arrian 2.16–2.24; Diodorus 17.40–17.46; Curtius 4.4.10–4.4.21; Plutarch *Alexander* 24).

Demonstrating an awesome power to rival the Persian king Xerxes, who in 480 BCE had made the sea land by bridging the Hellespont (today's Dardanelles), and the land sea by cutting a canal through the Athos peninsula in northern Greece, Alexander decided to join the island city of Tyre to the mainland. Alexander undertook to build a massive mole, or land bridge, to span the nearly kilometer-wide channel. The mole not only had to be long, it needed to be wide enough, roughly 65 meters according to the sources, to serve as a platform for giant siege towers. Fortunately, the old city of Tyre on the mainland furnished a plentiful supply of stone for the project, and timber was harvested from a nearby mountain. Alexander's men, who included soldiers but also masses drafted from nearby cities, started boldly bringing the land closer to Tyre and its horrified people, who had denied Alexander's request to sacrifice to Melqart on the assumption that they could not be taken.

Despite its rapid start, however, construction of the mole did not go smoothly. First there was the wind and weather, notoriously bad in the strait. Several times the mole simply collapsed under the assault of the elements. More frustrating still for the Macedonians, and potentially fatal to the entire enterprise, the Phoenicians of Tyre had superior naval forces. Alexander's dismissal of his Greek navy in 334 BCE, which some have hailed as a stroke of genius since he could apparently defeat the Persian navy by simply taking away its bases, is now seen as perhaps the greatest strategic blunder of Alexander's entire career. The first phase of the Siege of Tyre demonstrates Alexander's error as well as anything does. Enjoying their control of the sea, the Tyrians launched their ships to assault those constructing the mole. As Alexander's workers were busy with their tasks, the Tyrian ships approached the mole and attached the men with missiles, including those launched by on-board artillery, killing many and stopping construction in its tracks. The Tyrians also destroyed much of the mole by ramming a fire ship into it, causing a great conflagration and loss of life among the work crews. But as luck would have it – and luck seemed often on the side of Alexander – naval reinforcements did arrive for the Macedonians from those Greeks and Phoenicians who had gone over to Alexander's side after Issus. Alexander did not have the ships to safeguard his siege, but his new allies, jumping on the Macedonian bandwagon, did.

Once Alexander's naval reinforcements arrived, the Tyrians were still a long way from giving up. Once the mole got closer to the city, and Alexander began to make concerted attacks against the walls both from the mole and from his ships, the Siege of Tyre became a masterclass in both offensive and defensive siegecraft. Apart from being on an island, Tyre was fortified by walls in the order of 50 meters high, so Alexander constructed siege towers to match, which he wheeled to the end of the mole. Siege towers are not merely for allowing soldiers to climb over the top of enemy walls, but rather serve as high platforms for archers and slingers and, most importantly, artillery. From a great height, level with the defenders, Alexander's soldiers used the larger torsion artillery to hurl stones large enough to damage the walls, while using smaller artillery to fire bolts at the defenders on the battlements. The Macedonians also equipped their ships, including several ships lashed together to provide a larger platform, with artillery to batter the walls and defenders at many points.

The defenders were far from idle. Of all the sources on the siege, Diodorus offers us the fullest picture of the defensive countermeasures, which have led some to wonder whether he embellished his account with techniques gleaned from a tactical manual. Given the difficulty Alexander faced in taking the city even after achieving naval superiority and completing the mole, it is reasonable to think that the Tyrians did indeed have something up their sleeves. In addition to the standard measures of hurling stones, javelins, and fire on the attackers next to the walls, Diodorus describes great spinning wheels set up along the defenses to break the force of the Macedonian missiles. He also says that the Tyrians made use of soft materials to cushion the blows from stones and other projectiles. They hurled barbed tridents at the attackers to pull them off the towers to their deaths. Most horrifyingly, they filled shields with blazing hot sand to launch at the enemy. When Macedonian soldiers were struck with a shower of sand, the searing grains went inside their armor causing great agony and death, making the entire Macedonian force less eager to press the assault. So effective were the defenders, and so many attackers died, that Alexander was on the verge of calling off the siege, which would have dealt a serious blow to his prestige.

Alexander finally decided to launch one more concerted assault, surrounding the city on all sides with his ships after decisively defeating the Tyrian navy in an engagement at sea. The literary sources say that the king was inspired to make this final push because of the omen delivered by a giant sea-monster (a whale?) appearing near the mole, or even propelling itself on top of the mole, before disappearing beneath the waves. Whatever the meaning of this strange event, Alexander's attack met with success. Surrounded by Alexander's ships and siege towers, the Tyrian defenders began to suffer too many losses. The walls, too, were breached in many places after taking a continuous beating from catapults and battering rams. As was typical of Alexander's style of command, he stood out conspicuously among his force, easily identifiable in his resplendent armor as he urged his men in person. Once the walls were breached or surmounted, Alexander led the attack himself, facing great danger as he killed many defenders with his own hands. A man named Admetus, commanding the elite unit of the guards, was run though with a spear as he stormed the wall, only to be replaced in the van by Alexander himself, who held the position and was the first to secure a section of the Tyrian fortifications. Soon Alexander's troops were pouring into the city, killing any enemy they came across, even those running to the temples for sanctuary. In addition to the thousands of Tyrians who had died over the course of the six-month siege, Alexander executed some 2,000 others, apparently by crucifixion, to make a grisly example for any others who might oppose him.

The Siege of Tyre exemplifies many important features of Macedonian warfare. Most obviously, it showcases the tremendous advances in siege warfare in the late fourth century BCE. Both sides deployed innovative technologies, including siege towers, land- and ship-based torsion artillery, and countermeasures to lessen the artillery's effect. Alexander's spanning of the channel between Tyre and the mainland demonstrated both the Macedonian king's boldness and

the tremendous materiel and personnel resources he could command – no Classical Greek polis could have built this mole. Hellenistic warfare in the period after
Alexander would entail further conspicuous displays of great, world-scale
military power. Alexander's leadership style and self-presentation were on
display, notably in his personal leadership during the final assault, and in the
cruel punishments he inflicted on the defeated Tyrians. Both the city of Thebes,
which Alexander razed to the ground after it rebelled at the start of his reign, and
the Greek mercenaries on the Persian side at the Battle of the Granicus River,
whom Alexander had surrounded and butchered, had similarly experienced
Alexander's wrath. Fear and a sense of inevitability – no city could stand in his
way – were important themes bolstering Alexander's mission of conquest.
Finally, Alexander's weaknesses were on display at Tyre, too. He very nearly
lost the struggle by being outmatched at sea, a consequence of his controversial
dismissal of the Greek fleet. Only the lucky arrival of new naval allies saved the
day for the Macedonians. And did Alexander really need to spend so much blood
and treasure on this one city, which he simply could have isolated as he continued his campaign? Perhaps; but if he had lost, the Siege of Tyre would have
gone down as a colossal blunder.

The campaign of Gaugamela in 331 BCE, the final decisive battle between
Alexander and the Persian king, Darius III, began with Alexander turning down
a marriage proposal (Arrian *Anabasis* 3.7–3.16; Diodorus 17.53–17.61; Curtius
4.11–4.16; Plutarch *Alexander* 31–33).[7] In 333 BCE, Alexander had defeated
Darius and his great army at Issus and had managed to gain as hostages the
women of Darius' family after the Persian king ignominiously abandoned the
field. With Alexander firmly in control of Egypt and the entire Aegean and
Levantine coasts, Darius made an offer to cede this territory to Alexander

Figure 6.4 Satellite image of modern Tyre, in which the causeway built by Alexander is
          clearly visible.

Source: © 2018 DigitalGlobe. © 2018 Google. © 2018 ORION-ME.

formally and pay the Macedonian a handsome ransom for the return of the royal Persian women. Alexander refused and instead began to march towards the heart of the Persian Empire. As Alexander moved closer and closer to Darius' position, in what is now northern Iraq, just south of the Zagros Mountains, Darius made another offer, this time offering even more money and the entirety of the Persian Empire west of the Euphrates – a nearly unfathomable stretch of territory. Darius also pledged an enduring alliance and partnership with Alexander, to be sealed by the marriage of Alexander and Stateira, Darius' eldest daughter (who was already a hostage in Alexander's possession). Parmenio, the old veteran of Philip's wars and Alexander's senior military advisor, said that, "if I were Alexander, I would take the deal." Alexander's celebrated response was, "so would I, if I were Parmenio." Whether or not Alexander really spoke these words – they are almost too good to be true – they do reveal a lot about the Macedonian king and the nature of his campaign in Asia. Alexander inspired almost fanatical devotion in his soldiers and fear in his enemies because he was bold, often recklessly so. And his campaign against the Persian Empire had always been framed as a crusade, to punish the Persians for the sacrilege of burning Greek temples during the invasion of 480–479 BCE. Agreeing to terms, no matter how generous they were and no matter how sensible it was to accept, suited neither Alexander's personality nor his propaganda.

Once a battle was clearly imminent, Darius chose the spot carefully, at a site called Gaugamela ("camel's hump") not far from the modern city of Mosul. With the Zagros at his back, Darius groomed a broad plain for a pitched battle, giving his large army plenty of room to outflank and overwhelm the numerically inferior troops of Alexander. The Persians blamed their defeat at Issus on the narrowness of the battle area, which had prevented the Persians' numbers from making any difference to the outcome. In addition to choosing broad and level ground suited to his army's strengths, Darius laid spikes and other obstacles to trip up the Macedonian forces, and smoothed out lanes for the charges of his scythed-chariots, his most fearsome weapon. These tools of war, with blades protruding from their wheel-hubs, were legendary for the sickening wounds they inflicted on the Persians' enemies. Darius seems not to have cared that at the Battle of Cunaxa in 401 BCE, Greek hoplites had neutralized scythed-chariots simply by opening their ranks to let the chariots pass through the line, while the horses and drivers were killed at the Greeks' leisure. Darius was counting on these weapons to inflict significant damage on an enemy more professional and battle-tested than the Greek mercenaries of 401 BCE had been, which was not destined to end well for the Persians. More crucially, by relying on a defensive position, Darius ceded the tactical initiative to Alexander, just as the Persians had done at the Granicus River, Alexander's first battle in Asia, and as Darius himself did at Issus. As Gaugamela demonstrated yet again, no amount of prior planning and no defensive position proved adequate against a bold attack of Alexander and his combined-arms army.

At Gaugamela, Alexander needed to rely on boldness and superior tactics more than he had in past battles, where the equipment and skill of his Companions

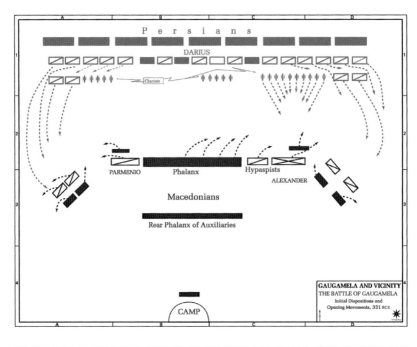

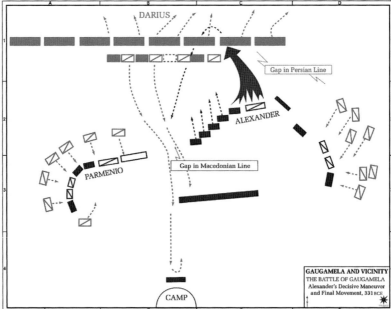

Figure 6.5 The Battle of Gaugamela, 331 BCE.

Source: public domain. Image produced by the Department of History, United States Military Academy.

and other heavy cavalry vastly outmatched his opponents. Darius' army in 331 BCE boasted overwhelming numbers of horsemen of the highest quality, from the central Asian territories in the eastern part of the empire, like Bactria and Sogdiana. Not only did these cavalry forces come from cultures steeped in centuries of equestrian culture, like the Macedonians, they were also heavily armed and armored, including even "cataphracts," fully armored horses and riders that resembled medieval knights. The Macedonian phalanx was still superior to Darius' infantry, but Alexander's heavy cavalry could no longer take for granted that they would outmatch their opponents. Darius' eastern cavalry units were stationed under Bessus, a satrap in the eastern empire and relative of Darius, on the left wing to counter Alexander and his Companions on the Macedonian right. Keeping Alexander and his most lethal forces in check, Darius planned to break gaps in the Macedonian line, ideally by charges of his scythed-chariots, into which his numerous cavalry would charge. It was a sensible plan. Fortunately for the Macedonians, they had a leader whose speed and innate sense of where to direct his attack proved decisive against even the awesome forces arrayed at Gaugamela.

Alexander's line at Gaugamela was largely typical. In the center was the phalanx, and on the wings were cavalry, Macedonians on the right, under the personal command of Alexander, Thessalians on the left, on the wing led by Parmenio. As usual, the elite infantry unit of the hypaspists was stationed between the phalanx and the heavy cavalry on the right. To mitigate flank attacks, Alexander also had units arrayed at an angle stretching behind the front line at the wings, with light-armed troops filling the gaps between these units and the main line. The Macedonians also had a reserve line of soldiers behind the main force, whereas in other battles Alexander seems not to have used reserves at all. The broad and flat plain at Gaugamela combined with the Persians' far greater numbers threatened the Macedonian army with inevitable outflanking, and indeed total envelopment, which Alexander's slightly modified battlefield arrangement was designed to resist. Nevertheless, the battle could not go on too long, or no measures taken by Alexander would suffice. Alexander simply did not have enough soldiers to win a battle of attrition.

Because the Persian line was so much larger than Alexander's, Alexander and his right wing lined up with Darius, who was stationed in the exact center of his own force. The Persian left, therefore, extended far beyond Alexander's right, which forced Alexander to move to the right once the battle began. As Alexander and his cavalry began to move, Parmenio and the rest of the army had to move right too, to prevent a gap opening in the Macedonian line. We know that the Macedonian left bore the brunt of the Persian attack since, at one point, the Persians managed to break through and even began plundering the Macedonian camp. The sources tell us that Parmenio sent an urgent message to Alexander at one point in the battle, begging him for help. Many scholars doubt that such a message could have reached the Macedonian king, but it is clear that the battle was on a razor's edge in Parmenio's part of the field. The decisive action, however, took place on the Macedonian right, after Alexander and the surrounding horsemen, by moving ever rightward, had drawn the enemy far enough from their original positions to create an opportunity for a shock attack.

To his own right, Alexander had a screen of mercenary heavy cavalry and some light cavalry, which eventually clashed with the extreme left of the Persian line that had been meant to outflank the Macedonians. As a struggle unfolded at the very edge of the line, a gap formed between Bessus' left wing and the Persian center, where Darius was commanding the battle. This was Alexander's moment. He saw the gap and ordered his Companions to charge into it, while Bessus' force was held at bay by the rest of the Macedonian right. Alexander punched through the Persian line near the center and wheeled to charge directly at Darius, just as he had done two years earlier at Issus. Some of our sources say that Alexander managed to hurl a spear and almost strike the Persian king. Whether or not the two actually got that close to each other, once he saw that his line had been penetrated and that the Macedonian cavalry was causing havoc, Darius fled in his chariot, again just as happened at Issus. Once their king had fled, and once the line had been breached and great numbers began to fall, the Persian army was eventually routed, but not before causing considerable casualties among the Macedonian force, particularly on Parmenio's left wing where the Persian breakthrough had taken place. Alexander wanted to end the war once and for all and set off in pursuit of Darius, but had to call off the chase with the coming of night. Darius would die later, still on the run and slain at the hands of his own relative, Bessus.

The ancient sources, so keen to present the genius of Alexander, make it seem that Alexander was destined to win at Gaugamela. He might have caught Darius, too, had Parmenio not sent a message begging for help, providing a clear contrast between the conservative and old-school military leadership of Parmenio and the bold new style of the Macedonian king. Ancient propaganda aside, Gaugamela could have gone very badly for the Macedonians. Had Parmenio's left wing had to hold out for much longer against the huge numbers marshaled against them, who were both outflanking the Macedonians and had broken through to the Macedonian camp, Alexander's left might have collapsed utterly. Even if Alexander had won the battle in such circumstances, he might have lost so many men that his entire campaign might have crumbled while Darius was still alive and still claimed to be the Persian king. But Alexander struck quickly and decisively enough to end the battle before he faced disaster. His movement to the right, drawing his enemy along with him, and his sense to see where a gap had formed and to know when the moment to strike had arrived, won the battle, despite long odds and terrain chosen by and favorable to Darius. The Persian army had many skilled and professional soldiers, especially among the heavy cavalry. But the Macedonians had Alexander, who, at Gaugamela just like all his other pitched battles, seized the tactical initiative.

Alexander's legend

To get a sense of the long shadow Alexander cast across the ancient world, we can turn to two towering figures of a later age, Pompey the Great and Julius Caesar, whose rivalry sparked a civil war that brought an end to the Roman Republic nearly 300 years after Alexander's death. Pompey, who achieved much renown as a military leader against foes like Spartacus and was granted an unprecedented level of power in order to stamp out piracy in the Mediterranean, wore his hair pushed back from his forehead in a distinctive way meant to mimic famous portraits of Alexander. Even Pompey's honorific title "magnus" or "the great" recalled Alexander's example (Plutarch *Pompey* 2). Julius Caesar, who became the sole ruler of Rome before his assassination on the Ides of March, lamented early in his career, while he was an official in Spain and came across an image of Alexander, that he had achieved nothing of note at an age when Alexander had already conquered the world. Caesar was so disgusted by his own lack of eminence in comparison to the famous Macedonian that he resigned his provincial post before the end of his term in order to return to Rome to secure a loftier position (Plutarch *Caesar* 11). More than just amusing anecdotes about well-known historical figures, these vignettes hit at an important truth: after 323 BCE, there was no one in the ancient world who generated awe and inspired fervent emulation more than Alexander. This legend did not take long to develop. Right after his death in Babylon, Alexander's body was hijacked by Ptolemy and taken to Egypt, to serve as the ultimate sign of Ptolemy's legitimacy as he built a new kingdom (Pausanias 1.6).

In order to evaluate Alexander's reception and the extent to which it is faithful to the real man and his achievements, we must first ask a deceptively simple question: why did he do it? In other words, what drove Alexander to push further and accumulate a greater empire than any Greek, or even anyone, had done before? In a time and place free of Christian ideals, such as loving one's enemies and the careful if controversial formulation of "just war" theories, conquest was perhaps less problematic than it is to many modern readers. When the mark of a good Greek man was to provide the most benefit to one's friends and the most harm to one's enemies, and the example set by every military, political, and cultural leader from Homer's heroes on down is that one should always "strive to be the best, better than all the rest," maybe Alexander was doing what anyone else would have done given the same material and mental resources. Yet a generation or two ago, some scholars, especially W. W. Tarn, ascribed to Alexander a loftier vision than mere conquest and glory.

Based on Alexander's behavior towards the end of his life, including especially a mass wedding at the Persian capital at Susa in which hundreds of Macedonians received noble Persian and Iranian brides, and his elevation of native Persian and Iranian military units at the perceived expense of the Macedonians, which caused a mutiny at Opis near Babylon, Tarn argued that Alexander had a grand cosmopolitan vision. Instead of the tribalism and nativism that plagued the Greek world, and indeed excluded Alexander from full "Greekness" in the eyes of many of his contemporaries, Alexander aspired to forge a "unity of mankind," in Tarn's phrasing, in which all human beings were conceived of as members of one people. In Tarn's influential view, therefore, Alexander was not just an ego-maniac bent on glory for its own sake. Military conquest was just the messy means to a far nobler end, a radical reorientation of the world that showed the way to Rome, the greatest cosmopolitan empire of the ancient world, and sowed the seeds for the spread of Christianity.

As expected, Tarn's view finds few adherents today. Far more plausible is A. B. Bosworth's argument that Alexander added ethnically diverse units to his army and encouraged intermarriage between Macedonians and various peoples of the former Persian Empire in order to forge a military force and even an ethnic group loyal only to Alexander instead of any geographical region or creed. If Alexander was cosmopolitan at all, it was not because of high-minded universalism, but because he wanted greater control over his empire and its peoples. Likewise, Alexander's adoption of Persian practices, including some of the physical trappings of Persian rulers, such as the royal diadem and the honor of *proskynesis*, the ritual bowing of his subjects, was a way to frame himself as the new Great King of Persia rather than just a foreign conqueror. That Alexan-der's embrace of the outward signs of Persian rule aroused tensions between the king and his fellow Macedonians owes less to the fact that the Macedonian sol-diers did not share Alexander's vision than to the general principle that it is exceedingly difficult to rule a large territorial empire comprised of many peoples. If anything, Alexander's failure to groom a clear successor and the dis-interest he showed in the day-to-day running of his new territories bespeaks a lack of grand strategic vision. Alexander also failed to put in place the adminis-trative structures necessary for governing a vast empire as foreign conquerors. The historian Barry Strauss puts it succinctly: "For [Alexander], government wasn't about institutions, much less about citizens. It was about a great man, his friends, and the army."[8] The empire, unsurprisingly, did not last long after the death of the great man.

While a master battlefield tactician and man of great physical courage, if not outright recklessness, in the face of grievous injury and probable death, I do not see in Alexander a particularly brilliant strategist or politician, certainly not on the level of his father, Philip, who rarely acted without an eye to the long game. The search for a deeper reason or meaning behind Alexander's unprecedented military campaigns largely misses the point. For a young king raised on Homer's epics, glory was its own reward, and I doubt any Greek or Macedonian would have disagreed. Like many before him, Alexander "strove to be the best, better than all the rest" (as a hero is famously encouraged in Homer *Iliad* 6.208). In many ways, he succeeded in spectacular fashion; in others, he fell short, at least by our standards. When he died in 323 BCE at the age of thirty-three, he was plan-ning to embark on a new war of conquest, at least as grand as his conquest of Asia had been. He aimed first to conquer Arabia, before turning his sights on the western Mediterranean. Even Alexander's contemporaries thought these plans went too far. Alexander's lust for battle and conquest far outstripped any interest or talent he had for governing, which in the end set the stage for decades of war between his generals, who fought over the pieces of his empire after 323 BCE.

What Alexander lacked in strategic vision, he more than made up for in terms of PR. In addition to taking along with him a court historian to chronicle his exploits, Alexander was quick to embrace any honors, particularly divine ones that came his way. He was also eager to demonstrate his greatness of soul, perhaps best exemplified by his kind treatment of Darius' female family members captured at Issus after Darius himself had fled from the field. The surest mark of Alexander's success in self-promotion comes not from the emulation practiced by later leaders like Pompey and Caesar – to say nothing of Alexander's immediate successors in the Hellenistic world – but in how modern military historians long embraced him as a genius, almost beyond reckoning in standard historical terms.

In his famous book on Alexander's generalship, Major General J. F. C. Fuller devotes several pages to a discussion of Alexander's "genius," the mysterious and unquantifiable quality that allowed Alexander to achieve what few others could even dream. Fuller cites no less a figure than Napoleon, himself commonly

Figure 6.6 An image of Alexander on his horse at the Battle of Issus, from the Alexander Sarcophagus, late fourth century BCE.

Source: Archaeological Museum of Istanbul. Photo credit: Erich Lessing/Art Resource, NY.

reckoned as a military genius, who said that it was not the Macedonian phalanx that penetrated to India, but Alexander. For Napoleon (and most military historians until very recently), Alexander was in a league with the likes of Hannibal, Caesar, and Napoleon himself, all of whom led by sheer force of will and personality as much as by tactical brilliance or logistical sophistication. While Fuller does devote many more pages to the more tangible elements of Alexander's leadership, there is no doubt that Fuller thinks there is something about such commanders that simply cannot be explained, let alone emulated.

This notion of genius can distort our perspective and encourages us to view Alexander as something more than human. N. G. L. Hammond, himself a war hero and perhaps the most prolific Greek historian of the twentieth century, entitled one of his last books *The Genius of Alexander the Great*. Make no mistake, Hammond did not choose this provocative title in order to challenge such an assumption, but rather to promote it. For Hammond, like many before him, Alexander could do virtually no wrong, including those military decisions – such as disbanding his own fleet while the Persians still controlled the Aegean – we might reasonably question or his most wanton acts of cruelty. Alexander's legend, however, has in recent decades inspired a spate or revisionist accounts. A. E. Bosworth's *Conquest and Empire*, first published in 1988, has probably been the most influential in reorienting the popular image of Alexander as a figure bent on conquest and domination instead of as a cosmopolitan visionary. The extreme end of revisionism is represented by John D. Grainger's 2009 *Alexander the Great Failure*, which treats Alexander as politically incompetent and criminally negligent by not taking steps to ensure a smooth succession of leadership. I think Grainger's critique goes too far in the anti-Tarn direction. If we judge Alexander by the standards of his own day and his own native country, the charismatic leadership of the king was always of central importance, and for Alexander to focus on deeds of conquest and bravery at the expense of long-term political stability and mundane administrative tasks can only have been expected. Alexander was a complex and flawed person, one equipped with the ancient world's most formidable war machine and one who used that war machine to strive to equal Homer's Achilles, who for centuries had served as the model for Greek manhood and heroism.

Notes

1 Representative of this genre is Gabriel (2010).
2 For further commentary on this passage, see Stylianou (1998, 342–346).
3 Markle (1977, 1978) provides a detailed discussion of the new Macedonian equipment and its use, based on a great deal of experimental archaeology and field tests.
4 Philip's use of cavalry at Chaeronea has been disputed. For an account of the dispute and an argument that a cavalry charge did take place, see Sears and Willekes (2016).
5 The excavation reports from Olynthus can be found in Robinson and Mylonas (1929–1952).
6 For a succinct discussion of these recruitment problems, see Sekunda (2007, esp. 334–335).

7 For the Battle of Gaugamela, we also have a rare, contemporary written source from Persia, from the so-called Astronomical Diaries. For this source, see van der Spek (2003).

8 Strauss (2012, 198).

Further reading

Bosworth, A. B. 1988. *Conquest and Empire: The Reign of Alexander the Great*. Cambridge.

One of the first studies to treat Alexander as a ruthless imperialist rather than simply as a charmed military genius.

Carney, Elizabeth and Daniel Ogden (eds.). 2010. *Philip II and Alexander the Great: Father and Son, Lives and Afterlives*. Oxford.

A stimulating collection of essays on the relationship (dynastic, military, etc.) between Philip II and Alexander.

Engels, Donald W. 1978. *Alexander the Great and the Logistics of the Macedonian Army*. Berkeley.

An essential exploration of how Alexander managed to campaign for as long and as far away from home as he did. Logistics tends to be an under-studied aspect of military history, but it is essential for understanding warfare.

Fuller, J. F. C. 1960. *The Generalship of Alexander the Great*. New Brunswick, NJ.

A seasoned military commander himself, Fuller wrote one of the standard accounts of Alexander's military genius.

Grainger, John D. 2009. *Alexander the Great Failure*. London.

This polemic argues that Alexander was in fact singularly unsuccessful, especially given his lack of strategic purpose and failure to secure a plan of succession for his sprawling empire.

Hammond, N. G. L. 1998. *The Genius of Alexander the Great*. Chapel Hill, NC.

A representative introduction of Alexander as a singular genius, a notion that has come under increasing scrutiny in recent years.

Hammond, N. G. L., G. T. Griffith, and F. W. Walbank. 1972–1988. *A History of Macedonia* (3 vols.). Oxford.

The definitive scholarly resource for ancient Macedonia.

Heckel, Waldemar. 2006. *Who's Who in the Age of Alexander the Great*. London.

A valuable resource that sorts out the immense and varied cast of characters connected to Alexander and his reign.

Heckel, Waldemar and John Yardley. 2004. *Alexander the Great: Sources in Translation*. Oxford.

A convenient and scholarly collection of the major literary sources for Alexander.

Holt, Frank L. 2012. *Into the Land of Bones: Alexander the Great in Afghanistan* (second edition). Berkeley.

Linking Alexander's campaign to contemporary events, Holt provides a stirring account of the most difficult part of Alexander's campaign in Asia.

King, Carol J. 2017. *Ancient Macedonia*. London.

An excellent and comprehensive resource, with up-to-date discussions and bibliography spanning the entire history of ancient Macedonia.

Kuhrt, Amélie, 2007. *The Persian Empire*. London.

A collection of texts and other sources illuminating the Persian Empire on its own terms, instead of the standard scholarly perspective that relies almost entirely on Greek sources.

Lendon, J. E. 2005. *Soldiers and Ghosts: A History of Battle in Classical Antiquity*. New Haven.

Lendon argues that developments in Greek warfare, including the Macedonian phalanx of Philip II, were inspired by the desire to emulate the heroes of Homer's *Iliad*.

Marsden, E. W. 1969. *Greek and Roman Artillery: The Historical Development*. Oxford.

A comprehensive account of ancient artillery, which developed a great deal in the time of Philip and Alexander.

Strauss, Barry. 2012. *Masters of Command: Alexander, Hannibal, Caesar, and the Genius of Leadership*. New York.

A comparison of three of antiquity's most famous military leaders, with exciting, up-to-date discussions about Alexander's tactics and strategy.

Tarn, W. W. 1948. *Alexander the Great* (2 vols.). Cambridge.

For decades, the leading work on Alexander and his empire, against which all modern histories of the period must respond. Tarn was a leading proponent of the idea that Alexander strove for a "brotherhood of mankind."

Trundle, Matthew. 2005. *Greek Mercenaries: From the Late Archaic Period to Alexander*. London.

A comprehensive and up-to-date discussion of mercenaries in the Archaic and Classical Greek world.

Willekes, Carolyn, 2016. *The Horse in the Ancient World: From Bucephalus to the Hippodrome*. London.

A comprehensive study of the horse and its use in antiquity, including much discussion about the Macedonian cavalry. Willekes combines a survey of the ancient sources with the observations gained through experiments with horses.

Winter, Frederick E. 1971. *Greek Fortifications*. Toronto.

The standard reference work for Greek fortifications and siegecraft.

Worthington, Ian. 2012. *Demosthenes of Athens and the Fall of Classical Greece*. Oxford.

A biography of Demosthenes, Philip's great Athenian rival, situating the orator's life and work in the historical context of the rise of Macedon and decline of the Classical Greek polis.

Worthington, Ian. 2014. *By the Spear: Philip II, Alexander the Great, and the Rise and Fall of the Macedonian Empire*. Oxford.

A recent and readable account by a leading scholar of Philip II and Alexander.

7   Warfare in the Hellenistic world

The coming of Rome

Introduction

Until recently, the Hellenistic Era – the period between the death of Alexander in 323 BCE and the Battle of Actium in 31 BCE – was relatively neglected by scholars of the Classical World. Even the name itself is in a sense dismissive and derogatory. Coined in the nineteenth century, "Hellenistic" means something like "Greekish," as opposed to "Hellenic," meaning "Greek."[1] Greekish, because after the conquests of Alexander the Great, Greco-Macedonian leaders, soldiers, and culture spread further than ever before, and interacted with already-existing local cultures to produce something new, something that was no longer purely "Greek." For a long time, the Hellenistic world was seen as somehow less than the preceding Archaic and Classical periods of Greek history and culture. Hellenistic art, for example, was routinely denigrated as baroque in comparison to the more restrained art of earlier periods.[2] In the sphere of warfare too, the Hellenistic world seemingly produced little to complement or improve upon the brilliant innovations of Philip and Alexander. Instead, Hellenistic warfare saw the emergence of exotic weapons like scythed-chariots, elephants, and fantastically large warships, providing a military analogue to the excesses of Hellenistic material culture. Furthermore, the most crucial development of Philip and Alexander, namely the heavy cavalry as the main striking force of the army, fell by the wayside, replaced by the reemergence of the phalanx as the be-all-and-end-all of Hellenistic warfare. The over-reliance on the unwieldy phalanx, even one with as much fearsome striking power as the Macedonian phalanx, proved disastrous for the Hellenistic kingdoms when they faced the much more versatile Roman legion.

Only lately have scholars begun to study the Hellenistic world on its own terms, instead of merely as a foil for the ages that preceded and followed it. Most importantly, many scholars now use methods such as papyrology and archaeological excavation to illuminate the local cultures with whom the Greco-Macedonian successors of Alexander interacted. This expanding field of study has revealed the complexity and tension between the persistence of local customs and the influence that flowed both ways between Alexander's successors and local peoples and structures. In short, the Hellenistic world was dynamic and

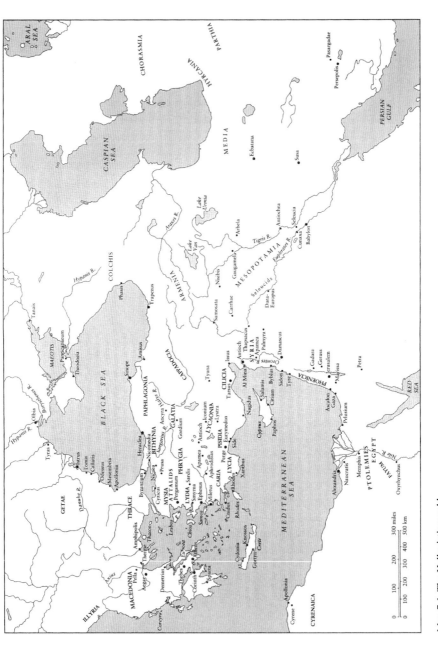

Map 7.1 The Hellenistic world.

Source: from *Readings in Greek History* (2nd edition) by D. B. Nagle and S. Burstein (2014). Map 8.2. p. 290. By permission of Oxford University Press, USA.

creative. Even from the perspective of strictly Classical scholarship, systems of thought as important as Stoicism and Epicureanism, which greatly influenced the Romans, emerged in a Hellenistic context. That said, many of the standard critiques of Hellenistic warfare hold true. Armies did rely too much on the phalanx, and the Roman legion did prove to be a superior system. Nevertheless, there were many interesting military developments in this period, including in the nature of command and power, and at the strategic and tactical levels.

This chapter will begin by exploring how the context of Hellenistic warfare differed from the other periods addressed in this book. Most obviously, gone were the days of the independent polis, completely in control of its own foreign policy and warfare. Instead, the Greco-Macedonian world was now largely divided up into huge kingdoms ruled by powerful kings, most of whom were descendants of Alexander's generals. The scale of warfare was therefore often far greater, with armies of many tens of thousands clashing, with huge swaths of the eastern Mediterranean at stake. At the same time, individual poleis did still exist, and engaged in their own limited campaigns, as they also jockeyed for position within the larger kingdoms. Next, we will consider how the unique challenges the Hellenistic powers faced in terms of recruiting, training, and fielding military forces. Macedonia furnished Philip and Alexander with manpower for the phalanx, and generations of Macedonian aristocrats steeped in equestrian culture meant that elite cavalry units could be formed relatively easily. Alexander's successors ruling in places like Egypt and Syria had to rely far more on local recruitment, and it became next to impossible to replicate the skill and effectiveness of the Companion Cavalry. There were some interesting tactical innovations in Hellenistic armies, including new cavalry types, and a new kind of hybrid soldier, called the *thureophoros*, which might have been adapted after contact with Italians or Gallic invaders. Also, the use of exotic weapons, though often causing more harm than good, was sometimes decisive. Since the Hellenistic world is the one with which the Romans came into contact – and conquered – we will compare the military systems of the Hellenistic kingdoms with the Roman legion, including how the legion overcame the phalanx in combat. Instead of case studies of individual battles, we will look at two standout Hellenistic leaders and how they waged war: Pyrrhus of Epirus and Hannibal of Carthage. The chapter – and book – will conclude with a brief look at the end of the Hellenistic world and the Roman Republic, and the birth of the Roman Empire.

Hellenistic kingdoms and the polis

The greatest failure of Alexander the Great was that he did not provide for an orderly succession to his rule, or really put any measures in place to keep his vast new empire together. As he lay dying of a sudden illness at Babylon in 323 BCE, he was asked to whom his kingdom should fall. "To the strongest," he apparently replied. Some sources also say that he envisioned the epoch-shaping struggles that would follow his death as his funeral games, a murderous and fitting tribute for a man bent only on glory and conquest (Arrian *Anabasis* 7.26).

As soon as Alexander was dead, his generals fought each other over his spoils. At first, the goal was to keep the empire intact under a single ruler. Only Ptolemy sensed the inevitable, that the empire would be divided up into several pieces. Ptolemy immediately headed to Egypt to rule it independently, and commandeered Alexander's body along the way to serve as a key piece of propaganda. Within a generation or two, the hope of a united empire vanished, and the Ptolemies in Egypt were joined by the Seleucids in Syria, the Antigonids in Macedonia, and some smaller kingdoms, such as Attalid Pergamum in Asia Minor. These "Successor Kingdoms" dominated the eastern Mediterranean until they were eclipsed by the expanding power of Rome in the second and first centuries BCE.

Like Alexander, his successors sought legitimacy by means of military prowess, not only in terms of commanding the loyalty of the men they ruled, but also in determining which territories they ruled. When Alexander first crossed into Asia, he is said to have hurled a spear into the earth, declaring Asia "spear-won territory." It mattered not that Alexander had no historic or familial claim to the rule of Asia. All that mattered was that he had the military strength to put himself in power. Success in war is what made kings, according to Alexander's philosophy. His successors shared that philosophy and needed to demonstrate that they were capable generals and brave soldiers. Angelos Chaniotis sums up the Hellenistic theory of military kingship by referring us to the Byzantine encyclopedia called the *Suda*. Under the entry for monarchical power, the *Suda* says, "Monarchical power [*baslieiai*] is given to men neither by nature nor by law; it is given to those who are able of commanding troops and dealing prudently with [political] matters." Alexander's successors, therefore, fought many wars, both in their struggles to secure kingdoms for themselves against their rivals and in their desire to maintain their royal legitimacy. In the Hellenistic world, peace offered few enticements for rulers.

A quirk of the Hellenistic era is that the designation "king" often seemed to be used as a title or rank, rather than indicating rule over a specific territory. Many Hellenistic kings were frequently without any territory at all, yet retained the title. And kings seemed to be the kings of whichever region they held by force of arms, often quite temporarily. What made them kings was their status as generals (or the sons of generals) of Alexander, and their ability to command large armies. In such a world, where militarily experienced and hardened Macedonians and Greeks roamed the Mediterranean at the head of tens of thousands of soldiers, warfare was bound to be endemic. And indeed it was.

While the major players in the Hellenistic world were the successors of Alexander, especially those like the Ptolemies, Seleucids, and Antigonids, who ruled large kingdoms, the independent poleis still existed, though obviously curtailed in terms of their foreign policy and frequently at the beck and call of the kings. The Greek ideal of citizen-soldiers continued to hold sway over these poleis, and although warfare was now on a scale far larger and engaged in for different reasons than in the days of the early hoplite phalanx, important cultural aspects of warfare persisted – or, in many cases, revived.

One of the most important rituals of many poleis was the military training of young men between the ages of 18 and 20, called *ephebes*, or "those coming of age." An inscription from the mid-fourth century BCE, found in the Athenian community, or *deme*, of Acharnae, north of the city itself, records the oath sworn by Athenian *ephebes* as they embarked on the two-year-long *ephebeia*, which included various types of military training along with stints of guard duty on the frontiers. The language of the oath suggests that this practice was already one of long standing at the time the inscription was made. The Athenian *ephebeia* declined somewhat during the Hellenistic period, and was at points restricted to the children of wealthy Athenians. The *ephebeia*, however, did remain a part of Athenian life, and in the mid-second century BCE came to allow more Athenian citizens to participate once again, as they had in earlier days.

Other poleis had *ephebeia* of their own, which remained strong throughout the Hellenistic period. Angelos Chaniotis, in his superb *War in the Hellenistic World*, singles out an oath sworn by the ephebes of the Creatan city of Dreros around 220 BCE.

I swear … truly I will never be benevolent to the Lyttians. And neither a trial nor an execution of verdicts will be protected by this oath; and I will be friendly towards the Drerians and the Knossians; and I will neither betray the city or the forts of the Drerians nor the forts of the Knossians; and I will betray no men to the enemies, neither men of Dreros, nor men of Knossos … I will not start a revolt, and I will always be an opponent of those who do; I will not participate in the organization of a conspiracy, neither in the city nor outside of the city, nor will I help someone else …

(Austin 91; trans. Austin)

Unlike the Athenian oath, which emphasized military training, the ephebes of Dreros swore in the name of local gods and heroes to remain loyal to their city, as well as to the allied city of Knossos, and to maintain eternal enmity towards Lyttos, a city with which they were at war. This oath is revealing in many ways. First of all, it reaffirms how important warfare, particularly as led by the body of citizens, remained in the consciousness of Hellenistic poleis. This is not an oath that reflects blind loyalty to a far-off king to fight his far-off wars, but rather attachment to the local polis and its parochial military concerns. The oath also demonstrates that, though Hellenistic kings fought huge wars over huge parcels of the Mediterranean world, individual poleis could still engage in smaller conflicts with each other.

Poleis could make war against or peace with each other on their own, without interference from the kings. Two poleis could even grant joint citizenship to the people in each respective polis, as is attested on many Hellenistic inscriptions. But despite these signs of local autonomy, kings often did intervene in disputes between poleis, often at the invitation of one polis trying to gain an advantage over the other. An inscription from Priene, on the western coast of Asia Minor, records a letter sent in 283/2 BCE by the king Lysimachus, who had control over much of Thrace and the Turkish coast, intervening in a territorial dispute between Priene and the island of Samos (Austin 53). In order to gain Lysimachus' backing, the people of Priene had voted him various honors, a ubiquitous Hellenistic practice, but the king sided with Samos anyway. The Hellenistic world was a complex one in which poleis maintained a level of agency in dealing with each other and with kings in order to gain advantages, while at the same time the kings who relied on the soldiers these poleis provided were bound to calculate carefully which poleis to support and in which ways.

A superb example of how Greek poleis could work for themselves both for and against Hellenistic kings, and Hellenistic kings could use Greek poleis for their own purposes, is the so-called Chremonidean War of *c.*268–265 BCE. Fought between an alliance of poleis including Athens and Sparta, along with king Ptolemy II, against Antigonus Gonatas of Macedonia, the Chremonidean War is so named because of Chremonides, the Athenian who proposed the military alliance preserved on a stone inscription:

> Since previously the Athenians, the Lacedaemonians, and their respective allies after establishing a common friendship and alliance with each other have fought together many glorious battles against those who sought to enslave the cities, which won them fame and brought freedom to the other Greeks; and now, when similar circumstances have afflicted the whole of Greece because of [those] who seek to subvert the laws and ancestral constitutions of each city, and King Ptolemy following the policy of his ancestor and of his sister conspicuously shows his zeal for the common freedom of the Greeks; and the people of Athens having made an alliance with him and the Greeks has passed a decree to invite (all) to follow the same policy…
>
> (Austin 61, lines 9–21; trans. Austin)

The inscription is a masterpiece of Hellenistic liberation propaganda, which borrowed from the language used to describe the Persian Wars in order to keep at least the pretext of Greek freedom in the forefront of diplomacy. In the inscription, the Athenians and Spartans trumpet their former alliances forged in order to resist those who would "enslave" the Greeks, a clear reference to the Hellenic alliance formed against Xerxes in 480 BCE, more than two centuries earlier. The terms of the alliance stipulate that all parties are to come to the defense of any alliance member that is attacked, but also that all members are to retain their own territory, continue to abide by their "ancestral" constitutions, and remain free and autonomous.

Despite the reality that many states, including Athens, could not expect to be truly autonomous in terms of foreign policy, and frequently had pro-Macedonian leaders in the government and even Macedonian troops garrisoned in the city, rhetorically the Greeks framed themselves as continuing to live in a world of free and independent poleis. If the Hellenistic kings wanted to secure Greek cooperation against their rivals, they needed to play along with this rhetoric, and even provide some tangible measures of at least internal, governmental autonomy to the poleis they hoped to entice. This could include removing the garrisons rival monarchs had installed in various poleis, to which the poleis tended to respond by declaring their new ally a savior and benefactor. Athens even added two new tribes to their traditional ten in honor of Antigonus I and his son Demetrius in 307/6 BCE after Demetrius "liberated" Athens from the control of Cassander and Ptolemy. The Athenian tribe list changed several more times, including the addition of Ptolemy III and Attalos I of Pergamum for various benefactions and military support, and the removal of Antigonus and Demetrius around 200 BCE when the Athenians went to war with Antigonid Macedonia. Despite their political and military eclipse, the Greek poleis, especially prestigious ones like Athens, held considerable sway for Hellenistic monarchs eager to present themselves in the tradition of great Greek leaders of the past.

A particularly Hellenistic way for independent poleis, especially smaller and relatively obscure ones, to gain leverage in a world of great powers was to form federal leagues. Leagues of various sorts had existed in the Classical period, but they tended to be dominated by single poleis. For example, the Spartans dominated the Peloponnesian League, and the Thebans were clearly on top in Boeotia. The leagues that rose to prominence in the Hellenistic period, mainly in the third

Figure 7.1 View from the Athenian Agora towards the Acropolis. On the left is the reconstructed Stoa of Attalos, originally built by the king of Pergamum, mid-second century BCE.

Source: author's photograph.

century BCE, were much more truly federal, and notably tended not to include major players. The most historically important of these leagues, and the one for which we have the best sources (especially since the great historian Polybius was a citizen), was the Achaean League, based in the northern Peloponnese.

The Achaean League grew to its greatest extent under the political and military leadership of Aratus of Sicyon, who rose to fame in 251 BCE at the age of twenty when he overthrew the tyrant ruling his native city, and joined the city to the Achaean League. As a general, Aratus gave even the Antigonid kings of Macedonia a run for their money. In 243 BCE, building on his reputation as an opponent of tyranny and champion of freedom, he drove the Macedonian military garrison out of Corinth, and seized the imposing fortress of Acrocorinth, which dominated the land route into the Peloponnese. Though Aratus aimed to unify the entre Peloponnese under a federal league, in order to safeguard Greek freedom and autonomy against the Macedonians, later in his career he spent most of his energy in struggles with a resurgent Sparta, led by a series of active and expansionist kings.

Philopoemen of Megalopolis succeeded Aratus as general of the Achaean League and became its most famous figure, and indeed one of the most famous Greek military leaders of the Hellenistic world. Perhaps his greatest victory came at the Battle of Mantinea in 207 BCE, the third major battle fought in this storied plain. Philopoemen was ready for this battle because he had gathered the citizen-soldiers from states in the league in order to train and drill them to a greater degree than was typical for citizen-soldiers. These citizens of the league's poleis made up the phalanx around which Philopoemen would marshal his army. Since Polybius says the men of this phalanx used sarissas instead of shorter hoplite spears, Philopoemen seems to have crafted a Macedonian phalanx. He supplemented these citizen-soldiers with mercenaries from various parts of the Greek world, which included specialized heavy-armed troops and light-armed skirmishers. The Achaean league also had a decent local cavalry force, which allowed Philopoemen to fight with fairly sophisticated combined-arms tactics. Though the Spartans also had skilled soldiers and lots of mercenaries – and even field artillery such as bolt-hurling catapults – Philopoemen and the Achaeans prevailed at Mantinea. Philopoemen personally killed the Spartan leader in single combat, a feat that was commemorated with a bronze statue at Delphi.

After several more years of back-and-forth struggle, Philopoemen eventually subjugated Sparta completely and made it a part of the Achaean League, rendering the league the greatest power in Greece. The Romans, however, soon came to dominate the league, first by taking many hostages (including the historian Polybius) at the end of the Third Macedonian War in 168 BCE, and finally by destroying Corinth and dissolving the league utterly in 146 BCE. Still, the Achaean League was a major player in the eastern Mediterranean for a century, despite being an equal alliance of relatively obscure poleis that needed to contend with the great kingdom of Macedonia and the formidable Spartans.[3]

Figure 7.2 Dedicatory statue base of Philpoemen at Delphi, early second century BCE.
Source: author's photograph.

Hellenistic armies

Despite the fanfare surrounding the Macedonian phalanx, the most important tactical innovation of Philip and Alexander was the use of heavy cavalry to decide battles quickly, while the phalanx mainly held the enemy in place and tried to open up gaps in the enemy line into which the horses could gallop. The Macedonians were able to field so many and such excellent horsemen because of generations of skilled aristocratic horsemanship, built into the DNA of upper-class Macedonians. No amount of drill, training, or breeding could completely replace a rich equestrian culture. The further in time and geography the successors moved from Philip and Alexander's Macedonia, the more difficult it became to raise cavalry forces of the size and quality of those that had conquered the Persian Empire. Hellenistic armies certainly had cavalry forces, sometimes very large and well-equipped ones; but more often than not, Hellenistic cavalries played a secondary role in battle. The wedge formation that allowed Alexander to smash through enemy formations seems to have been abandoned in favor of rectangular formations that required far less drill. Hellenistic cavalry forces usually fought each other on the flanks of the armies, instead of delivering decisive blows. In the Hellenistic period, the Macedonian phalanx took center stage.[4]

The phalanx, however, was also increasingly difficult to build to full strength. Despite Alexander's overtures towards recruiting local troops for the phalanx near the end of his reign, and despite the Hellenistic monarchs' willingness to draw on local resources for their armies, Greco-Macedonian soldiers were still preferred for the phalanx. Egypt, with its rich supply of papyri, provides the best evidence for how Hellenistic rulers tried to establish a base population of Greco-Macedonians large enough to allow for a proper phalanx. The Ptolemies in Egypt granted parcels of land on which soldiers could settle, themselves serving as citizen-soldiers for the phalanx should they be needed. These settlers would also produce children, who would be raised in the Greco-Macedonian tradition and be eligible for the phalanx once they came of age.[5] But land for new settlers was not in limitless supply, and the Hellenistic practice of separating Greco-Macedonian rulers from local subjects meant that recruitment for the phalanx was always a challenge, and heavy losses of Greco-Macedonian soldiers in battle often proved irreplaceable.

Hellenistic kings ruled huge territories and fought with commensurately huge armies. Perhaps the greatest battle of the period, the Battle of Raphia fought between Ptolemy IV and Antiochus III in 217 BCE, saw some 70,000 or more soldiers fighting on each side (Polybius 5.79–5.86). Though Raphia was the biggest, Hellenistic battles regularly involved several tens of thousands fighting across massive fronts. Given the difficulty in recruiting Greco-Macedonian soldiers in far-flung regions of the eastern Mediterranean, especially as the decades wore on, Hellenistic kings turned to local troops to meet their personnel needs. But, although Alexander proposed incorporating native Iranians into the phalanx, his successors usually employed local soldiers in their own special units, fighting in their own native styles and with their own unique equipment, with the Greco-Macedonian phalanx serving as the core of a much larger army.

These local troops could be of many different types, from heavy infantry such as the spearmen native to Egypt, to various types of light-armed troops such as the javelin-throwers and archers from various places around the Mediterranean. One particularly effective type of native soldier was the cataphracts, or fully armored horses and riders from the Middle East and central Asia that were later used by the Parthians and Sassanid Persians, and prefigured medieval knights. The Seleucid rulers of Syria and much of the eastern stretches of Alexander's empire were usually well-equipped with cataphracts. The regions conquered by Alexander furnished other exotic weapons, including scythed-chariots and, most famously, elephants. While such weapons could inspire fear and made for an impressive spectacle on the battlefield, against disciplined troops they enjoyed only limited success, and often proved more dangerous for the side employing them than for the enemy. Well-drilled formations could open gaps through which scythed-chariots could pass harmlessly, as in fact happened with Alexander's own army at Gaugamela. And elephants were notoriously difficult to control and were prone to stampeding and trampling soldiers in their own armies.

Aside from local troops, another way for rulers to field large armies was to hire mercenaries, both non-Greek and Greek. Many perceive the Hellenistic period as one in which mercenaries played the predominant role in warfare, but this is an exaggeration. Nevertheless, mercenaries were plentiful and Hellenistic rulers could draw upon great wealth in order to hire many soldiers. Just as Darius had employed Greek hoplites to serve in his armies against Alexander in the early stages of Alexander's campaign in Asia, so too did Hellenistic kings supplement their large Greco-Macedonian and local armies with Greek heavy infantry, who continued to be prized as skilled and effective warriors. One of the more curious developments of the period following Alexander's death was the creation of a permanent mercenary base on Cape Tainaron, the southernmost tip of the Peloponnese. Near the end of his life, Alexander ordered his satraps to discharge their mercenaries, many of whom then set up shop in Cape Tainaron to offer their services to all-comers (Diodorus 17.111). At many points in Hellenistic history, we hear of generals traveling to Tainaron to recruit soldiers for various campaigns.

To return to the Greco-Macedonian soldiers themselves, including those who fought in the phalanx and the cavalry, there is some disagreement as to whether they were equipped in the same way as Alexander's troops had been. Some literary sources suggest that the sarissas used by the phalanx became even longer, stretching to more than 5 or 6 meters, rendering the phalanx even more unwieldy than it had been in the fourth century BCE. The visual evidence, however, sometimes tells a different story. One of our best sources is the monument the Roman consul Aemilius Paullus dedicated at Delphi after his victory over the Macedonian king Perseus at Pydna in 168 BCE. On this monument, the Macedonians are shown equipped with shields not dissimilar to hoplite shields, but for being slightly narrower in diameter and more concave. Such shields would have been heavier than the *peltē* shields used by the phalanx of Philip and Alexander, which were held by a strap over the neck and shoulders to allow the soldiers to grip the sarissa with both hands. Heavy cavalrymen are also sometimes depicted as being protected by large round shields, whereas Alexander's Companions did not typically have shields at all.

The most distinctive innovation among Hellenistic Greco-Macedonian soldiers was the *thureophoros*, meaning "door-carrier" because of the distinctive shape of his shield. This type of soldier is depicted on the Aemilius Paullus monument and in other places as carrying a single-grip flat shield of a large oval shape, and bearing a thrusting spear in his right hand. The *thureophoros*, representing a medium-armed fighter capable of more battlefield maneuverability and better suited for single combat than a member of the phalanx, might have been adapted from the Gauls, against whom the Macedonians fought in the third century BCE. Another possible source of inspiration was the soldiers of Italy, whom the Macedonians encountered in the early third century BCE during the campaigns of Pyrrhus of Epirus, whom we will discuss below.[6]

Despite the sources that suggest a degree of military innovation, most literary depictions of Hellenistic battle, especially as found in historiographical sources such as the Greek Polybius and the Roman Livy, emphasize the heavy phalanx and its effectiveness in frontal assaults on level terrain. Cavalry and light-armed troops played a role in most battles, but usually only on the flanks, against

Figure 7.3 Frieze from the Monument of Aemilius Paullus, depicting Macedonian and Roman soldiers, 167 BCE.

Source: Archaeological Museum of Delphi. Photo credit: Foto Marburg/Art Resource, NY.

similar troop types, and during skirmishes before battle was joined in earnest. Hellenistic kings pitted their phalanxes against one another and relied on them even against the Romans.

Apart from pitched land battle, the Hellenistic period witnessed the continuation of many trends begun in the fourth century BCE. With great resources at their command, Alexander's successors made use of great siege trains and expert military engineers. Demetrius, the son of Antigonus, who was the forebear of the Antigonid dynasty in Macedonia, was given the nickname "Poliorketes," which means "the Besieger." He earned the title because of his famous – yet ultimately unsuccessful – siege of Rhodes, for which he employed the famous "helopolis," or "city-taker," a siege tower of unprecedented size. The most famous Hellenistic military scientist is probably Archimedes, the Greek inventor who lived in Syracuse. To protect his city against the Romans in the third century BCE, he is said to have devised various novel weapons, including a crane that could lift ships out of the water and smash them on the rocks, and a giant mirror that could focus a beam of light to set ships ablaze. Fascinating as Archimedes' inventions are, they made little impact on warfare in general.

Phalanx vs. legion

The Greek historian Polybius, who was taken from Greece to Rome as a hostage in 167 BCE and wrote his history largely to explain to his fellow Greeks how Rome was able to conquer the world, famously said that in a frontal charge the Macedonian phalanx is virtually unstoppable.[7] The sheer striking power of a broad hedge of massive pikes, arrayed to a depth of sixteen ranks, surely stopped many opposing armies in their tracks – if they even came to blows at all. The triumph of the Roman legion over this formation is one of the great accomplishments of the Roman Republic, and is due to two weaknesses inherent in the Macedonian formation. First, the Hellenistic kingdoms had a very difficult time recruiting enough soldiers to bring the phalanx to full strength, while any significant loss of men in battle might prove irreplaceable. The Romans, by contrast, had seemingly bottomless personnel reserves on which to draw. Second, though irresistible in a frontal assault, the phalanx was unwieldy and vulnerable to flank attacks and broken terrain. The more versatile Roman legion proved too much for the phalanx, especially since heavy cavalry no longer played a central role in Hellenistic armies. Polybius' take on the superiority of the legion is instructive:

> The Roman legion does not attempt to equal the front of the phalanx and charge it head-on with all of its soldiers at once, but some of its divisions are held back while others clash with the enemy. Now, whether the phalanx drives back those upon whom it charges, or is itself driven back, in both cases its order is dissolved. For whether pursuing a retreating enemy or withdrawing from an advancing enemy, it leaves behind the rest of its force, and when this happens the enemy's reserves can fill in the gaps and take the ground the phalanx had been holding. The enemy can then attack no longer

against the front, but against the flanks and rear of the phalanx … The Roman formation, by contrast, is flexible. For each Roman, when he is fully armed, can rush to where he is needed, being equally well suited for every place, time, and appearance of the enemy.

(Polybius 18.32)

Despite his detailed descriptions of tactics, Polybius was convinced that the Romans did not prevail because of tactics alone; rather, the Roman social and political system too was superior to those of the Greeks and the Hellenistic kingdoms. Aside from having a mixed constitution that blended elements of monarchy, aristocracy, and democracy, the Roman Republic of Polybius' day fought its wars with citizen militias, legions raised primarily from farmers who worked their own lands in Italy and returned to those lands once a campaign was finished. By around 200 BCE, increasingly long campaigns outside Italy led the Roman army to become more professionalized, but still built around citizens who in theory had to meet certain property qualifications. Only in the decades after Polybius was writing did the lowest classes of Roman citizens officially gain the right to join the legions, and this was due to the increasing military demands of a growing empire and perhaps a land shortage leading to a shortage of those meeting the old property requirements (though the extent of this land shortage is disputed today). But in the early second century BCE, when Rome began to fight wars against the Hellenistic kingdoms, there were lots of Roman citizens eligible for service in the legions, far more than were available to the Hellenistic kings. The personnel and financing needs of Roman military campaigns were met more easily because of Rome's system of formal alliances with other states in Italy. The citizen legions were supplemented by equal or slightly greater numbers of auxiliary troops that came from Rome's allies, states that did not yet enjoy full citizenship but had some rights and privileges because of their formal ties to Rome. These allies funded their own soldiers, who not only supplemented Rome's numbers in the field but also shielded Rome from the effects of losing too many of its own men. These allies also often provided the bulk of the specialized troops, including cavalry.

As a complete military system, integrated into Roman society, the legion had a great advantage over the Macedonian phalanx and Hellenistic armies. Although soldiers in any one Hellenistic phalanx could number in the tens of thousands, a decisive defeat in a single battle might kill enough soldiers to render a Hellenistic king unable to field a new army, thus ending the war in a single blow. The Romans, on the other hand, could draw upon a recruitment base of unprecedented size and replace even entire armies lost in battle. Furthermore, given a Macedonian leader's propensity to lead from the front, as a very sign of his legitimacy to lead, generals and kings often fell in battle, which also ended his side's war effort.

After the Battle of Cannae in 216 BCE, in which Hannibal had annihilated the combined army of two consuls during the Second Punic War, any state other than Rome would likely have folded, having lost tens of thousands of its soldiers in a single afternoon. The Romans, though, simply raised more armies and expanded the theater of the war to defeat Hannibal and the Carthaginians in the Carthaginians' own territory, a staggering feat of logistics and sheer stubbornness. The Romans performed a similar feat a generation earlier, during the First Punic War, when they, though notorious land-lubbers, built and staffed a navy from scratch to defeat the Mediterranean's preeminent naval power. The Romans even replaced whole fleets lost at sea in order to continue the war against Carthage. No Hellenistic kingdom could compete against such resources, certainly not for the decades-long wars the Romans were willing to fight.

Where the Hellenistic system encouraged military leaders to run the greatest risks, often leaving kingdoms without capable commanders or even kings, the Roman political system provided a ready supply of experienced generals and officers who tended not to throw themselves into the front lines. Roman aristocrats embarking on political careers were expected to serve on many campaigns, starting as junior officers and working their way up politically and militarily along Rome's tightly controlled *cursus honorum*, or course of offices. By the time a Roman was elected to a senior post such as the praetorship or the consulship, he was experienced in combat and command. Furthermore, if a Roman leader was killed, the *cursus honorum* ensured that many other eager and experienced soldiers were waiting in the wings. In comparison to the Roman legionary system, therefore, the Hellenistic kingdoms found it difficult to recruit soldiers, were unable to replace heavy losses, and relied too much on brash aristocrats and kings to lead their armies.

In terms of tactics, the legions outmatched Hellenistic armies. Most soldiers in the Roman legion carried as their main offensive weapon a short sword, the famous *gladius hispaniensis* (Spanish sword), a slashing and thrusting weapon with a blade about 60 centimeters long. Since the soldiers of the Macedonian phalanx of the Hellenistic period wielded two-handed sarissas often more than 6 meters long – ten times the length of the Roman sword – one could be forgiven for wondering just how Roman soldiers could even reach their Macedonian opponents, let alone kill enough of them to win a battle. But in fact it was the sword's modest length that made it such an effective hand-to-hand weapon and gave the legionary far greater individual and collective mobility than his counterparts.

As we have seen throughout this book, ancient soldiers always had to balance mobility with security. Heavier armor, larger shields, and denser formations offered protection against the enemy's weapons, but tended to limit the types of terrain on which an army could operate and rendered the individual soldier virtually ineffective on his own. To all appearances, Roman soldiers were heavily armored. They carried a large rectangular or oval shield called a *scutum*, reinforced by a boss in its center. They also wore cuirasses made of mail (or lesser materials if the soldier was not wealthy enough), a heavy belt to protect the groin, a metal helmet, and often greaves, or leg-guards. The legionary's defensive equipment was as heavy as a Greek hoplite's, yet, while the legionary could fight in a dense formation, he did not have to.

The scutum was held with a single grip, unlike both the double-grip hoplite shield and the shield of the Macedonian phalanx, secured over the neck and shoulders by a strap. So while the shield was large enough to offer substantial protection, and could even be braced against the ground, the single grip allowed the legionary much more freedom of movement, to the point that the shield, and especially its boss, could be used as an offensive weapon in its own right. And while the short sword did not hold enemies at bay like the long hoplite spear or the far longer sarissa did, up close it was a devastating weapon, and Roman soldiers were well-trained in its use. The legionary's defensive equipment provided good protection against the spear points of the enemy. The cut and thrust effectiveness of the short sword meant that, if the legionary could close with his enemy and fight toe-to-toe, he would almost certainly defeat a soldier of the phalanx. The Roman legionary achieved perhaps the perfect blend of safety and mobility.

On paper, a legion was comprised of 4,200 soldiers. A consular army (a force commanded by a consul, one of Rome's two senior annual magistrates) typically consisted of two legions, supplemented by roughly equal numbers of non-Roman auxiliary troops who provided the bulk of cavalry and other arms in which the Romans did not specialize. At the time of Rome's encounter with the Hellenistic kingdoms, in the field the legion was divided into three lines based on age. The youngest men stood in the first line, and were called the *hastati*, or spearmen, even though they were equipped with the sword. The soldiers of the second line were called the *principes*, or the mainstay of the force. The third line soldiers, the oldest men in the army, were called the *triarii*, or third-liners, and were equipped differently than the others, making use of a thrusting spear much like a hoplite's. The first two lines supplemented their swords with the heavy javelin called the *pilum*, which was hurled at the enemy before the two sides clashed in an effort to break up the opposing formation and to pierce and cling to enemy shields to make them useless. Not only were two-thirds of the Roman legion held back from the front line, a clear contrast to the phalanx, which tended not to make use of reserves, the three lines themselves seem not to have formed a continuous front. Instead, the Roman soldiers were divided up into "maniples" of 120 men, or 2 "centuries" of 60 men each. These maniples had gaps between them, covered by the maniples of the line behind, the maniples of which were arrayed in a staggered formation with the line in front. Only the triarii stood in a solid line, representing the last bastion of the legion with their spears. The triarii also differed in being grouped in half-strength maniples of one century each. In front of the 3,000 soldiers making up these 3 lines fought 1,200 light-armed skirmishers known as *velites*, or swift ones, who were too poor to afford proper legionary equipment and thus fought solely with ranged weapons, before retiring through the gaps in the maniples once the opposing armies had joined battle in earnest. This manipular legion must have struck Rome's Hellenistic enemies as a strange beast indeed, but it proved to be nimble on the battlefield and rendered the Macedonian phalanx tactically obsolete.

Two battles between Rome and the Antigonid kingdom of Macedonia from the first half of the second century BCE well illustrate the triumph of legion over phalanx. At Cynoscephalae in Thessaly, in 197 BCE, the legions of the proconsul Titus Flamininus defeated the Macedonian king Philip V in pitched battle (Polybius 18.19–18.27; Livy 33.3–33.3.10; Plutarch *Flamininus* 7–8). When the two sides met unexpectedly in the morning fog, Philip held the high ground, a tremendous advantage. But since battle was joined unexpectedly and haphazardly, neither side deployed in a particularly orderly fashion. The upshot was that Philip's army was divided and did not advance against the Romans in a single front. At a key stage in the battle, the right wing of Philip's phalanx was pushing the Romans down the hill, while the Roman right was advancing up the slope against Philip's left, which was being driven back before the Romans' elephants. As the Roman right wing moved up the hill to a position beyond where the Macedonian right wing had charged down the hill, an enterprising Roman officer moved several maniples from the Roman right to advance laterally across the battlefield and hit the Macedonian right in the rear, annihilating the formation. The divisibility of the legion, in the thick of battle, was something beyond the capabilities of the phalanx. Furthermore, the phalanx was utterly unable to react when the Romans appeared behind them. Titus Flamininus thus destroyed Philip's army and drove the Macedonians from Greece, a crucial step towards Rome's domination of the eastern Mediterranean.

Thirty years later, in 167 BCE, the last gasp of an independent Macedonian kingdom came at Pydna, in the shadow of Mt. Olympus (Livy 44.33–44.42; Plutarch *Aemilius Paullus* 11–22). Philip's son, Perseus, started making trouble again, and the Romans sent Aemilius Paullus to deal with him. The Battle of Pydna began in a relatively flat plain, where the Macedonian phalanx was most effective. Faced with an unbroken hedge of spears, the Roman army initially had a very tough time of it. In desperation, some soldiers tried to break off the Macedonians' spear points by hand, in an effort to close for hand-to-hand combat. One commander of an auxiliary unit threw his standard into the midst of the phalanx, inspiring his soldiers to fight like men possessed to claim it back. Despite their heroic effort, these allies of Rome managed only to be skewered on the Macedonians' sarissas. The phalanx continued to advance. In this battle, the phalanx was largely a victim of its own success. As the Macedonians pushed the Romans back, the fight moved from the plain to the more broken ground of the foothills emanating from Olympus. Once hills, valleys, and other topographical obstacles got in the way of the Macedonian line, gaps began to form in the phalanx. Though on the verge of defeat, the Roman soldiers noticed these gaps and took advantage of them, pouring in to hit the Macedonian soldiers from the side. Once the legionaries got inside the forest of sarissas, the Macedonians were defenseless, and fell in great numbers, further destabilizing the phalanx. Soon the Macedonian army broke down, and the Romans pursued and killed their enemies all the way to the sea and north towards the city of Pydna itself. This was the last major battle between legion and phalanx, and it resulted in Macedonia and Greece both being made official Roman provinces. It was only a matter of time before the entirety of the Hellenistic world fell under Roman control and the Hellenistic way of war fell into irrelevance.

At both Cynoscephalae and Pydna, the Macedonian phalanx, making use of a frontal charge on favorable ground, enjoyed initial success against the Roman legion. But in both cases the phalanx's inflexibility proved too great a disadvantage, while the flexibility of the legion as a formation and the versatility of the individual legionary as a hand-to-hand fighter won the day. Combined with Rome's advantages in terms of manpower and being able to draw on a large reserve of experienced commanders, the Hellenistic kingdoms just could not keep up. Tactically and socially, the Roman system proved superior.

Case studies: Pyrrhus of Epirus and Hannibal of Carthage

Instead of focusing on individual battles, for this chapter's case studies let's consider the careers of two famous Hellenistic generals. Both Pyrrhus of Epirus and Hannibal of Carthage encapsulate the strengths and weaknesses of the Hellenistic way of war, especially as manifested in conflict with the growing power of Rome.[8] Pyrrhus, a relative of Philip and Alexander, was a dashing Hellenistic warrior-king and the first Greco-Macedonian leader to fight pitched battles against the Romans. Pyrrhus won his battles on the field, but lost the war because of Rome's stubborn refusal to give in; hence, "Pyrrhic victory." Hannibal, though a Carthaginian and thus arguably not a Hellenistic leader at all, was nevertheless a general in the Hellenistic tradition and was a masterful practitioner of combined-arms warfare at a time when most other generals relied solely on the phalanx. But like Pyrrhus, Hannibal was unable to parlay battlefield victories over the Romans into decisive victory in a war.

Like other Hellenistic kings, for Pyrrhus "king" was used more or less as a title or rank, rather than signifying kingship over a particular territory. As his name implies, he was linked to Epirus, a region across the Pindus mountain range in western Greece, and did rule there; he was a king of the Molossian people and eventually the whole of Epirus. But he was also proclaimed king in many of the places to which he brought his army. For example, for a time he was co-ruler (with Lysimachus) of Macedonia, having been proclaimed king by the Macedonian soldiers of Demetrius Poliorketes. For several years, Pyrrhus also ruled Sicily, even while still being king of Epirus and maintaining claims to other regions.

Pyrrhus consciously emulated the leadership style of Alexander, his distant relative through Alexander's mother, Olympias. Plutarch's biography of Pyrrhus has several stories of the ambitious general leading from the front in battle, and taking himself to different parts of the line in order to rally his troops in the face of stiff opposition. Perhaps his most famous act of derring-do was his single combat against one of Demetrius' generals, Pantauchus. Although Pyrrhus was unable to kill Pantauchus, because Pantauchus' soldiers came to the rescue, Pyrrhus did inflict two wounds and clearly won the duel. Pyrrhus' actions so inspired his own soldiers that they rallied and routed the enemy. Even the enemy soldiers were impressed by Pyrrhus' deed, and began comparing him explicitly to Alexander (Plutarch *Pyrrhus* 7–8). Pyrrhus knew well how to gain power in

Figure 7.4 Marble bust of Pyrrhus.

Source: Museo Archeologico Nazionale, Naples. Photo credit: Scala/Ministero per i Beni e le Attività culturali/Art Resource, NY.

an age in which battlefield prowess was central to a king's legitimacy. As a means to remain as a legitimate ruler, and to keep his soldiers usefully occupied, like many other Hellenistic rulers Pyrrhus campaigned nearly constantly.

Pyrrhus is most famous as the Greco-Macedonian leader who first came into large-scale military conflict with Rome, initiating a century-and-a-half of military conflict that ended with all of mainland Greece and Macedonia being made provinces of Rome's expanding empire. Pyrrhus crossed the Ionian Sea in 280 BCE at the request of Terentum, a Greek city in the heel of Italy that was embroiled in a struggle with Rome. In addition to an advance force of 3,000, Pyrrhus entered Italy with an army of 20,000 infantry, 3,000 cavalry, 2,000 archers, 500 slingers, and 20 elephants. In its ratio of infantry to cavalry, along with other arms, Pyrrhus' army harkened back to the true combined-arms tactics of Alexander. With this force, Pyrrhus fought a pitched battle against the army of the Roman consul Laevinus near the city of Heraclea.

The Battle of Heraclea was a close-run thing. Pyrrhus began by leading his own cavalry against the cavalry of the Romans, consisting mostly of Rome's Italian allies, commanding in person from the front and cutting a dashing figure. After Pyrrhus was almost killed by an enemy's lance, he disguised himself as a regular soldier and dismounted to lead his phalanx in person. Plutarch says that control of the field changed hands no less than seven times and that Pyrrhus' army very nearly buckled when they thought Pyrrhus himself had been killed. When Pyrrhus took off his helmet to reveal himself to his line, he rallied the troops enough to drive the Romans from the field and secure victory. The final stroke was delivered by the Thessalian cavalry, the heavy lancers who had fought so well with Alexander. The battle was costly for both sides. Depending on which conflicting source one believes, the Romans lost 15,000 men, while Pyrrhus lost 13,000. Alternatively, the Romans lost 7,000, and Pyrrhus 4,000. In either case, though Pyrrhus won, it was not the sort of lopsided victory common in the ancient world. He had defeated the Romans in the field, but at the expense of the core of his army.

Despite Pyrrhus' losses, the Romans' were far greater. And Pyrrhus had won the battle and taken the field. In Pyrrhus' Hellenistic world, such a victory should have resulted in the surrender of the other side, or at least an attempt to sue for terms. There was an unwritten rule that decisive victories in pitched battles typically led to such a result, compounded by the fact that Hellenistic powers could not easily replace thousands of soldiers killed or captured. A victory against the forces of Demetrius, for example, had led to Demetrius' own troops acclaiming Pyrrhus king. Unfortunately for Pyrrhus, he was not fighting a typical Hellenistic enemy. The Romans, for all their impressive organization, tactics, and equipment, enjoyed the advantages of a massive population base from which to recruit replacement soldiers, and sheer stubbornness.

After his victory at Heraclea, Pyrrhus sent an envoy to the Roman Senate to propose terms. To prevent his fellow senators from acquiescing, the legendary Appius Claudius Caecus ("the blind") was brought into the Senate on a litter to deliver a rousing speech against conceding to Pyrrhus' terms. Appius' appeal worked, and the Romans resolved either to convince Pyrrhus to leave Italy or to continue fighting. The two sides met again at Asculum in 279 BCE, after the Romans raised an entirely new army, now under the command of the consul Fabricius. On the first day of the two-day battle, the Romans managed to force a confrontation on the rough ground along a river, where Pyrrhus could not use his cavalry or elephants to their full effect. On the second day, however, Pyrrhus succeeded in drawing the Romans into a broad plain, where his combined-arms force was more effective. Pyrrhus occupied the rough ground with light-armed troops and placed more light-armed troops in the gaps between his elephants. He took advantage of the level ground by sending the full weight of his phalanx against the Romans, who for their part hacked furiously at the long sarissas to little avail. What finally broke the Romans was the charge of Pyrrhus' elephants. Though victorious on the field, once again this battle was costly for Pyrrhus. Compared to the Romans' 6,000 killed, Pyrrhus lost 3,500, more than half of Rome's casualties and representing soldiers far more difficult to replace. Plutarch says that, after being congratulated for his victory, Pyrrhus quipped, "one more victory like that over the Romans will destroy us completely." Abandoning any real hope of conquering or establishing a permanent foothold in Italy, Pyrrhus moved on to other things, including a stint as the military governor of Sicily, before returning to Epirus.

Pyrrhus' expedition to Italy demonstrated some of the fundamental differences between the Roman and Hellenistic way of war. Pyrrhus, in his personal courage, continuous campaigning, and combined-arms approach to warfare, was every inch the ideal Hellenistic general in the mold of Alexander the Great. He surpassed many of his contemporaries in his tactical approach that emphasized cavalry, a military arm that had declined sharply in numbers and quality in the generations after Alexander. And, like other Hellenistic rulers, Pyrrhus assumed a battlefield victory would translate into terms favorable to his side, willingly accepted by the Romans, who should acknowledge their own defeat. The Romans, however, refused to play by Pyrrhus' rules and were able to recover from two battlefield losses by drawing on a far broader base of citizen-soldiers and allies. Pyrrhus won the battles, but lost the war, not necessarily because he was good at tactics and bad at strategy, but because he was playing an entirely different game than the Romans. Rome's unparalleled ability to withstand losses and its prodigious stubbornness were on display to an even greater extent against Hannibal in the Second Punic War.

Many readers might wonder why I have chosen Hannibal for the second case study. Though one of the most famous commanders of the ancient world, and active during the Hellenistic period, Hannibal was a Carthaginian rather than a Greek or Macedonian. Carthage was a powerful North African city in what is now Tunisia, settled by Phoenicians, a Semitic people from the Levant, and from whom the Romans derived the term "Punic." Nevertheless, Hannibal idolized and emulated Alexander the Great and Pyrrhus of Epirus, and was taught the military art by Greek tutors hired by his father for just such a purpose. Furthermore, Hannibal's military success and failures fit the pattern of Hellenistic leaders struggling against the rising power of Rome and its legions.

If the Roman army had a major weakness, it was in cavalry. The Romans themselves had never been avid horsemen, and most of the horses that fought along with the legions were supplied by Rome's allies. To be sure, many of these allied cavalry contingents were of high quality, but none came close to matching the skill and effectiveness of Macedonian heavy cavalry, such as that employed by Alexander. None, that is, until Hannibal recruited cavalrymen from neighboring peoples in North Africa, especially the Numidians. Using a combined-arms force of mostly mercenaries from a variety of nationalities, Hannibal was able to coordinate heavy and light infantry, and heavy and light cavalry, in such a way as to rival Alexander as a battlefield tactician and to outclass the Roman legions in battle after battle. If the Hellenistic period encouraged the proliferation of military manuals, military science, and military experts, Hannibal represents the pinnacle of these developments. Had his antagonist been a Hellenistic monarch – or even the Great King of Persia – Hannibal might well have met with the sort of success Alexander enjoyed. But, like Pyrrhus, Hannibal found the Romans to be intractable and possessed of too many citizens and allies.

According to legend, Hannibal as a boy was made to swear an oath of eternal enmity with Rome by his father, Hasdrubal, who had been a leading general during the First Punic War between Rome and Carthage (264–241 BCE). That war had been fought largely at sea, forcing Rome to develop a navy from scratch, and on the island of Sicily, where Rome made great inroads at Carthaginian expense. For the Second Punic War (218–201 BCE), Hannibal decided on the bold step of invading Italy itself, by marching an army overland across the Alps, during the cold months of fall at that. Like Alexander, who had inherited his own father's crusade against Persia and brazenly crossed into Asia into the teeth of the enemy, Hannibal took up his father's cause and brought war to the enemy's own lands. Also like Alexander, Hannibal counted on shock and sheer audacity, combined with battlefield wizardry, to break his foe. He would put all of his Greek military education to good use.

Alexander used a relatively small, but well-trained and equipped, force to subdue a much larger enemy. He did so by employing bold, knock-out punches, often at the expense of high casualties on his own side. At the Battle of Gaugamela in 331 BCE, for instance, Alexander placed all his hopes in a decisive cavalry strike, which was only made possible by his phalanx keeping the Persian army at bay and suffering huge losses and even a breakthrough by the Persians. Gaugamela was a decisive victory for Alexander. More controversially, he led his army across the Gedrosian Desert at the end of his campaign, which resulted in great loss of life. The sources say Alexander chose this route out of a desire to do what no one else had done. A bold action, to be sure, but perhaps also an irresponsible one. Hannibal's legendary crossing of the Alps evinces a similar military outlook. On the one hand, his entrance into Italy was completely unexpected and took the Romans off guard, which proved a tremendous advantage in the early phase of the campaign. On the other hand, by crossing in colder months instead of waiting until the following spring and summer, Hannibal suffered far greater losses to his army than he needed to, essentially half of his force. Also like Alexander, Hannibal's tactical boldness won him several pitched battles. However, where Alexander simply replaced Darius as the Great King of Persia once Darius' army was defeated at Gaugamela, and where Hellenistic kings replaced one another and annexed territory by virtue of battlefield victories, Hannibal was unable to turn tactical boldness into strategic success.

Hannibal arrived in Italy with about 20,000 soldiers, mostly mercenaries and allies picked up along the way, to which he added some Italian allies once he defeated Roman armies in battles like Trebia and Lake Trasimene. Hannibal's combined-arms force consisted of heavy-armed infantry, the cream of which were the Libyans, light infantry, and heavy and light cavalry, the best of which were the expert light horsemen of Numidia. By Hannibal's day, many Hellenistic commanders relied too much on their phalanx, not only because they seemed to have forgotten the tactics that won Alexander an empire, but also because good cavalry was hard to come by outside of the aristocratic equestrian traditions of places like Macedonia and Thessaly. Hannibal, though, had excellent cavalry, and he used it to great effect in combination with his well-trained infantry. Nowhere were these combined-arms tactics better displayed than at the Battle of Cannae in 216 BCE, one of history's most celebrated clashes.

On a plain in southeast Italy, Hannibal fought with the combined armies of both Roman consuls. Hannibal's force of around 50,000 (he had supplemented his army with local allies during his first 2 years in Italy) was outnumbered by a Roman army of a staggering 85,000 men. Cannae demonstrated both Rome's great strength and its great weakness. The huge citizen and allied pool from which Rome could recruit soldiers meant that the Republic could raise an army the size of that fielded at Cannae. At the same time, much of this force consisted of raw recruits, citizen-soldiers who had seen little or no military action before facing the Carthaginians. Hannibal, by contrast, relied on a core of professional soldiers, carefully drilled and hardened by many months in the field and several victories against Rome. As the Roman consuls massed their legions into an unusually deep formation designed to punch through Hannibal's line, Hannibal arrayed most of his infantry in a convex formation, bulging out towards the Romans. On the wings of the infantry, Hannibal placed his best soldiers, the Libyans. On his army's flanks, Hannibal placed his cavalry, lined up opposite the Roman and allied cavalry on the legions' flanks.

When the battle began, after skirmishing between the light-armed troops of both sides, the Carthaginian cavalry clashed with their Roman counterparts and soon drove them from the field. As the legions slammed into Hannibal's line, Hannibal's soldiers gave ground, turning their convex line into a concave one, drawing in the inexperienced legionaries until the Libyans on Hannibal's wing were at the Romans' flanks. The Romans' fate was sealed when the Libyans began to envelop the legionaries in a pincer formation, and Hannibal's victorious cavalry returned to the fight by appearing in the Romans' rear. Hannibal had achieved a total envelopment, and his soldiers went to work killing the trapped Romans, an exhausting process that took most of the day. In the end, Rome lost 48,000 killed and 20,000 taken prisoner, casualty numbers rarely exceeded in the

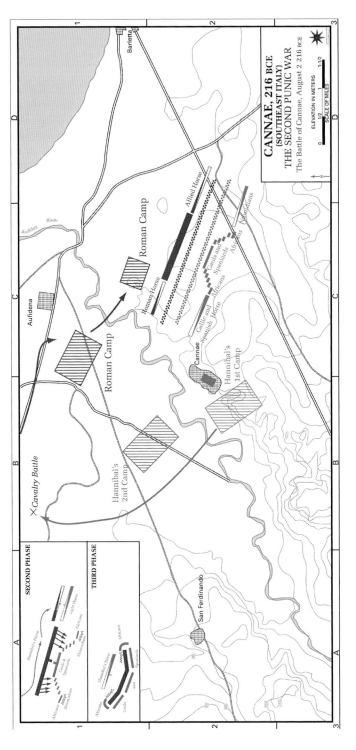

Figure 7.5 The Battle of Cannae, 216 BCE.

Source: public domain. Image produced by the Department of History, United States Military Academy.

history of warfare, including in the modern age of powder, mechanization, and machine guns. Using combined-arms tactics that would have made Alexander proud, and an experienced and nimble army of professionals, Hannibal had won a decisive victory that in any other circumstance should have meant the end of the war.

One of the most perplexing questions in ancient history is why Hannibal did not march on Rome after his spectacular victory at Cannae. Barry Strauss suggests several possibilities. First, Rome was a couple of weeks' march from Cannae, so it would have taken Hannibal's battle-weary army some time to reach the city. Second, Rome was surrounded by a massive wall and would therefore have been extremely difficult to take by storm, especially since Hannibal did not have an advanced siege train (in contrast to many other Hellenistic generals). Third, Hannibal's strategy seemed to center not on taking Rome itself, but on dislodging allies from Rome, which he thought would surely happen once word of Cannae spread. But, more than anything, Hannibal probably expected Rome to surrender, or at least admit defeat and accept a diminished role in the western Mediterranean, after experiencing one of the greatest military defeats of all time and losing tens of thousands of soldiers. Hannibal perhaps simply found it inconceivable that Rome would, or even could, continue the fight, and would accordingly be ready to bargain, especially after its Italian allies defected to Carthage. Given the frequency with which alliances shifted and territory changed hands in the Hellenistic world, especially after great battles, Hannibal's assumption was a rational one.

Rome, famously, did not give in. It not only raised new legions, it also took the war to Carthaginian territory, first by campaigning in Spain, and eventually by invading North Africa itself and dislodging Carthage's African allies, including the Numidians, who had formed much of the backbone of Hannibal's invasion force. Hannibal's most innovative and dogged Roman enemy was Scipio, eventually to be given the title "Africanus" after he defeated Hannibal in battle at Zama in 202 BCE and forced the capitulation of Carthage the following year. Hannibal's military career was not over, despite this great setback. Instead, he served as a general for several more years, including in the employ of the Seleucid king Antiochus III. But the personal charisma that had held his army together, even while crossing the Alps and spending many years in enemy territory, and the military expertise that allowed him to envelop and annihilate the Roman army at Cannae were not enough to overcome the systemic advantages enjoyed by Rome. Although Scipio was a brilliant and charismatic general, Rome did not rely on sheer force of personality. If Scipio had failed at Zama, someone else would have risen through the ranks to finish the job. Hannibal's crusade was Hannibal's alone, and when he could not deliver, the enterprise withered and died. Hellenistic tactical prowess and the Hellenistic model of charismatic leadership, so important for Alexander and his successors, faltered against the Roman *cursus honorum* and the bottomless manpower of the legions.

Conclusion: the end of the Hellenistic world – and the Roman Republic

The last reigning Hellenistic monarch did not die until 30 BCE. You probably know her name: Cleopatra. Though Cleopatra is remembered in popular culture as an Egyptian queen – a role she thoroughly embraced – she was a Macedonian, descended from one of Alexander's generals and successors, Ptolemy. When she died, along with her lover and ally, the famous Roman Marc Antony, not only did the last Hellenistic kingdom lose its independence, the Roman Republic fell too. In its place, the Roman Empire emerged, led by the last man left standing after decades of civil war. Octavian, the grand-nephew and adopted heir of Julius Caesar, is better known as Augustus, a title he adopted in 27 BCE. Octavian, the first Roman emperor, won sole power by defeating Antony and Cleopatra in the Battle of Actium, a naval engagement fought on the west coast of mainland Greece. As a reward for his victory, in addition to having no clear rivals for control of an empire that stretched across the entire Mediterranean, Octavian took the great Ptolemaic kingdom of Egypt as his own private property. In Rome even today you can see the results of Octavian's conquest in the many Egyptian obelisks that adorn the city's piazzas.

An important thing to remember when thinking about the transition from the Hellenistic period to the Roman Empire (and from Classical Greece to the Hellenistic period, for that matter) is that the people living in the Greek east did not suddenly cease to be Greek (or any other culture or nationality to which they belonged). Instead, the Romans were the new political masters, just as the Hellenistic kings had been after Alexander's conquests. Greek culture and identity persisted, including in the realm of warfare. The Roman poet Horace, writing during the reign of Augustus, said: "*Graecia capta ferum victorem cepit et artes intulit agresti Latio,*" which translates to, "Captive Greece captured her rude conqueror, and brought the arts to rustic Latium" (Horace *Epistles* 2.1.156). Horace's point is that, while Rome might have conquered politically and militarily, an affinity for Greek culture took hold of many Romans, leaving the Greeks the cultural conquerors of Rome. Early in his career, Julius Caesar lamented that he had not lived up to the spectacular example set by Alexander the Great. Various powerful Romans of the Late Republic, most infamously Crassus, tried to emulate Alexander and others by fighting the Parthians, the successors to the Persian Empire, and losing many Roman soldiers in the process. Augustus clearly looked to Greece for inspiration. He commissioned the poet Vergil to write Rome into the heroic past of the Greeks, which Vergil did by composing the *Aeneid* and telling the story of the ancestors of Rome's flight from Troy as the Greeks stormed the city.

Notes

1 "Hellenistic" was introduced to academic discourse by the German scholar Johann Gustav Droysen in 1836 with the publication of his seminal work, *Geschichte des Hellenismus.*

2 "Hellenistic Baroque" is also frequently employed as a term to describe a particular style of Hellenistic art, especially in sculpture. See the interesting discussion in Schultz (2011).

3 Philopoemen was a remarkable tactician and introduced many new ways of fighting, especially with light-armed troops and unconventional measures, including night raids. For his military innovations, see Williams (2004).

4 It is a comment on the poor nature of many of our sources for Hellenistic warfare that the two standard reference works on ancient warfare can come to nearly opposite conclusions about the role of the cavalry. Sekunda (2007) argues that the heavy cavalry remained the main striking force. On the other hand, Serrati (2013) offers the – to my mind – more correct view that cavalry declined precipitously in importance and the infantry became the military mainstay.

5 Because of its dry climate, Ptolemaic Egypt provides a wealth of evidence for administrative practices in the form of documents on papyri. For a recent study of how papyri can shed light on military settlement, see Sänger (2015).

6 Often *thureos* is just translated as shield, making *thureophoroi* simply "shield-bearers." But in various places, the *thureos* seems to be a particular kind of shield and the *thureophoroi* a particular kind of specialized troop, for which several images, such as the Aemilius Paullus monument, seem to provide evidence. Plutarch (*Philopoemen* 9) contrasts the *thureos*, a shield appropriate for light-armed troops, with the *peltē* held by soldiers in the Macedonian phalanx. Polybius (10.29.6) indicates that the *thureophoroi* were specialized troops, contrasted with those carrying the heavier *aspsis*. Several sources suggest that the *thureos* might have originated among the Gauls. See, for example, the inscription recorded by Plutarch (*Pyrrhus* 26), celebrating Pyrrhus' dedication of *thureoi* taken from defeated Gauls.

7 Polybius (18.28–18.32) offers a lengthy digression on the respective natures of the phalanx and legion and the superiority of the latter. This entire passage is essential reading for military historians.

8 The best ancient source for Pyrrhus is Plutarch's biography of him. Hannibal's campaign is treated in detail by both Polybius (esp. book 3, which covers up to Cannae, while much of the rest of his treatment of the war survives only in fragments) and Livy (books 21–30).

Further reading

Austin, M. M. 2006. *The Hellenistic World from Alexander to the Roman Conquest: A Selection of Ancient Sources in Translation* (second edition). Cambridge.

An important collection of the scattered sources for the Hellenistic period, including much epigraphic evidence to supplement literary works.

Chaniotis, Angelos. 2005. *War in the Hellenistic World: A Social and Cultural History.* Malden, MA.

An exploration of the many themes pertinent to warfare beyond tactics and strategy, this book sheds a great deal of light on the Hellenistic world in general.

Eckstein, Arthur M. 2006. *Mediterranean Anarchy, Interstate War, and the Rise of Rome.* Berkeley.

This book focuses on the role of the Greco-Macedonian powers of the eastern Mediterranean in spurring Roman imperialism and the eventual Roman conquest of the Hellenistic world.

Erdkamp, Paul (ed.). 2007. *A Companion to the Roman Army.* Oxford.

An edited collection of chapters on the Roman army, including its development during the Republic and its clash with the Hellenistic kingdoms.

Errington, R. M. 1969. *Philopoemen*. Oxford.

A standard resource for understanding the life and times of one of the Hellenistic world's most important military leaders.

Grainger, John D. 2016. *Great Power Diplomacy in the Hellenistic World*. London.

A recent study on a vital but relatively under-studied aspect of Hellenistic history, with obvious importance for military history.

Green, Peter. 1993. *Alexander to Actium: The Historical Evolution of the Hellenistic Age*. Berkeley.

A sprawling and detailed narrative of 300 years of Hellenistic history. This book is very readable, but unfortunately neglects much of the scholarship and sources pertaining to the Near Eastern territories Alexander conquered.

Griffith, G. T. 1968. *The Mercenaries of the Hellenistic World*. Groningen.

A standard reference work on Hellenistic mercenaries.

Gruen, Erich S. 1984. *The Hellenistic World and the Coming of Rome* (2 vols.). Berkeley.

Still an essential resource for understanding Greco-Roman interactions during the Hellenistic period, including in the sphere of warfare.

Kuhrt, Amelie and Susan Sherwin-White. 1987. *Hellenism in the East: The Interaction of Greek and Non-Greek Civilizations from Syria to Central Asia after Alexander*. London.

A groundbreaking work focusing on the Near East on its own terms, drawing on Near Eastern sources from literature to archaeology, to illuminate the complex relationship between Greco-Macedonians and native populations after Alexander.

Kuhrt, Amelie and Susan Sherwin-White. 1993. *From Samarkhand to Sardis: A New Approach to the Seleucid Empire*. Berkeley.

Expanding on their earlier work, Kuhrt and Sherwin-White provide a model for scholars seeking to move beyond Greco-Roman sources in examining how Near Eastern peoples reacted and adapted to Greco-Macedonians.

Lendon, J. E. 2005. *Soldiers and Ghosts: A History of Battle in Classical Antiquity*. New Haven.

Provides a lively account of the Battle of Pydna between the Romans and Macedonians, including a useful overview of the Roman manipular legion that encountered the Macedonian phalanx.

Ma, John. 2000. "Fighting Poleis of the Hellenistic World." In Hans van Wees (ed.), *War and Violence in Ancient Greece*. Swansea. 337–376.

An important look at war at the micro-level during the Hellenistic period. Even though most studies focus on great power politics, individual poleis continued to exercise agency and fought many wars with each other, and with and against the great powers.

Parke, H. W. 1970. *Greek Mercenary Soldiers, from the Earliest Times to the Battle of Ipsus*. Oxford.

The standard work on Greek mercenaries.

Sage, Michael M. 2008. *The Roman Republican Army: A Sourcebook*. London.

A convenient, annotated collection of crucial sources for the Roman army that fought the Macedonian phalanx and the Hellenistic kingdoms.

Strauss, Barry. 2012. *Masters of Command: Alexander, Hannibal, Caesar, and the Genius of Leadership*. New York.

In this comparison of three famous ancient commanders, Strauss provides an exciting account of Hannibal's military career and situates him in the broader context of Greco-Roman warfare.

Walbank, F. W. 1957–1979. *A Historical Commentary on Polybius* (3 vols.). Oxford.

A necessary resource for scholars using Polybius, one the Hellenistic period's most important literary sources and one of the best ancient sources for warfare in general.

Select bibliography

Allison, Graham. 2017. *Destined for War: Can America and China Escape Thucydides's Trap?* New York.

Anderson, J. K. 1970. *Military Theory and Practice in the Age of Xenophon*. Berkeley.

Arrington, Nathan. 2015. *Ashes, Images, and Memories: The Presence of the War Dead in Fifth-Century Athens*. Oxford.

Austin, M. M. 2006. *The Hellenistic World from Alexander to the Roman Conquest: A Selection of Ancient Sources in Translation* (second edition). Cambridge.

Balot, Ryan, Sarah Forsdyke, and Edith Foster (eds.). 2017. *The Oxford Handbook of Thucydides*. Oxford.

Barry, William. 2016. "Alone in the Village: Hesiod and his Community in the *Works and Days*." *Classical Philology* 111: 305–329.

Beal, Richard Henry. 1992. *The Organisation of the Hittite Military*. Heidelberg.

Beckman, Gary. 1999. *Hittite Diplomatic Texts*. Atlanta.

Best, Jan G. P. 1969. *Thracian Peltasts and their Influence on Greek Warfare*. Groningen.

Bosworth, A. B. 1988. *Conquest and Empire: The Reign of Alexander the Great*. Cambridge.

Bryce, Trevor. 2005. *The Kingdom of the Hittites*. Oxford.

Buck, Robert J. 1994. *Boiotia and the Boiotian League, 432–371 B.C.* Edmonton.

Buckler, John. 1985. "Epameinondas and the 'Embolon'." *Phoenix* 39: 134–143.

Buckler, John. 2003. *Aegean Greece in the Fourth Century BC*. Leiden.

Burckhardt, Jacob. 1963. *History of Greek Culture*. New York.

Butera, C. Jacob. 2010. *"The Land of the Fine Triremes:" Naval Identity and Polis Imaginary in 5th Century Athens*. PhD. Dissertation, Duke University, Durham, NC.

Carney, Elizabeth and Daniel Ogden (eds.). 2010. *Philip II and Alexander the Great: Father and Son, Lives and Afterlives*. Oxford.

Cartledge, Paul. 1987. *Agesilaos and the Crisis of Sparta*. Baltimore.

Cartledge, Paul. 2007. *Thermopylae: The Battle that Changed the World*. New York.

Caven, Brian. 1990. *Dionysius I, War-Lord of Sicily*. New Haven.

Chadwick, John. 1976. *The Mycenaean World*. Cambridge.

Chaniotis, Angelos. 2005. *War in the Hellenistic World: A Social and Cultural History*. Malden, MA.

Clarke, Michael. 2004. "Manhood and Heroism." In Robert Fowler (ed.), *The Cambridge Companion to Homer*. Cambridge. 74–90.

Cline, Eric H. ed. 2010. *The Oxford Handbook of the Bronze Age Aegean*. Oxford.

Cline, Eric H. ed. 2014. *1177 B.C.: The Year Civilization Collapsed*. Princeton.

Connor, W. Robert. 1972. *The New Politicians of Fifth-Century Athens*. Princeton.

Davis, Jack. L. and Sharon R. Stocker. 2016. "The Lord of the Gold Rings: The Griffin Warrior of Pylos." *Hesperia* 85: 627–655.

Davis, Jack. L. and Sharon R. Stocker. 2017. "The Combat Agate from the Grave of the Griffin Warrior at Pylos." *Hesperia* 86: 583–605.

Devine, A. M. 1983. "EMBOLON: A Study in Tactical Terminology." *Phoenix* 37: 201–217.

Diesner, H. J. 1959. "Peisistratidenexkurs und Peisistratidenbild bei Thukydides." *Historia* 8: 12–22.

Doerries, Bryan. 2015. *The Theater of War: What Ancient Greek Tragedies Can Teach Us Today*. New York.

Doumas, Christos. 1992. *The Wall-Paintings of Thera*. Athens.

Drews, Robert. 1993. *The End of the Bronze Age: Changes in Warfare and the Catastrophe ca. 1200 B.C.* Princeton.

Driessen, Jan M. and C. MacDonald. 1984. "Some Military Aspects of the Aegean in the Late Fifteenth and Early Fourteenth Centuries B.C." *Annual of the British School at Athens* 79: 49–56.

Eckstein, Arthur M. 2006. *Mediterranean Anarchy, Interstate War, and the Rise of Rome*. Berkeley.

Engels, Donald W. 1978. *Alexander the Great and the Logistics of the Macedonian Army*. Berkeley.

Erdkamp, Paul (ed.). 2007. *A Companion to the Roman Army*. Oxford.

Errington, R. M. 1969. *Philopoemen*. Oxford.

Finley, M. I. 1954. *The World of Odysseus*. New York.

Flower, Michael A. 2012. *Xenophon's Anabasis or the Expedition of Cyrus*. Oxford.

Flower, Michael A. (ed.). 2017. *The Cambridge Companion to Xenophon*. Cambridge.

Fowler, Robert (ed.). 2004. *The Cambridge Companion to Homer*. Cambridge.

Fuller, J. F. C. 1960. *The Generalship of Alexander the Great*. New Brunswick, NJ.

Gabriel, Richard A. 2010. *Philip II of Macedonia: Greater than Alexander*. Washington, DC.

Gomme, A. W., A. Andrewes, and K. J. Dover. 1945–1981. *A Historical Commentary on Thucydides* (5 vols.). Oxford.

Grainger, John D. 2009. *Alexander the Great Failure*. London.

Grainger, John D. 2016. *Great Power Diplomacy in the Hellenistic World*. London.

Green, Peter. 1993. *Alexander to Actium: The Historical Evolution of the Hellenistic Age*. Berkeley.

Griffith, G. T. 1968. *The Mercenaries of the Hellenistic World*. Groningen.

Gruen, Erich S. 1984. *The Hellenistic World and the Coming of Rome* (2 vols.). Berkeley.

Hale, John R. 2009. *Lords of the Sea: The Epic Story of the Athenian Navy and the Birth of Democracy*. London.

Hall, Edith. 1989. *Inventing the Barbarian: Greek Self-Definition through Tragedy*. Oxford.

Hall, Jonathan M. 2006. *A History of the Archaic Greek World: ca. 1200–479 BCE*. Malden, MA.

Hamilton, Charles D. 1979. *Sparta's Bitter Victories: Politics and Diplomacy in the Corinthian War*. Ithaca.

Hammond, N. G. L. 1998. *The Genius of Alexander the Great*. Chapel Hill, NC.

Hammond, N. G. L., G. T. Griffith, and F. W. Walbank. 1972–1988. *A History of Macedonia* (3 vols.). Oxford.

Hanson, Victor Davis. 1999. *The Other Greeks: The Family Farm and the Agrarian Roots of Western Civilization* (second edition). Berkeley.

Hanson, Victor Davis. 2005. *A War Like No Other: How the Athenians and Spartans Fought the Peloponnesian War*. New York.

Hanson, Victor Davis. 2009. *The Western Way of War* (second edition). Berkeley.

Heckel, Waldemar. 2006. *Who's Who in the Age of Alexander the Great*. London.

Heckel, Waldemar and John Yardley. 2004. *Alexander the Great: Sources in Translation*. Oxford.

Holladay, A. J. 1988. "Further Thoughts on Trireme Tactics." *Greece & Rome* 35: 149–151.

Holt, Frank L. 2012. *Into the Land of Bones: Alexander the Great in Afghanistan* (second edition). Berkeley.

Horden, P. and N. Purcell. 2000. *The Corrupting Sea: A Study of Mediterranean History*. Malden, MA.

Hornblower, Simon. 1991–2008. *A Commentary on Thucydides* (3 vols.). Oxford.

How, W. W. and J. Wells. 1912. *A Commentary on Herodotus* (2 vols.). Oxford.

Hunt, Peter. 1998. *Slaves, Warfare, and Ideology in the Greek Historians*. Cambridge.

Kagan, Donald. 1969. *The Outbreak of the Peloponnesian War*. Ithaca.

Kagan, Donald. 2009. *Thucydides: The Reinvention of History*. London.

Kagan, Donald. 2012. *A New History of the Peloponnesian War*. Ithaca.

Kagan, Donald and Gregory F. Viggiano (eds.). 2013. *Men of Bronze: Hoplite Warfare in Ancient Greece*. Princeton.

Kallet, Lisa. 1999. "The Diseased Body Politic, Athenian Public Finance, and the Massacre at Mykalessos." *American Journal of Philology* 120: 223–244.

King, Carol J. 2017. *Ancient Macedonia*. London.

Kirk, G. S. (ed.). 1985–1993. *The Iliad: A Commentary*. Cambridge.

Kitchen, K. A. 1982. *Pharaoh Triumphant: The Life and Times of Ramesses II, King of Egypt*. Mississauga, ON.

Konecny, A. 2001. "Katekopsen ten moran Iphikrates. Das Gefecht bei Lechaion im\ Frühsommer 390 v. Chr." *Chiron* 31: 79–127.

Konijnendijk, Roel. 2016. "Mardonius' Senseless Greeks." *Classical Quarterly* 66: 1–12.

Krentz, Peter. 2000. "Deception in Archaic and Classical Greek Warfare." In Hans van Wees (ed.), *War and Violence in Ancient Greece*. Swansea. 167–200.

Krentz, Peter. 2010. *The Battle of Marathon*. New Haven.

Kuhrt, Amélie, 2007. *The Persian Empire*. London.

Kuhrt, Amelie and Susan Sherwin-White. 1987. *Hellenism in the East: The Interaction of Greek and Non-Greek Civilizations from Syria to Central Asia after Alexander*. London.

Kuhrt, Amelie and Susan Sherwin-White. 1993. *From Samarkhand to Sardis: A New Approach to the Seleucid Empire*. Berkeley.

Latacz, Joachim. 1977. *Kampfparänese, Kampfdarstellung und Kampfwirklichkeit in der Ilias, bei Kallinos und Tyrtaios*. München.

Latacz, Joachim. 2005. *Troy and Homer: Towards a Solution of an Old Mystery*. Oxford.

Lazenby, John F. 1985. *The Spartan Army*. Warminster.

Lazenby, John F. 1987. "The Diekplous." *Greece & Rome* 34: 169–177.

Lazenby, John F. 1993. *The Defence of Greece, 490–479 B.C.* Warminster.

Lazenby, John F. 2004. *The Peloponnesian War: A Military Study*. London.

Lee, John W. I. 2007. *A Greek Army on the March: Soldiers and Survival in Xenophon's "Anabasis."* Cambridge.

Lendon, J. E. 2005. *Soldiers and Ghosts: A History of Battle in Classical Antiquity.* New Haven.

Lendon, J. E. 2010. *Song of Wrath: The Peloponnesian War Begins.* New York.

Lewis, Sian (ed.). 2006. *Ancient Tyranny.* Edinburgh.

Lissarrague, François. 1990. *L'autre guerrier: archers, peltastes, cavaliers dans l'imagerie attique.* Paris.

Lorimer, H. L. 1947. "The Hoplite Phalanx with Special Reference to the Poems of Archilochus and Tyrtaeus." *Annual of the British School at Athens* 62: 76–138.

Lovén, Bjørn. 2011. *The Ancient Harbours of the Piraeus.* Athens.

Ma, John. 2000. "Fighting Poleis of the Hellenistic World." In Hans van Wees (ed.), *War and Violence in Ancient Greece.* Swansea. 337–376.

Markle, Minor M., III. 1977 "The Macedonian Sarissa, Spear, and Related Armor." *American Journal of Archaeology* 81: 323–339.

Markle, Minor M., III. 1978. "Use of the Sarissa by Philip and Alexander of Macedon." *American Journal of Archaeology* 82: 483–497.

Marsden, E. W. 1969. *Greek and Roman Artillery: The Historical Development.* Oxford.

Marsden, E. W. 1971. *Greek and Roman Artillery: Technical Treatises.* Oxford.

Martin-Mcauliffe and John K. Papadopoulos. 2012. "Framing Victory: Salamis, the Athenian Acropolis and the Agora." *Journal of the Society of Architectural Historians* 71: 332–361.

Matthew, Christopher A. 2009. "When Push Comes to Shove: What Was the "Othismos" of Hoplite Combat?" *Historia* 58: 395–415.

Meiggs, Russell. 1972. *The Athenian Empire.* Oxford.

Mitchell, Lynette. 2013. *The Heroic Rulers of Archaic and Classical Greece.* London.

Morley, Neville. 2014. *Thucydides and the Idea of History.* London.

Morris, Ian. 1987. *Burial and Ancient Society: The Rise of the Greek City-State.* Cambridge.

Morris, Ian. 1996. "The Strong Principle of Equality and the Archaic Origins of Greek Democracy." In J. Ober and C. Hedrick (eds.), *Demokratia: A Conversation on Democracies, Ancient and Modern.* Princeton. 19–48.

Morris, Ian and Barry Powell (eds.). 1997. *A New Companion to Homer.* Leiden.

Morrison, J. S., J. F. Coates, and N. B. Rankov. 2000. *The Athenian Trireme: The History and Reconstruction of an Ancient Greek Warship* (second edition). Cambridge.

Ober, Josiah. 2005. *Athenian Legacies: Essays on the Politics of Going on Together.* Princeton.

Ober, Josiah. 2007. "I Besieged that Man: Democracy's Revolutionary Start." In Kurt A. Raaflaub, Josiah Ober, and Robert W. Wallace (eds.), *Origins of Democracy in Ancient Greece.* Berkeley. 83–104.

Papagrigorakis Manolis J., C. Yapijakis, P. N. Synodinos, and E. Baziotopoulou-Valavani. 2006. "DNA Examination of Ancient Dental Pulp Incriminates Typhoid Fever as a Probable Cause of the Plague of Athens." *International Journal of Infectious Diseases* 10: 206–214.

Parke, H. W. 1970. *Greek Mercenary Soldiers, from the Earliest Times to the Battle of Ipsus.* Oxford.

Parkinson, Richard Bruce and Louise Schofield. 1994. "Of Helmets and Heretics: A Possible Egyptian Representation of Mycenaean Warriors on a Papyrus from el-Amarna." *Annual of the British School at Athens* 89: 157–170.

Pounder, Robert L. 1983. "A Hellenistic Arsenal in Athens." *Hesperia* 52: 233–256.

Pritchard, David M. 1998. "The Fractured Imaginary: Popular Thinking on Military Matters in Fifth Century Athens." *Ancient History* 28: 38–61.

Pritchard, David M. (ed.). 2010. *War, Democracy and Culture in Classical Athens*. Cambridge.

Pritchett, W. K. 1974. *The Greek State at War, Part II*. Berkeley.

Pritchett, W. K. 1985. *The Greek State at War, Vol. 4*. Berkeley.

Pulak, Cemal. 2005. "Who Were the Mycenaeans Aboard the Uluburun Ship?" In R. Laffineur and E. Greco (eds.), *Aegeans in the Central and Eastern Mediterranean. Proceedings of the 10th International Aegean Conference. Athens, Italian School of Archaeology, 14–18 April 2004*. Liège. 295–312.

Pulak, Cemal. 2010. "Uluburun Shipwreck." In E. Cline (ed.) *The Oxford Handbook of the Bronze Age Aegean*. Oxford. 862–876.

Raaflaub, Kurt A. 2007. "The Breakthrough of *Dēmokratia* in Mid-Fifth-Century Athens." in Kurt A. Raaflaub, Josiah Ober, and Robert W. Wallace (eds.), *Origins of Democracy in Ancient Greece*. Berkeley. 105–154.

Raaflaub, Kurt A. 2008. "Homeric Warriors and Battles: Trying to Resolve Old Problems." *Classical World* 101: 469–483.

Robinson, David M. and George E. Mylonas. 1929–1952. *Excavations at Olynthus*. Baltimore.

Roisman, Josef. 1993. *The General Demosthenes and his Use of Military Surprise*. Stuttgart.

Sage, Michael M. 2008. *The Roman Republican Army: A Sourcebook*. London.

Sänger, Patrick. 2015. "Military Immigration and the Emergence of Cultural or Ethnic Identities: The Case of Ptolemaic Egypt." *Journal of Juristic Papyrology* 45: 229–253.

Schultz, Peter. 2011. "Style, Continuity, and the Hellenistic Baroque." In Andrew Erskine and Lloyd Llewellyn-Jones (eds.) *Creating a Hellenistic World*. Swansea. 313–344.

Sears, Matthew A. 2010. "Warrior Ants: Elite Troops in the *Iliad*." *Classical World*. 103: 139–155.

Sears, Matthew A. 2011. "The Topography of the Pylos Campaign and Thucydides' Literary Themes." *Hesperia* 80: 157–168.

Sears, Matthew A. 2013. *Athens, Thrace, and the Shaping of Athenian Leadership*. Cambridge.

Sears, Matthew A. and Carolyn Willekes. 2016. "Alexander's Cavalry Charge at Chaeronea, 338 BCE." *Journal of Military History*, 80: 1017–1035.

Sekunda, Nicholas. 2007. "Military Forces A: Land Forces." In Philip Sabin, Hans van Wees, and Michael Whitby (eds.), *The Cambridge History of Greek and Roman Warfare* (vol. 1). Cambridge. 325–356.

Serrati, John. 2013. "The Hellenistic World at War: Stagnation or Development?" In Brian Campbell and Lawrence A. Tritle (eds.), *The Oxford Handbook of Warfare in the Classical World*. Oxford. 179–198.

Shapiro, Beth, Andrew Rambaut, and M. Thomas P. Gilbert. 2006. "No Proof that Typhoid Caused the Plague of Athens (A Reply to Papagrigorakis et al.)." *International Journal of Infectious Diseases* 10: 334–335.

Snodgrass, A. M. 1967. *Arms and Armour of the Greeks*. London.

Spalinger, Anthony J. 2005. *War in Ancient Egypt*. Malden, MA.

Ste. Croix, G. E. M. de. 1972. *The Origins of the Peloponnesian War*. Ithaca.

Strauss, Barry. 1987. *Athens after the Peloponnesian War: Class, Faction, and Policy, 403–386 B.C.* Ithaca.

Strauss, Barry. 1996. "The Athenian Trireme, School of Democracy." In J. Ober and C. Hedrick (eds.), *Demokratia: A Conversation on Democracies, Ancient and Modern.* Princeton. 313–326.

Strauss, Barry. 2004. *The Battle of Salamis: The Naval Encounter that Saved Greece – and Western Civilization.* New York.

Strauss, Barry. 2007. *The Trojan War: A New History.* New York.

Strauss, Barry. 2012. *Masters of Command: Alexander, Hannibal, Caesar, and the Genius of Leadership.* New York.

Stylianou, P. J. 1998. *A Historical Commentary on Diodorus Siculus, Book 15.* Oxford.

Tarn, W. W. 1948. *Alexander the Great* (2 vols.). Cambridge.

Trundle, Matthew. 2005. *Greek Mercenaries: From the Late Archaic Period to Alexander.* London.

van der Spek, Bert. 2003. "Darius III, Alexander the Great and Babylonian Scholarship." In Wouter Henkelman and Amelie Kuhrt (eds.), *A Persian Perspective: Essays in Memory of Heleen Sancisi-Weerdenburg.* Leiden. 289–346.

van Wees, Hans. 1992. *Status Warriors: War, Violence, and Society in Homer and History.* Amsterdam.

van Wees, Hans. 2001. "The Myth of the Middle-Class Army: Military and Social Status in Ancient Athens." In L. Hannestad and T. Bekker-Nielsen (eds.), *War as a Cultural and Social Force.* Copenhagen. 45–71.

van Wees, Hans. 2004. *Greek Warfare: Myths and Realities.* London.

Vickers, Michael J. 2008. *Sophocles and Alcibiades: Athenian Politics in Ancient Greek Literature.* Stocksfield.

Walbank, F. W. 1957–1979. *A Historical Commentary on Polybius* (3 vols.). Oxford.

Westlake, H. D. 1968. *Individuals in Thucydides.* London.

Whitehead, David. 2002. *How to Survive under Siege, by Aineias the Tactician. A Historical Commentary with Translation and Introduction.* London.

Whitehead, Ian. 1987. "The Periplous." *Greece & Rome* 34: 178–185.

Willekes, Carolyn, 2016. *The Horse in the Ancient World: From Bucephalus to the Hippodrome.* London.

Williams, Mary Frances. 2004. "Philopoemen's Special Forces: Peltasts and a New Kind of Greek Light-Armed Warfare (Livy 35.27)." *Historia* 53: 257–277.

Winter, Frederick E. 1971. *Greek Fortifications.* Toronto.

Worthington, Ian. 2012. *Demosthenes of Athens and the Fall of Classical Greece.* Oxford.

Worthington, Ian. 2014. *By the Spear: Philip II, Alexander the Great, and the Rise and Fall of the Macedonian Empire.* Oxford.

Yadin, Yigael. 1963. *The Art of Warfare in Biblical Lands.* New York.

Index

Page numbers in *italics* denote figures